"In this book Torrey Seland applies postcolonial theory to better comprehend Philo's works in the political and social context of Alexandria and the Greco-Roman world. His argument throughout the book suggests Philo was influenced by the colonizing power of the Roman Empire. As an esteemed Philonic scholar, Seland once again offers a fresh reading of Philo as a Jewish interpreter of the Torah of his time and broadens our perspectives on his writings."
—PER JARLE BEKKEN, Professor, Nord University, Norway

"In *Reimagining Philo*, Seland offers a compelling reinterpretation of Philo as a thinker negotiating the tension between Jewish identity and Roman imperial power. Drawing on postcolonial categories, he explores how Philo employs mimicry and hybridity in ways characteristic of colonized subjects. This approach opens exciting new paths for understanding Philo's corpus and its sociopolitical embeddedness."
—KEN SCHENCK, Provost, Campus Edu, USA

"In an innovative study Torrey Seland introduces an original, postcolonial reading of Philo of Alexandria. Seland argues that Philo became radicalized in his view of Rome as a colonial power, and shows how Philo, although belonging to the elite, wrote from the perspective of the oppressed. Using mimicry and hybridity to analyze Philo's expositions, Seland presents a new understanding of the political context of Philo's texts."
—HALVOR MOXNES, Professor Emeritus, Faculty of Theology, University of Oslo, Norway

"In this provocative reappraisal of Philo, Torrey Seland moves the Jewish thinker away from being an abstract engager of Graeco-Roman philosophies to living as a Jewish resident of Alexandria during the disrupted 30s and 40s CE. Adopting a postcolonial perspective, Seland unfolds Philo's Alexandrian social world, as experienced under the Roman imperial presence. This approach opens exciting new reading strategies and vistas for Philo, wielded with consummate skill by the author. A highly stimulating read!"
—JAMES R. HARRISON, Distinguished Professor, Australian University College of Divinity

Reimagining Philo

Reimagining Philo

Philo of Alexandria Writing Back from the Empire

TORREY SELAND

CASCADE Books · Eugene, Oregon

REIMAGINING PHILO
Philo of Alexandria Writing Back from the Empire

Copyright © 2025 Torrey Seland. All rights reserved. Except for brief quotations in critical publications or reviews, no part of this book may be reproduced in any manner without prior written permission from the publisher. Write: Permissions, Wipf and Stock Publishers, 199 W. 8th Ave., Suite 3, Eugene, OR 97401.

Cascade Books
An Imprint of Wipf and Stock Publishers
199 W. 8th Ave., Suite 3
Eugene, OR 97401

www.wipfandstock.com

PAPERBACK ISBN: 979-8-3852-4503-1
HARDCOVER ISBN: 979-8-3852-4504-8
EBOOK ISBN: 979-8-3852-4505-5

Cataloguing-in-Publication data:

Names: Seland, Torrey, author.

Title: Reimagining Philo : Philo of Alexandria writing back from the empire / Torrey Seland.

Description: Eugene, OR: Cascade Books, 2025. | Includes bibliographical references and indexes.

Identifiers: ISBN 979-8-3852-4503-1 (paperback). | ISBN 979-8-3852-4504-8 (hardcover). | ISBN 979-8-3852-4505-5 (ebook).

Subjects: LCSH: Philo, of Alexandria—Criticism, interpretation, etc.

Classification: B689 S45 2025 (print). | B689 (epub).

Scripture quotations marked (NRSV) are from the New Revised Standard Version Bible © 1989 Division of Christian Education of the National Council of the Churches of Christ in the United States of America. Used by permission. All rights reserved worldwide.

09/22/25

Contents

Preface vii
Acknowledgments ix
Abbreviations xi

PART 1: PHILO AND HIS SOCIAL WORLD

1. Reimagining Philo of Alexandria: An Introduction 3
2. Philo and Roman Alexandria: Reimagining Philo's Setting and Social World 23
3. Philo's Writings: Reimagining Relevant Reading Strategies 47
4. Philo and Practical Politics: Reimagining Philo the Politician 73

PART 2: FOUR EXEMPLARY CASES

5. Reimagining Philo on the Diaspora, Metropolis, and Apoikia: A Case of Political Mimicry 97
6. Reimagining Philo and the Mysteries: A Case of Mimicry and Hybridity? 120
7. Reimagining Philo on the Clubs and Associations in Alexandria: A Case of Cultural Criticism Seen from a Postcolonial Perspective 143
8. Reimagining Philo's Views of Magic: A Study of Cultural Criticism as Antimagical Apologetic 164

Epilogue	199
Bibliography	205
Index of Modern Authors	231
Ancient Document Index	235

Preface

THIS VOLUME REPRESENTS AN experimental approach in multiple respects. The application of postcolonial categories, models, and perspectives to the study of Philo of Alexandria may elicit skepticism from certain readers: Is Philo not considered one of the most assimilated Jews of the Diaspora? Is he not to be characterized as the first-century Jew most influenced by Greco-Roman philosophies, an eclectic thinker significantly shaped by philosophical currents such as Platonism, Stoicism, and Epicurean philosophy, to name the most prominent?

The influences on Philo from contemporary philosophical traditions are undeniable. However, it would be erroneous to characterize Philo's primary intellectual profile solely through such a lens. Philo was also a devout adherent of Judaism, maintaining fidelity to his religious heritage. Consequently, he should be interpreted and understood as a Torah observant Jew, a scholar of Judaism, and an apologetic thinker and author of his era, engaging with diverse intellectual currents of his time.

However, some additional factors should be considered when attempting to understand Philo. He was also a politician. Residing in Alexandria during the significant upheavals of 38–39 CE and serving as a leader of a Jewish delegation traveling to Rome to negotiate the problematic conditions in Alexandria, he gained new insights into the superpower Rome, the *colonizing* Roman Empire. Inherent in these experiences are not only the tumultuous events of Alexandria but also the encounters with Emperor Gaius Caligula, who offered little more than scorn and abuse to the Jews when Philo met him to present the Jewish situation of Alexandria.

Therefore, this volume endeavors to examine the nature of the colonizing Roman Empire, its dealings with the Jewish issues of Alexandria, and the potential impact of these factors on Philo's perception of the Empire as a colonized Jew. A primary thesis posits that Philo's perspective was irrevocably altered after his sojourn in imperial Rome; he developed a new understanding of the empire, as well as the Jewish conditions and roles within that world.

Such a perspective may be considered one-sided. However, regarding him primarily as a philosopher, whose main impressions in Rome were limited to an expanded knowledge of the current philosophies of that city, is equally one-sided. Philo's experiences in Rome affected him in multiple ways, and this volume explores how his cultural criticism of the Roman Empire evolved after 38 CE.

Acknowledgments

THE PRESENT VOLUME CONSISTS of two parts. The first one deals with important aspects and issues of Philo's world, trying to depict and understand these in light of some post-colonial categories and perspectives. The second part consists of four studies, of which three have been previously published, but are here presented and used in a somewhat reworked form. The chapter on Philo and the mysteries has not been previously published, but is an extended version of an article, hopefully to be published later.

I am grateful to the following institutions for their permission to use the following publications of mine in the present volume:

"'Colony' and 'Metropolis' in Philo: Examples of Mimicry and Hybridity in Philo's Writing Back from the Empire?" In *Études Platoniciennes VII Philon d'Alexandrie. Les Belles Lettres* 7 (2010) 13–36. Used by permission.

"Philo as a Citizen: Homo Politicus." In *Reading Philo: A Handbook to Philo of Alexandria*, edited by Torrey Seland, 47–74. Grand Rapids: Eerdmans, 2014. Used by permission.

Establishment Violence in Philo & Luke: A Study of Non-Conformity to the Torah & Jewish Vigilante Reactions. Biblical Interpretation Series 15. Leiden: Brill, 1995. Used by permission.

"Philo and the Clubs and Associations of Alexandria." In *Voluntary Associations in the Graeco-Roman World*, edited by John S. Kloppenborg and Stephen G. Wilson, 110–27. London: Routledge, 1996. Used by permission.

"The Expository Use of the Balaam Figure in Philo's *De vita Mosis*." In *The Studia Philonica Annual* XXVIII. 2016 / *Studies in Hellenistic Judaism: Studies in Honor of David Runia*, edited by Greg E. Sterling, 321–348. Atlanta: SBL Press, 2016. Used by permission.

"Philo, Magic and Balaam: Neglected Aspects of Philo's Exposition of the Balaam Story." In *The New Testament and Early Christian Literature in Greco-Roman Context. Studies in Honor of David E. Aune*, edited by John Fotopoulos, 333–46. Supplements to Novum Testamentum 122. Leiden: Brill, 2006. Used by permission.

Abbreviations

As for abbreviations of Biblical, Philonic, and other Jewish Scriptures, I have used the abbreviations recommended by *The SBL Handbook of Style*, 124–30. 2nd ed. Atlanta: SBL Press, 2014.

For abbreviations of scholarly book series and journals, I have used the abbreviations recommended by *The SBL Handbook of Style*, 171–216. 2nd ed. Atlanta: SBL Press, 2014. All of these abbreviations used in footnotes are written in full in the Bibliography.

PART 1

Philo and His Social World

I

Reimagining Philo of Alexandria

An Introduction

AN INTRODUCTORY CASE

THE RELATIONS BETWEEN THE Jews and other peoples in Alexandria—including the imperial authorities—escalated into a series of severe conflicts in the period of 38–41 CE.[1] By then, the Jews had a history in Alexandria going back centuries,[2] and relations between the Jews, the native Egyptians, and the so-called Greeks, who represented more a political than an ethnic category, had witnessed some changing circumstances and various degrees of relationship over the years. However, after they had sailed in smooth waters, so to speak, during the first decades of the Common Era (CE), a storm arose in 38 CE, endangering the social conditions and lives of many Jews. To Philo of Alexandria, who had been living in the city all his life and was now approaching the age of sixty,[3] the events of 38–41 CE probably changed his view of the colonizing power,

---

1. For the description to follow, I draw on a former presentation of mine: See Seland, "Philo as a Citizen," 63–68.

2. See e.g., Smallwood, *Jews Under Roman Rule*, 220–35; Modrzejewski, *Jews of Egypt*; and Gambetti, "Jewish Community."

3. We do not know the exact dates of Philo's birth and death, but most scholars today seem to consider his lifetime spanning the years between ca. 20 BCE to ca. 50 CE.

the Roman Empire, forever. What happened in Alexandria has been described as a pogrom against the Jews.[4] The extensive details of the events involved cannot be addressed here; however, an outline of the conflicts as presented by Philo[5] can be sketched thus: In his treatise *In Flaccum*, Philo presents a positive portrayal of the local governor, Flaccus, albeit only to a certain extent (*Flacc.* 1–5). Flaccus, who benefited from the patronage of Tiberius Caesar, encountered an altered political landscape upon the death of Tiberius and the ascension of Gaius Caligula to the imperial throne. Gaius was not an individual from whom Flaccus could anticipate a favorable disposition; consequently, he recognized that his procuratorship was imperiled. According to Philo (*Flacc.* 16–24), Flaccus was drawn into a conspiracy against the Jews by three somewhat enigmatic figures named Dionysius, Lampo, and Isidorus. Subsequently, Flaccus, as per Philo's narrative, became antagonistic toward the Jews in Alexandria (*Flacc.* 24), initially discriminating against them in an indirect manner and later more overtly. One significant episode in this conflict occurred when King Agrippa (10 BCE–44 CE), the grandson of Herod the Great, arrived in Alexandria from Rome. Flaccus's advisors provoked his jealousy, asserting that the entire visit constituted an affront to the local governor. Flaccus, however, did not directly or publicly disparage Agrippa, but permitted what Philo terms "the mob" to defame the king. They mocked Agrippa, parading a mentally ill individual named Carabas, attired as a king, whom they hailed as Marin, Lord (*Flacc.* 36–39). Although Flaccus possessed the authority to intervene, he refrained from doing so, thus, in Philo's assessment, demonstrating his tacit approval of the demeaning scheme.

Thus, the mob proceeded to ravage Jewish synagogues. Some were burned, whereas others were desecrated by the installation of images of Gaius (*Flacc.* 41; *Legat.* 134). Still, Flaccus did nothing to prevent these acts, leading Philo to conclude that they were carried out, if not on the order of Flaccus, at least with his consent. Flaccus then, proceeded more openly against the Jews (*Flacc.* 53–54), issuing an edict in which, still according to Philo, he "denounced us as foreigners and aliens (ξένους καὶ ἐπήλυδας) and gave us no right of pleading our case but condemned us

---

4. Seland, "Philo as a Citizen," 65. For a criticism of this term, see Gambetti, "Attack."

5. "as presented by Philo" is the point here. A historical reconstruction of "what really happened" is difficult, and historians disagree on many details. See, for example, Gambetti, *Alexandrian Riots*; Harker, *Loyalty and Dissidence*; Smallwood, *Jews Under Roman Rule*; and more recently Schwartz, "Philo and Josephus"; and Gruen, "Caligula."

unjudged" (*Flacc.* 54). This represented "the destruction of our citizenship (τὴν τῆς ἡμετέρας πολιτείας ἀναίρεσιν), so that when our ancestral customs and our participation in political rights (μετουσίας πολιτικῶν), the sole mooring on which our life was secured, had been cut away, we might endure the worst misfortunes..."

The resulting devastation (*Flacc.* 55–96; *Legat.* 120–131) of the conditions of the Jews in Alexandria has been labeled the first Jewish ghetto in history.[6] The Jewish population, previously residing in all five sectors of the city, albeit predominantly in two sectors, was subsequently confined to a single sector. Their residences and workplaces were subject to damage and looting, and numerous individuals were impeded from pursuing their regular occupations. The resultant scarcity and overcrowding prompted many to attempt to escape; however, according to Philo, they were apprehended and executed, some by immolation, and others by crucifixion. The leadership of the Jewish community, comprising thirty-eight individuals, was arrested, divested of clothing, and subjected to lacerations with "scourges commonly used for the degradation of the vilest malefactors" (*Flacc.* 75, see 80). Jewish dwellings were searched for armaments, but according to Philo, none were discovered. Flaccus appears to have assumed a more active role in these events, and Philo interpreted the occurrences politically, particularly flagellation, as the most severe dishonoring of the Jewish population. The account of these Alexandrian conflicts preserved in Philo's *In Flaccum* concludes with the arrest, subsequent deportation, and execution of Flaccus, a narrative corroborated by other sources.

Upon the assumption of duties by the new governor, C. Virasius Pollio, the situation de-escalated. The Jewish population was likely permitted to return to their residences, resume their occupations, and reconsecrate their synagogues. However, tensions and instability persisted, prompting both sides of the conflict to appoint delegations to present their respective cases to Emperor Gaius Caligula in Rome.

Philo's work *De Legatione* is his account of these embassies sent to the emperor in Rome, representing both sides of the conflict: the Jews, and their opponents. The chronology of events in Rome is, at best, "uncertain and controversial."[7] According to Philo's accounts, the delegation initially received a brief audience with the emperor, who pledged to examine the

---

6. Smallwood, *Jews Under Roman Rule*.
7. Smallwood, *Jews Under Roman Rule*, 243.

case more thoroughly later. However, several months elapsed before the second hearing occurred. During this interim period, Gaius issued a decree for a statue of himself to be erected in the Jerusalem temple, an event Philo elaborates on in *Legat.* 184–198 and 207–348. When the meeting between the emperor and the embassies eventually transpired, the emperor granted them an audience in a garden, engaging in conversation while inspecting the grounds and a residence on the premises. The entire scenario demonstrated that Gaius exhibited minimal interest in their case: "In a sneering, snarling way he said: Are you the god-haters who do not believe me to be a god, a god acknowledged among all the other nations but not to be named by you?" (*Legat.* 353). The opposing delegation utilized the opportunity to defame the Jewish representatives. The Jewish contingent voiced their objections; however, as the group proceeded through the garden, the emperor continued his inspection of a residence, posing a limited number of inquiries while allocating insufficient time to consider their responses. The interaction with the emperor transpired in a manner that induced profound apprehension in Philo and his delegation, causing them to perceive a significant threat to their personal safety, expecting "nothing else but death" (*Legat.* 367). The emperor brought the meeting to an end, declaring that "they seem to me to be people unfortunate rather than wicked and to be foolish in refusing to believe that I have got the nature of a god" (*Legat.* 367).

Thus, the delegation to Rome failed to achieve positive results. Neither Philo nor Josephus documents any further ruling by the Emperor Gaius Caligula in this matter. Consequently, we leave Philo's narrative here[8] and proceed to a presentation of my focus and methodology in the present study.

MY FOCUS AND QUEST FOR METHODOLOGY

Through the application of postcolonial lenses, this research aims to examine Philo from novel perspectives. Specifically, it endeavors to reanalyze the works of the late Philo and reconsider our understanding of Philo in relation to certain aspects of his social milieu, as articulated in his conceptualization of specific cultural issues and values.

---

8. For a further presentation of these events of 38–41 CE, readers may consult these studies: Seland, "Philo as a Citizen," 63–72; Gambetti, *Alexandrian Riots*; and Harker, *Loyalty and Dissidence*. See also Chapter 4 below.

The central thesis of this volume posits that Philo's attitudes towards the Roman empire underwent a transformation in the 30s and 40s CE. As he observed the Romans' treatment of Jews in his native Alexandria and during his sojourn in Rome circa 38–42 CE, he began to express more overt criticism of the Romans in his writings. However, several of his earlier works also contain a negative disposition towards the Romans. To elucidate this reconstruction and reconceptualization from Philo's perspective, this study will employ insights derived from postcolonial theories and research.

Some Postcolonial Perspectives

Hence, the research and composition of this book do, in numerous aspects, constitute an exploration of novel and previously unexamined domains regarding the methodologies and perspectives to be applied in the current research on Philo. By employing analytical frameworks from postcolonial studies, this research endeavors to examine Philo from new perspectives. Accordingly, to a certain extent, this represents an exercise of conceptual reinterpretation.[9]

Postcolonial Perspectives

Consequently, this study will focus on the potential applications and challenges of employing postcolonial perspectives in the analysis of Philo of Alexandria. To the best of the present author's knowledge, postcolonial perspectives had not been utilized in any study of Philo prior to the publication of the author's article in 2011.[10] Hence, I would like to continue in the vein initiated in this article.

In Greco-Roman Alexandria, the Jewish population used various strategies to preserve their cultural identities. However, in numerous

---

9. Postcolonial concepts and perspectives have not been used much in studies of Philo. Niehoff, one of those not using such categories and perspectives, states, almost *en passant*, that "there is no sign that Philo is in principle opposed to the institution of the Roman Principate and that his views were shaped by his Jewish identity. To assume that Philo is 'anti-imperialist' is to apply modern values." Niehoff, *Philo of Alexandria*, 56. Although Niehoff employs the term "anti-imperialist" rather than "postcolonial" (or comparable terminology), her assertion remains subject to critique. If the application of "modern values" serves as the criterion for rejecting or accepting various viewpoints, it is probable that the majority of scholars would be subject to criticism.

10. See Seland, "'Colony' and 'Metropolis'" to be partly reused in Chapter 5 below.

instances, they were compelled to choose between adaptation and adoption. Philo may be characterized as an acculturated Jew, yet he was not assimilated. Acculturation entails a degree of adaptation to the dominant culture, whereas assimilation represents a more comprehensive process involving not only adaptation but also substantial adoption of local and prevalent cultural aspects to achieve maximal integration into the relevant society.[11]

Postcolonial studies, or what has been referred to above as the application of postcolonial perspectives, represent a relatively recent development in both biblical and related scholarly disciplines. According to Neil Lazarus, "Before the 1970s, there was no field of academic specialization that went by the name of 'post-colonial studies.'"[12] In earlier times, when a term like "postcolonial" (or "post-colonial") was applied, it was "a periodizing term, a historical and not an ideological concept."[13] However, since the early 1980s, this scene has completely changed: postcolonial perspectives are now utilized across a diverse range of academic disciplines, extending beyond literary and historical studies to encompass fields such as anthropology, political science, philosophy, economics, and geography, among others. In recent decades, particularly in the twenty-first century, studies focusing on Christian views of the empire and its role have been published routinely within biblical scholarship.[14] However, far from all studies of the empire are using postcolonial models and perspectives.[15] But postcolonial studies pertaining to the Bible, particularly to the New Testament, is experiencing rapid growth, constituting an extensive field that requires continuous monitoring and updating. Within New Testament studies, the application of postcolonial perspectives has predominantly focused on political issues, frequently manifesting in research categorized as studies or examinations of specific individuals(e.g.,

---

11. For a further discussion of this terminology and the social processes involved, see Seland, "'Conduct Yourselves Honorably.'"

12. Lazarus, "Introducing Postcolonial Studies," 1.

13. Lazarus, "Introducing Postcolonial Studies," 2.

14. For such a short period, there is no 'history of biblical postcolonial studies,' but a few review articles might be mentioned: Crowell, "Postcolonial Studies and the Hebrew Bible"; Diehl, "Anti-Imperial Rhetoric"; Diehl, "Empire and Epistles"; and Diehl, "'Babylon.'" The following study is also informative: Moore, "Paul After Empire."

15. Such studies are not at least triggered by several volumes edited by Richard A. Horsley: Horsley, ed., *Paul and Empire*; Horsley, ed., *Paul and Politics*; Horsley, *Paul and the Roman Imperial Order*; and Horsley, *In the Shadow of the Empire*. For postcolonial studies of Paul, see several articles in Stanley, ed., *Colonized Apostle*.

Jesus's, Paul's, etc.) and their perspectives and attitudes toward the Roman Empire. Studies of intertestamental literature, not to say of Josephus[16] or Philo,[17] applying political and/or postcolonial perspectives are still surprisingly few, and the whole project of applying postcolonial perspectives in New Testaments studies has not been universally accepted, but has faced some criticism.[18]

Postcolonial Reading as a Style of Inquiry

The predominant lack of postcolonial studies of political issues pertaining to imperial Roman governance and culture, as evidenced in numerous studies of Philo and in a multitude of New Testament studies, is regrettable. Cultural issues relevant to postcolonial analyses are far more diverse than perspectives on the emperor and his rule or on the emperor cult as religious and political phenomenon. Consequently, numerous other issues and aspects of cultural life warrant further consideration. New Testament studies as well as studies of Philo continue to progress in this regard. Accordingly, the case studies presented in Part 2 of this volume adopt a significantly broader cultural focus. Ashcroft, Griffiths, and Tiffin state in their introductory book on *Post-Colonial Studies*[19] that

> Post-colonialism (or often postcolonialism) deals with the effects of colonization on cultures and societies. As originally used by historians after the Second World War in terms such as the post-colonial state, 'post-colonial' had a clearly chronological meaning, designating the post-independence period. However, from the late 1970s the term has been used by literary and social critics to discuss the various cultural effects of colonization.

Consequently, a diverse range of colonization manifestations can be observed, from the colonization of a state to military occupation and the establishment of new settlements to what may be termed the colonization of cognition, which occurs when indoctrination and ideologically

---

16. Some info on Josephan studies is offered here: Barclay, "Empire Writes Back."

17. See Seland, "'Colony' and 'Metropolis,'" parts of which is to be used in Chapter 5 below.

18. For some recent criticisms, see e.g., Kim, *Christ and Caesar*; and McKnight and Modica, eds., *Jesus Is Lord*. However, their criticism is directed more at empire studies than postcolonial studies. See here also Stanley, ed., *Colonized Apostle*.

19. Ashcroft et al., *Post-Colonial Studies*, 168.

constrained curricula are implemented in educational institutions.[20] Furthermore, to illustrate how postcolonial perspectives can be applied to various settings, I might again exemplify this by drawing upon a recent application of postcolonial perspectives within biblical studies. Mongstad-Kvammen distinguishes between four main perspectives. The term "Bible" might, to some extent, be substituted with "Philo":[21]

> The first perspective is that texts within the Bible can be understood as reflecting opposition towards a suppressive regime. These texts are written from the perspective of the colonised. Thus, a postcolonial analysis of the Bible focuses on its historic role as an oppositional text.
>
> On the other hand, there are also texts within the Bible from the perspective of the colonizer. Hence, the second perspective is that the Bible can be read as a colonising text . . .
>
> A third perspective within postcolonial biblical scholarship is to examine the role the Bible has had in the Western colonisation of Africa, South America and Asia. . . .
>
> The fourth perspective is an analysis of western interpretations of the Bible and the social and political background for these interpretations. Central issues are: How has the omnipresence of the Western empires had an impact on Western scholars and their interpretations of the Bible?

Hence, we might say that postcolonial studies of the Bible can be applied from four different angles: two focusing on its history and two more contemporary and still under development. The first examines critical issues *in the texts*, that is, how the author (and/or the sources drawn upon) negotiates the author's social situation, whether political, social, economic, or otherwise. This is the view I am applying to Philo's works. The second angle concerns the fact that some biblical texts, especially in the Old Testament, deal with other peoples and their cultures in a colonizing way. The third, however, deals with how biblical texts *have been used* in more modern times, that is, in times of European colonization, asking what role the Bible has played for colonizers. A fact often pinpointed here and problematized is that the age of colonization was also a time of great missionary endeavors. Finally, the fourth angle focuses on how and in

---

20. Consult here Victor, *Colonial Education*.

21. Mongstad-Kvammen, *Toward a Postcolonial Reading*, 5–6. Mongstad-Kvammen here draws especially upon Segovia, *Decolonizing Biblical Studies*.

what ways the interpreters of the Bible, both then and now, were and are influenced by their imperial social settings and preferences.

The view of Mongstad-Kvammen referred to here is heavily influenced by F. F. Segovia. What I have called a postcolonial perspective, Segovia labels a "postcolonial optic" or a "lens."[22] He argues that a wider range of cultural issues and aspects must be considered. His first point is most relevant here:

> A first dimension of a postcolonial optic in biblical criticism involves an analysis of the texts of ancient Judaism and early Christianity that takes seriously into consideration their broader sociocultural contexts in the Near east and the Mediterranean Basin, respectively, in the light of an omnipresent, inescapable, and overwhelming sociopolitical reality—the reality of empire, of imperialism and colonialism.

Moreover, he conceptualizes the reality of empire as a structural phenomenon, primarily defined and manifested in terms of what he designates as "a primary binomial opposition": on one hand, a political, economic, and cultural center, and on the other hand, a number of peripheries (politically, economically, and culturally) subordinated to the center. This reality, he suggests, "is of such reach and such power that it inevitably affects and colors, directly or indirectly, the entire artistic production of center and margins, of dominant and subaltern, including their respective literary productions."[23] It should go without saying, that this view is not only applicable to biblical studies, but also to studies of ancient literature in general, and to Philo in particular. The shadow of the empire was felt—in various ways admittedly—in and by all colonized societies.

Hence a "postcolonial perspective" is not a strict method; R. S. Sugirtharajah says that "it is an instrument of method of analyzing situations where one social group dominated another," but he also uses labels as "a style of inquiry" or "a collection of critical and conceptual attitudes, an apt description would be to term it criticism."[24]

Returning to Philo and the present study, it is evident that the primary focus will be on the first approach, that is, on studying texts: examining how Philo addressed various issues and aspects of his

---

22. Segovia, *Decolonizing Biblical Studies*, 125–31.
23. Segovia, *Decolonizing Biblical Studies*, 126.
24. Sugirtharajah, "Charting the Aftermath," 9.

Greco-Roman social environment in Alexandria. The extent to which Philo can be characterized as a colonized author, responding from within the Empire, will be explored. This study analyzes Philo as a colonized author, investigating features that support this proposition through selected test cases. Concurrently, the research will demonstrate that the second approach must also be considered: Philo can, to some degree, be viewed as a colonizer in his attempts to persuade his opponents. These issues will be revisited in the subsequent test cases.

Postcolonialism and the Jewish Diaspora

Many of the most prominent postcolonial scholars, both within biblical studies and in the broader field of postcolonial studies, have been—and to a significant extent continue to be—individuals who have personally experienced colonization in their native countries, whether in South America, Africa, or Asia.[25] Not a few of them have migrated to Western countries, that is, to Europe or the United States, hence now living in a Diaspora situation. The impact of Diaspora conditions might thus be present in their personal lives as well as in their studies.[26]

Migration Studies

The phenomenon of the Diaspora has been a central focus in much recent postcolonial literature. This body of literature has frequently emphasized the question of migrant identities, the role of mimicry, and, particularly, the hybrid forms of resultant identities. Avtar Brah[27] has suggested that "at the heart of the notion of diaspora is the image of a journey. Yet not every journey can be understood as diaspora." Yet, at the same time, diasporic journeys are essentially about settling down, about putting roots "elsewhere."[28] John McLeod states that it is not possible to speak about one diaspora identity but of a plurality of identities.[29] Diaspora communities are composite communities. This phenomenon may

---

25. A brief look at the list of contributors to Sugirtharajah, ed., *Postcolonial Biblical Reader*, make this observation very pertinent.
26. Segovia, "Biblical Criticism and Postcolonial Studies."
27. Brah, *Cartographies*.
28. Brah, *Cartographies*, 182.
29. McLeod, *Beginning Postcolonialism*, 234–40.

be attributed to the transformative effects of migration on individuals' perspectives and cognitive processes. Furthermore, McLeod also says that "migration alters how migrants think about their home and host countries."[30] Home often becomes glorified or mystified, and after some time, it becomes a place of no return because it will then be a different place than that they once left. This may have several consequences, but to many the inevitable result is that the migrants and their descendants get a feeling of 'in-between,' and the result is a hybridization of their identity. They are no longer at home in their 'homeland,' and are not indigenous to their place of settlement. Hence it may come as no surprise that migration as such has come into focus.[31]

R. S. Sugirtharajah states in his book on *Postcolonial Criticism and Biblical Interpretation* that "in postcolonial discourse, diaspora has become a key word."[32] But in this kind of literature, *diaspora* also gains some further and more specified connotations:[33] "It is about the ambivalence and contradictions of being at home in many places, and among many peoples and many experiences . . . In postcolonial terms, diaspora signifies the formation of identities based on diversity and difference and is not necessarily seen in terms of reconnecting with a reverential notion of homeland."

Nevertheless, Sugirtharajah also sees this living in-between as challenging and inherent with possibilities. In this space of in-between something new may be created.

Regarding our comprehension of the circumstances surrounding the Egyptian Jewish Diaspora, perspectives from social science disciplines and contemporary postcolonial discourses may offer valuable insights. The phenomenon of migration played a crucial role in the formation of the Jewish Diaspora during the Greco-Roman period.[34] Concurrently, when applying postcolonial perspectives derived from literature focusing on modern societies, it becomes imperative to examine the potential unique aspects of the Egyptian Jewish Diaspora during Philo's era. With this consideration in mind, this study will narrow its focus to Philo in

---

30. McLeod, *Beginning Postcolonialism*, 241, with a reference to V. S. Naipaul.

31. Here see the overview provided in de Jonge, "Greek Migrant Literature"; see also Harland, ed., *Travel and Religion*.

32. Sugirtharajah, *Postcolonial Criticism and Biblical Interpretation*, 184.

33. Sugirtharajah, *Postcolonial Criticism and Biblical Interpretation*, 184.

34. See Lightstone, "Migration and Emergence."

order to address two significant issues prevalent in postcolonial research: mimicry and hybridity.

Diaspora Studies

Diaspora studies represent an emerging field of scholarly inquiry, still in its nascent stage; however, postcolonial perspectives have already demonstrated significant relevance for understanding the phenomenon of diaspora.[35] The phenomenon of the diaspora has been examined using various lenses. It is not only a historical issue or phenomenon but also a significant aspect of contemporary society. As such, it has been investigated from historical, sociological, and social-anthropological perspectives. Recently, postcolonial categories and perspectives have been extensively employed in the study of the diaspora.[36] While certain scholarly works on the history of the Jewish Diaspora do not delineate the conditions inherent in the concept of Diaspora, social science research emphasizes the definition and characterization of this phenomenon.

As stated above, Avtar Brah has suggested that "at the heart of the notion of diaspora is the image of a journey. Yet, not every journey can be understood as diaspora." However, at the same time, diasporic journeys are essentially about settling down, about putting roots elsewhere.[37] Hence, both the issues of settling down and home become important. On settling down in the Diaspora, home becomes ambiguous: "Where is home? On the one hand, 'home' is a mythic place of desire in the diasporic imagination. In this sense, it is a place of no return, even if it is possible to visit the geographical territory seen as the place of 'origin.' On the other hand, home is also the lived experience of locality."[38] This dual attitude to home is obviously present in a statement of Philo (*Flacc.* 46) where he states that Jerusalem is considered as their 'metropolis,' while at the same time, "yet those which are theirs by inheritance from their fathers, grandfathers, and ancestors even farther back, are in each case accounted by them to be their

---

35. See e.g., for brief introductions: Sugirtharajah, *Postcolonial Criticism and Biblical Interpretation*, 179–99 (Chap. 7: Hermeneutics in transit: Diaspora and interpretation); McLeod, *Beginning Postcolonialism*, 234–75; see also Ashcroft et al., *Post-Colonial Studies*, 61–62.

36. Knott and McLoughlin, eds., *Diasporas*.

37. Brah, *Cartographies*, 182.

38. Brah, *Cartographies*, 192.

fatherland (πατρίδας νομίσοντες) in which they were born and reared"[39] The significance of the concept of home is frequently associated with the process of integration in the new place of settlement; however, not all individuals immigrating to a diaspora possess an equivalent sense of connection to their homeland.[40] Brah states that

> The problematic of 'home' and belonging may be integral to the diasporic conditions, but how, when, and in what form questions surface, or how they are addressed, is specific to the history of a particular diaspora. Not all diasporas inscribe homing desire through a wish to return to a place of 'origin.' For some, such as the South Asian groups in Trinidad, cultural identification with the Asian subcontinent might by far be the most important element.[41]

Another scholar I would like to point to here is Robin Cohen.[42] He has endeavored to establish a typology of diaspora and proposes that one might categorize within it five distinct types of diaspora: victim diasporas, labor diasporas, trade diasporas, imperial diasporas, and cultural diasporas. While acknowledging that certain diasporic groups may exhibit dual or multiple forms or undergo changes in character over time, this typology is nevertheless considered highly relevant for a study of the ancient Jewish Diaspora. Cohen suggests that when examining some well-known diasporas, one might characterize them as follows:

the Jewish, African, and Armenian:	victim diasporas
the British:	imperial diasporas
the Indian:	labor diasporas
the Chinese and Lebanese:	trading diasporas
the Caribbean abroad:	a cultural diaspora[43]

Various types are observable in the context of ancient Jewish settlements in the Western Diaspora. Periods of forced exile resulted in victim diaspora populations, while subsequent eras, such as the Ptolemaic

39. On the question of the Diaspora Jews' relations to their homeland, see also Safrai, "Relations Between the Diaspora and the Land of Israel."
40. See here also my earlier work on acculturation and assimilation; Seland, "'Conduct Yourselves.'"
41. Brah, *Cartographies*, 193.
42. Cohen, *Global Diasporas*.
43. Cohen, *Global Diasporas*, x.

and Seleucid periods, as well as under Roman rule, witnessed imperial diasporas, including instances of enslavement. Additionally, migrations occurred due to potential trade and labor opportunities, alongside relocations motivated by diverse, often unspecified factors, including religious and cultural considerations. Archaeological evidence from papyri discovered at numerous Egyptian sites demonstrates the presence of Jews across multiple social strata and occupations within Egyptian society.[44]

Furthermore, drawing on the work of W. Safran,[45] Cohen can also suggest a more elaborate list of typical features of a diaspora. Most of these features, he suggests, should be present if we were to label any community a diaspora community: the persons concerned, or their ancestors, may have been dispersed; they might have a kind of collective memory about their homeland; they believe they are not fully integrated within their new host societies; their ancestral homeland is, to some extent, idealized, and they feel a certain commitment to it, perhaps even thinking that one day they might return. Cohen spells this out more in the ensuing list:[46]

Common Features of a Diaspora

1. Dispersal from an original homeland, often traumatically, to two or more foreign regions;
2. alternatively, the expansion from a homeland in search of work, in pursuit trade or to further colonial ambitions;
3. a collective memory and myth about the homeland, including its location, history and achievements;
4. an idealization of the putative ancestral home and a collective commitment to its maintenance, restoration, safety and prosperity, even to its creation;
5. the development of a return movement that gains collective approbation;
6. a strong ethnic group consciousness sustained over a long time and based on a sense of distinctiveness, a common history and the belief in a common fate;

---

44. See Tcherikover et al., eds., *Corpus Papyrorum Judaicarum*; and Horbury and Noy, ed., *Jewish Inscriptions*.
45. Safran, "Diasporas."
46. Cohen, *Global Diasporas*, 26.

7. a troubled relationship with host societies, suggesting a lack of acceptance at the least or the possibility that another calamity might befall the group;

8. a sense of empathy and solidarity with co-ethnic members in other countries of settlement; and

9. the possibility of a distinctive creative, enriching life in host countries with a tolerance for pluralism.

This list presents valuable insights; however, it should not be utilized as an absolute framework for determining the classification of a settlement as a diaspora community. Rather, it should be interpreted and employed as an inventory of social aspects frequently observed in diaspora communities, thereby facilitating a deeper understanding of the dynamics within these populations. It is important to note that certain factors may diminish in significance over time. For instance, first-generation individuals often exhibit a distinct attitude toward their homeland compared with subsequent generations. Additionally, the collective memory and myths surrounding the homeland tend to weaken over time, and relationships with host societies may evolve, among other factors.

Regarding Jewish Diasporas, however, there are two aspects that are not encompassed by this general model. Furthermore, these aspects are crucial for comprehending the attitudes of Diaspora Jews: the significant role of a common religious center and its location, and the role of its legitimating 'religious' literature. Jews asserted that they had only one temple, the Jerusalem temple—One God, and one temple (*CApion* 2:23; *Ant.* 3:5.4). Additionally, they possessed their religious literature, represented primarily by the Law (the Torah), the Prophets (the Nebi'im), and the Writings (the Ketuvi'im). The significance of these Scriptures is evident, among other factors, in their translation into Greek in the mid-second century BCE. Concurrently, this also demonstrates the transformation of descendants of immigrants, as the knowledge of Hebrew had diminished to such an extent that their Scriptures necessitated translation into Greek. The Jews were also granted several privileges by the Romans that facilitated the maintenance of connections with their homeland: the Romans permitted them to congregate in their synagogues on the Sabbath and to remit the tax to be transmitted to the temple in Jerusalem (*Legat.* 311–317; Josephus, *Ant.* 14:216; and 16:160–166), so that many undertook pilgrimages to Jerusalem (*Prov.* 2:64; *Spec.* 1:69–70). These aspects, along with some other privileges[47] provided by the Roman imperial leaders, influenced their lives as a diaspora people, even as a colonized diaspora people, and were pivotal in keeping their identity intact over the years, decades, and centuries.

My Specific Postcolonial Optics: Mimicry and Hybridity

The characterization by Borgen[48] concerning Philo: "A conqueror, on the verge of being conquered" is masterly formulated. A greater focus here, however, will be the extent to which Borgen's formulation is close to a postcolonial expression, even though a postcolonialist scholar would probably use other terms. The primary issues inherent in Borgen's formulation are that Philo appropriated certain aspects of contemporary culture, utilized them, expounded them, and transformed them to some extent, endeavoring to reinterpret his own cultural context in light of the other. A postcolonial scholar might ask: Does this not approximate what one could term mimicry, and might not the potential outcome (frequently, though not invariably) be what could be described as hybridity—that is, a transformed entity emerging from that which was mimicked, resulting in something similar to, yet distinct from, the original? In essence, Philo attempted to prevail by adopting and adapting certain aspects of the Greco-Roman world to ensure his survival as a colonized Jew. This study aims to utilize this characterization as a point of departure, while maintaining the postcolonial concepts of mimicry and hybridity as key terms in elucidating the process by which Philo adopted and adapted elements of Greco-Roman culture in his presentation of Judaism.

In numerous postcolonial literary works, the concepts of mimicry and hybridity elucidate several of the processes under consideration here. The term *mimicry* originates in the field of biology. This can denote the resemblance of one organism to another, conferring upon the mimicking organism certain advantages or protection from predators. Alternatively, in certain instances, it may be advantageous for a predator to resemble its prey; consequently, the metaphorical expression "a wolf in sheep's clothing" occasionally serves as an apt description.[49] In postcolonial and anti-imperial studies, the conceptualization of this term is significantly

47. E.g., the allowance to gather in their Synagogues and celebrate the Sabbath, etc. See here Rajak, "Was There a Roman Charter for Jews?"; Williams, ed., *Jews*; Rajak, "Was There a Roman Charter for the Jews?"; Trotter, "Going and Coming Home."

48. See Borgen, "Philo of Alexandria. A Critical," 150.

49. See more on this in Wickler et al., "Mimicry."

influenced by the framework established by Homi K. Bhabha.[50] To some extent, a colonizer might encourage the colonized subjects to mimic the colonizer, but there might also have evolved a strategy on the side of the colonized to survive, or even attempt to conquer the culture of the colonizer by enlarging on common aspects shared by the colonized and the colonizer. But it is often emphasized that "by adopting the colonizer's cultural habits, assumptions, institutions and values, the result is never a simple reproduction of those traits. Rather the result is a 'blurred copy' of the colonizer that can be quite threatening."[51] Here, the concept of hybridity enters. Hybridity denotes the new transcultural forms that may develop in the meeting of the colonizer and colonized, especially as the latter mimics the former. Mimicry may take many forms: linguistic, cultural, political, racial, and so on.[52] Furthermore, the concept of hybridity has also proved valuable in understanding the context of the diaspora.[53] Hence, I suggest that this is a relevant pair of concepts to apply when investigating Philo's reconstructions and conceptualization of aspects of his social world in his writing back from the Empire.

According to Homi K. Bhabha,[54] "colonial mimicry is the desire for a reformed, recognizable Other, as a subject of difference that is almost the same, but not quite. Which is to say, the discourse of mimicry is constructed around an ambivalence . . . Mimicry emerges as the representation of a difference that is itself a process of disavowal."

Reimagining Philo and the Empire: Postcolonial Perspectives?

Recently, the hermeneutic of postcolonialism has been increasingly applied in historical studies of antiquity, even including a few studies of Philo of Alexandria and his social world. However, if we exclude studies of the New Testament, there are still few studies available dealing with first-century CE Judaism. Yet, things are also changing here.[55] Dealing with Philo, the first study focusing on Philo in light of *mimicry* and

---

50. Bhabha, *Location*.
51. Ashcroft et al., *Post-Colonial Studies*, 125.
52. Ashcroft et al., *Post-Colonial Studies*, 108.
53. McLeod, *Beginning Postcolonialism*, 236–50.
54. Bhabha, *Location*, 122.
55. As examples from the last two decades, one might mention DeSilva, "Using the Master's Tools"; Barclay, "Empire Writes Back."

hybridity in postcolonial models' was probably an article published in 2010.[56]

However, two more recent studies of Paul the apostle and the Roman Empire have drawn upon Philo's works as relevant for understanding the world of Paul. Here, Goodenough's notion of "coded messages" or "hidden transcripts" has come into favor again. In light of the fact that a conception of 'coded messages' also may play a role in postcolonial understanding of how 'the Empire writes back' against its colonizers,[57] these studies are also interesting. James R. Harrison's study deals with *Paul and the Imperial Authorities at Thessalonica and Rome*, as the title of his study runs.[58] Harrison dealt with *Somn.* 2:83–92 and finds Goodenough's view relevant for understanding Rom 13.

Another scholar who has taken this debate a few steps further is Christoph Heilig.[59] He also provided a relevant discussion of several passages in Philo's *De Somniis*. I will have to return to this work. Finally, I might mention that Katell Berthelot has a presentation of postcolonial perspectives in her great book called *Jews and their Roman Rivals*.[60]

Working Hypothesis: Philo, the Colonized Colonizer, Writing Back from the Empire

The Jewish scholar Samuel Sandmel has said that "in Philo, the Greek philosophical tradition is absorbed to the maximum; on the other hand, Philo was as loyal to Judaism as any personality in the age with which we deal, and, indeed, as any personality in subsequent times."[61] According to Peder Borgen, however, Philo was a Jew on the border of being absorbed by the Greco-Roman culture:[62] "A conqueror, on the verge of being conquered."[63] This attitude, it must be added, was not—according to

---

56. Seland, "'Colony' and 'Metropolis.'" Related to Philo's world is also Victor, *Colonial Education*.

57. See Ashcroft et al., *Empire Writes Back*.

58. Harrison, *Paul and the Imperial Authorities*, esp. 28–34 and 305–8.

59. Heilig, *Hidden Criticism*.

60. See Berthelot, *Jews and Their Roman Rivals*, 19–22. See also Greenberg, "'Ἀγωνιάσωμεν.'"

61. Sandmel, *Judaism and Christian Beginnings*, 280.

62. See Borgen, "Philo of Alexandria," 150.

63. This characterization has been adopted by Runia, "How to Read Philo"; see esp. 190; see Runia, "Philo, Alexandrian and Jew," 16: "can hardly be bettered."

Borgen—because Philo compromised his Judaism or merged Hellenism and Judaism, but because of his efforts to conquer Greco-Roman culture by asserting that all the good to be found therein, in fact, stemmed from Judaism. "Consequently, being so extreme in his claims, he was on the verge of ending at the other extreme, that of being overcome by the ideas he wished to conquer. In this way, Philo's extreme form of particularism was on the point of ending up in a universalism where Jewish distinctiveness was in danger of being lost."[64] The question of universalism and particularism in Philo's ideology should not be considered as settled.[65]

The notion of Philo "writing back from the Empire" is influenced by the book of Ashcroft, Griffiths and Tiffin, *The Empire Writes Back*.[66] Much postcolonial literature has focused on how people and life in the colonies have been depicted, described, and evaluated in literature written from the center, from the imperial point of view; Ashcroft, Griffiths, and Tiffin try to broaden the horizon by focusing on how the Empire wrote back—that is, how writers in and from the colonies wrote. According to the view of these authors, which has not escaped criticism,[67] one might distinguish between three groups or stages of postcolonial literature: first, the "literate elite whose primary identification is with the colonizing power."[68] In our context, one might think about the Roman leaders Cicero, Pliny, and Tacitus as belonging to these elites. Second, there is the literature produced under imperial license or by "'natives' and 'outcasts' who have entered a privileged class endowed with values and time to write from their perspective."[69] Here one might think—with some qualifications—about the Jewish historian Josephus, who, though being a Jew, was brought to Rome by the (future) emperor and enjoyed the privileged life of being a member of the elite at the imperial center, writing historical works trying to explain to Romans the history of the Jews and what had really happened in Palestine before and during the great war of 66–70 CE.[70] Then lastly, we might have those being colonized and feeling oppressed, writing from the oppressed and colonized perspective. In my

---

64. Borgen, "Philo of Alexandria," 154.
65. See Birnbaum, *Place of Judaism*.
66. Ashcroft et al., *Empire Writes Back*.
67. McLeod, *Beginning Postcolonialism*, 28–32.
68. Ashcroft et al., *Empire Writes Back*, 5.
69. Ashcroft et al., *Empire Writes Back*, 5.
70. For a brief assessment of Josephus, see Feldman, "Josephus (PERSON)." For Josephus as writing back from the Empire, see Barclay, "Empire Writes Back."

opinion, but again, with some qualifications, we should read Philo from this last perspective; at least this is the perspective I would like to apply in my reading of some social issues as conceptualized by Philo. Hence, what follows is, to some extent, an experiment. In trying to look at some issues in the work of Philo through postcolonial lenses, I will try to see if Philo can stand out more clearly to us as a figure in Greco-Roman Alexandria. It is my hypothesis that he will.

My procedure is thus to present in Part 2 how Philo characterized and conceptualized some of the social phenomena of his time. These phenomena are presented and used as test cases for the aforementioned hypotheses. The four test cases to be given a closer investigation are Philo on the Jewish Diaspora, Metropolis, and Apoikia (Chapter 5); Philo and his Judaism conceptualized in terms of mystery (Chapter 6); Philo on the clubs and associations of his times (Chapter 7); and Philo on issues of magic (Chapter 8).

2

Philo and Roman Alexandria

Reimagining Philo's Social World and Locations

> "Egypt once held the sovereignty over many nations, but now is in slavery. The Macedonians in their day of success flourished so greatly that they held dominion over all the habitable world. But now they pay to the tax collectors the yearly tributes imposed by their masters."
>
> JOSEPH IN *ON JOSEPH* 135.

INTRODUCTION

THIS CHAPTER INTRODUCES SPECIFIC sociopolitical aspects and issues deemed pertinent to comprehending the discourse in subsequent chapters. Considering the focus on postcolonialism, this chapter will not present a comprehensive overview of all aspects of Philo's life, work, and thoughts, but rather will identify select social issues considered particularly relevant for the present volume, giving appropriate attention to recent representative research. Consequently, we first examine the key aspects of the Roman Empire in Alexandria. Subsequently, we briefly discuss certain issues pertaining to Philo's social position in Alexandria, addressing topics such as his familial background and status, education, and functions(s) in contemporary society.

At the time of Philo, Jews had a long history of being inhabitants of Egypt and Alexandria. Whether one traces their presence back to the sixth century BCE influx of Jewish refugees or the conquest of Alexander the Great in the fourth century, there had been Jews in Egypt for centuries. When Alexander established Alexandria in 331 BCE, the city's prospects also attracted Jews. In the first century CE, there was a large Jewish community.[1] Alexandria may have had some five hundred thousand to six hundred thousand inhabitants, and of these, some 180 thousand may have been Jewish.[2] Although living in Egypt, their ties with Jerusalem and Palestine remained strong, and communication was made easier by the fact that for about a hundred years (301–198 BCE), Palestine was one of the Ptolemies' foreign possessions.[3] There is no doubt that many Jews left Palestine for various reasons, such as trade opportunities, work emigration, or chances for adventure. There is no need to present the details of this history.[4] The main purpose is to pinpoint the various backgrounds of the Diaspora Jews of first-century CE Alexandria.

THE ROMAN EMPIRE IN PHILO'S ALEXANDRIA

How was the Roman Empire manifested in Alexandria during the time of Philo—that is, how was the Empire materialized in Philo's city? This perspective encompasses not only how the Empire organized its presence, but also how the inhabitants of Alexandria could experience on a daily basis that they were part of a greater Empire, being subjugated by the colonizing people originating from the other side of the Mediterranean Sea, despite Egypt's not being a colony in a strict legal sense.

1. For a fuller description of the history of the Jews in Egypt, consult these works: Tcherikover, *Hellenistic Civilization*; Smallwood, *Jews Under Roman Rule*; Modrzejewski, *Jews of Egypt*; Barclay, *Jews in the Mediterranean Diaspora*; and Schimanowski, *Juden und Nichtjuden*. The Introduction in volume 1 of Tcherikover et al., eds., *Corpus Papyrorum Judaicarum* is also indispensable.

2. Delia, "Population."

3. Borgen, "Judaism."

4. Borgen, "Judaism in Egypt"; Stern, "Jewish Diaspora"; and the more comprehensive presentation in Smallwood, *Jews Under Roman Rule*, 120–43.

Alexandria was founded by Alexander the Great in 331 BCE. During the reign of the Ptolemies, Alexandria became the principal city in the region and evolved into a cultural and educational center of Hellenism in Egypt. In 31 BCE, the Romans assumed control of Egypt, and the Roman presence became more firmly established in the city: "From now on, the resources of Egypt and Alexandria had to serve the needs and aims of the new rulers and their home base, Rome."[5] Therefore, this study focuses on the manifestation of the Roman imperial presence in Egypt, with an emphasis on Alexandria.

The Roman Imperial Presence

The Roman Empire was present throughout the world of Philo. It was heard, seen, and coped with every day of his life: at home, in the synagogue, and in the streets; in business, law, and politics. From the presence of the Roman prefect and his administration in Alexandria to the many statues and temples in the city, the Roman empire was inescapable.[6] F. Fernando Segovia, who is one of those who has worked much with postcolonial perspectives in biblical interpretation, has characterized the reality of empire, that is, its imperialism and colonialism, as "an omnipresent, inescapable, and overwhelming reality."[7] Concerning the nature of the Roman Empire, Greg Woolf writes:

> The Roman Empire invites metaphors. Ancients often used a biological analogy: each empire or state had its youth, maturity, and old age. One modern historian has used the metaphor of the vampire bat, seeing the empire as a means through which the Romans sucked the life out of peasants and slaves upon whose labor the empire depended. The Roman Empire does not seem to me much like an organic entity, unless it is an epidemic spreading throughout a host population feeding off the energies of the infected until it burns itself out. Analogies from natural science seem to capture the patterns of empire better. The

---

5. Borgen, "Judaism," 1068.
6. Moxnes, "'He Saw the City Was Full of Idols.'"
7. See Segovia, *Decolonizing Biblical Studies*, 125; see further Carter concerning the New Testament: "The Roman Empire provides the ever-present political, economic, societal, and religious framework and context for the New Testament's claims, language, structures, personnel and scenes." Carter, *Roman Empire*, 1. The same could be said about the relationship of the empire to the world of Philo.

Roman Empire was like a great tidal wave sweeping up more and more water before dissipating its energy.[8]

Over time, the Roman Empire incorporated diverse populations and their respective states, extending its dominion from Britain to the frontiers of the Parthian Empire. Despite its longevity and influence, the Roman Empire eventually faced an inevitable decline and ceased to exist as a dominant force, becoming relegated to the annals of history as a former imperial power. The onset of the seventh century CE marked a period of decline in the Roman Empire's influence and power. However, in the first century CE, it was a great and colonizing empire.[9]

Greek and Roman Colonization

Contemporary scholarship on these topics predominantly emphasizes that colonialism in antiquity underwent significant transformations from the Greek to the Roman period. Furthermore, notable changes and developments occurred within each of these epochs. The objective here is not to delve extensively into this historical narrative, but rather to elucidate certain salient structures that may prove beneficial in the interpretation of Philo.

In the *Greek world*, colonialization changed greatly from archaic to classical times and the heights of Hellenism, but some aspects remained.[10] Scholars emphasize that colonialism was not intended for trading purposes. That is a modern concept. However, in the main, the great Greek colonizing movement was caused by overpopulation and the desire for land.[11] Furthermore, it should be kept in mind that there were no states or nations at this time, no centers, but many independent cities, so-called city-states, many of which had several small colonies. During the archaic period, most colonies were founded by cities that decided to send out a group of colonists to settle elsewhere. These colonies were from the outset politically independent, "but maintained cultural and

---

8. Woolf, *Rome*, viii.

9. On the Roman colonies, see this review article: Isaac, "Roman Colonies (Judea)."

10. For the following paragraphs, see Seland, "'Colony' and 'Metropolis,'" 14–15. For a discussion of many aspects of early and later colonization, see Bradley and Wilson, eds., *Greek and Roman Colonization*; Malkin, "Postcolonial Concepts."

11. Graham, *Colony and Mother City*, 5.

particularly religious ties with the metropolis."[12] A city, which was itself a colony, could also be a mother city to its own colonies, thus being part of a wider network of cities and colonies. It thus belongs to the picture of ancient Greek colonialism that Greek overseas settlements could become increasingly imperialistic and colonialist in the modern sense.[13] During the Hellenistic era, the nature of political structures thus changed, and colonies were integrated into and within kingdoms. These tendencies increased during Roman times.

The history of Roman colonialization also comprises a long history, from Rome's conquest of Italy to much later in the life of the Roman Empire.[14] In early times, colonialization was part of a military strategy to secure the power of Rome; later, it was more a means of relieving poverty at Rome by allowing land redistribution, thus increasing Roman manpower for the emperors in their need to secure the empire, especially in the distant provinces and at the borders. Thus, at the time of the empire, the colonies were overwhelmingly of military character.[15] As such, these colonies also had several cultural purposes and impacts. According to E. T. Salmon, "the avowed aim of these imperial colonies was to provide discharged legionaries with farms and thereby integrate them into the civilian life of the Empire."[16] Furthermore, as they were peopled with former soldiers who received Roman citizenship, the colonies became culturally important promoters of Roman influence, such as the Latin language and the imperial cult, and they familiarized the natives with Roman customs and institutions. But Salmon also emphasizes their continuing strategic role for the emperors: "the ex-legionaries, or in some cases ex-praetorians, peopling the colonies were guardians of the Empire in whose armed forces they had so long served, and they could help the standing army either to repel invaders from without or to repress insurgents from within."[17] Accordingly, at the time of Philo, the military nature of the colonies and their imperialistic nature could not be denied.[18]

---

12. Wilson, "'Ideologies' of Greek Colonization," 25.

13. Wilson, "'Ideologies' of Greek Colonization," 51.

14. On the various phases of this history, see Patterson, "Colonization and Historiography."

15. See here especially Salmon, *Roman Colonization*, 145–57.

16. Salmon, *Roman Colonization*, 145.

17. Salmon, *Roman Colonization*, 150.

18. See also Levick, *Roman Colonies*, 184–94.

Imperialism: Ancient and Modern

Perhaps it is helpful to pause a little here and present a few comments on the similarities and dissimilarities between old and new empires. According to Craige B. Champion and Arthur M. Eckstein, the Romans had no word that corresponds to the modern term 'imperialism'; "the word 'imperialism' is itself a modern coinage, which only began to gain currency after 1870."[19] Imperialism was considered a phenomenon of international politics after the industrial revolution of the eighteenth and nineteenth centuries. However, in modern postcolonial research, this concept has been developed further.

To go further back, however, after Augustus, the goal of the Roman Empire was more one of maintenance and control than one of expansion. The period of imperial expansion was primarily from 200 to 50 BCE.[20] Scholars of antiquity have also discussed what kind of imperialism Roman imperialism was, and various models have been proposed, as modern postindustrial understanding does not work well in a Roman setting. Terms or models like 'hegemonian,' or ones based on military conquest, economic exploitation, territorial acquisition, or direct annexation have been proposed.[21] What these scholars agree on is that one must distinguish between modern and ancient imperialism. Hence, it is to be emphasized that 'imperialism's is to be used as an analytical term; remembering, however, that for some or perhaps most people, it is both an emotionally and ideologically loaded term. Champion and Eckstein thus define 'imperialism' as "an unequal power relationship between two states in which the dominant state exercises various forms of control, often forcibly, over the weaker state."[22] Rome did not have many colonies, and Egypt or Alexandria were not colonies, according to Roman law. 'Colony' may, however, also be considered an analytical or heuristic term, and here we might turn to modern postcolonial studies and their definitions of terms.

With the introduction of postcolonial perspectives in the research of, for example, the works of Philo, a variety of vocabulary has also been introduced. First, imperialism and colonialism must be distinguished.

19. Champion and Eckstein, "Introduction," 2.

20. Champion and Eckstein, "Introduction," 3.

21. See Champion and Eckstein, "Introduction: The Study of Roman Imperialism," 3. See also on p. 4 where they briefly discuss the metrocentric, the pericentric and the systemic forms of imperialism. On these see also Mattingly, *Imperialism, Power, and Identity*, 15–22.

22. Champion and Eckstein, "Introduction," 3.

Imperialism is an ideological concept which upholds the legitimacy of the economic and military control of someone over others.[23] Colonialism, on the other hand, represents a special form of imperialism, and usually denotes the establishment of a settlement of a group of people in a new location. In a way, one might say that 'colonization' in its traditional postindustrial way is now over; on the other hand, there are still various forms of imperialism at work in the world at large.[24] If one admits that there are various kinds of imperialism, such as cultural imperialism, economic imperialism, and media imperialism, then there are also various kinds of colonialization, such as ideological colonialization or colonialization of the mind.

There is also a certain ambiguity in the use of the label 'post(-)colonialism,' whether it is hyphenated or not. R. S. Sugirtharajah here influences my own use of this term.[25] He pinpoints that postcolonialism as a methodological category and as a critical practice has two aspects attached to it: "First, to analyze the diverse strategies by which the colonizers constructed images of the colonized; and second, to study how the colonized themselves made use of and went beyond many of those strategies in order to articulate their identity, self-worth and empowerment."[26] When studying Philo from a postcolonial perspective, my focus is on the latter: how he was writing back from the empire. Hence I use the unhyphenated version of 'postcolonialism' "as signifying a reactive resistance discourse of the colonized who critically interrogate dominant knowledge systems in order to recover the past."[27] In some ways and in many contexts, 'postcolonialism' can be substituted with 'anti-imperialism' as a better term.[28] As shown above, 'colonialism' changed its nature with the passing of Hellenistic times into the period of the Romans; hence, postcolonialism and anti-imperialism can be used interchangeably, but I prefer the former.

Roman Administration

Following Octavian's victory over Marcus Antonius at the Battle of Actium in 31 BCE, an event that precipitated the subsequent suicides of

23. Loomba, *Colonialism/Postcolonialism*, 7–8.
24. See here Ashcroft et al., *Post-Colonial Studies*, 6–36.
25. Sugirtharajah, "Charting the Aftermath," 7–32.
26. Sugirtharajah, "Charting the Aftermath," 7.
27. Sugirtharajah, "Charting the Aftermath," 8.
28. Segovia admits that he finds the expression "imperial-colonial" more and more attractive. Segovia, "Biblical Criticism and Postcolonial Studies," 154.

both Marcus Antonius and his consort Cleopatra, queen of Egypt, Octavian was able to assume control of and restructure Egypt as a Roman province.[29] Later, Octavian was remembered as Emperor Augustus, who ruled until 14 CE. In reorganizing Egypt, he also maintained direct influence over that province[30] by himself appointing the main Roman leader in the province. This means that the emperor wanted to keep a strong hand over Egypt, an emphasis that was further strengthened as the governor was not selected from the senatorial ranks but from the equestrian ranks, and as no members of the senatorial ranks or from the emperor's family were allowed to enter Egypt.[31]

From now on, Egypt was Roman, under Roman law and influence.[32] However, the Roman authorities preferred not to interfere with the local administrative structures more than they considered necessary, and we hear next to nothing about nationalistic protests against the occupying Roman colonial superpower, except about the Jews and their protests in the first century CE.[33] Furthermore, "the Roman administrative structures were minimal, keeping the costs of empire low, because most tasks were outsourced to local collaborators, and because the aims of Roman rule were equally minimal: to maintain order or at least to prevent outright conflict, to maintain the flow of taxes and military recruits, and to ensure continuing submission."[34]

However, Egypt was to become a central granary, supposed to deliver up to one-third of the grain required by the Rome population. Hence, it became extremely important to that city. Therefore, close control was considered relevant and necessary. The province was divided into three, later four, *epistrategoi*, which were administered by Roman officials

---

29. For a history of the last years of the Ptolemaic kingdom, see Hölbl, *History of the Ptolemaic Empire*, 179–256.

30. On the concept and phenomenon of *provincia*, see Lintott, *Imperium Romanum*, 22–32.

31. Lintott, *Imperium Romanum*, 126–28; Brown, "Egypt, History of (Greco-Roman Period)," 372.

32. Various issues of Roman Egypt are dealt with in this important handbook: Riggs, ed., *Oxford Handbook of Roman Egypt*. See also Mattingly, *Imperialism, Power, and Identity*; Garnsey and Saller, *Roman Empire*; Champion, ed., *Roman Imperialism*; Lewis, *Life in Egypt*, and general presentations of the history of the Roman Empire, such as, e.g., Woolf, *Rome*.

33. See Ando, "Administration of the Provinces."

34. Morley, *Roman Empire*, 59.

appointed directly by the emperor.[35] A more important administrative unit was the several more *nomoi*, each administered by *strategoi* or governors, and several other Roman officials. The emperor closely supervised their work by keeping officials in office for just a few years. Three Greek cities were given somewhat greater autonomy: Alexandria, Naukratis, and Ptolemais Hermou; however, it was a significant feature of imperial rule that the *boule* (council) of Alexandria was banned.

The Prefect

The *Prefect* of Egypt (*praefectus Alexandreae et Aegypti*) thus had his powers delegated directly from the emperor: "Egypt was probably the most populous province in the empire, and contributed more than any other to the revenues, partly in grain that provided much of Rome's essential food, and its exploitation was a public enterprise of which the prefect was the managing director."[36] He was the military leader too,[37] in command of three legions; he also had unlimited power in the civilian sector. He could create and issue *edicts* and had supreme judicial powers, including the authority to issue capital punishment.[38] He was also responsible for levying various taxes, and for corn deliveries from Egypt. His place of residence was located in Alexandria; hence, imperial power was made-visible in Alexandria by the presence of both the prefect, his administration, and all the other social aspects that belonged to the presence of such an authority as the physical buildings, the almost court-like personnel, as well as the feasts, parties, and other social gatherings associated with the presence of the Prefect in the city. For Alexandria's citizens, aspects such as taxes and educational ideals were also important in assessing the nature of imperial power.

Taxes

Colonizing power is often felt most intensively through the taxes levied on the population.[39] According to Andrea Jördens, "Most of the officials

---

35. Here I rely upon the summarizing descriptions in Herklotz, "Aegypto Capta."
36. Brunt, "Administrators," 124.
37. Brunt, "Administrators," 131–32.
38. Brunt, "Administrators," 132–36.
39. See Ando, "Administration of the Provinces," 185–88.

in the province of Egypt worked in the financial sector, specifically with the collection and management of state income."[40] In the first decades of Roman occupation, the collection of certain taxes was also farmed out for a specific number of years to local tax collectors by way of auctions.[41] In addition to the cash to be paid regularly as a *tributum capitis*, Jördens lists a *tributum soli* imposed by the state, which for Egypt consisted of the vast grain supplies earmarked for Rome. Furthermore, taxes were paid to the emperor on special occasions, and many other taxes were imposed on income of various kinds, as were fees to be paid for certain services, such as for legal procedures. A certain poll tax, called *laographia*, was levied on all male Egyptians aged fourteen to sixty-two years; privileged groups could, however, receive reduced rates or even be completely exempt (see below). Inability to pay the required taxes could result in imprisonment. We also have evidence that some tried to escape paying taxes by fleeing Egypt, as some papyri from there demonstrate.[42]

Educational Issues

In investigations of colonialism in modern times, education is sometimes emphasized as a central means of colonizing the minds of the conquered people. Royce M. Victor says that "colonizers used education as one of the major devices to propagate the cultural values, ethos and lifestyle of the colonizer. Education also has become a major way of eliminating indigenous elements of civilization, including language, social values, and religion."[43] However, this understanding should not be rapidly transferred to the Roman world. Behind such a statement may be certain presuppositions of what colonialism involved that should not be transferred to the ancient world and the mentality of the Roman colonizers en bloc. Neville Morley states that "the belief of later historians, especially in nineteenth-century Britain, that Roman imperialism was driven by a mission to bring civilization to the unenlightened barbarians was entirely misplaced."[44] Hence, some reservations in applying ideals from later colonization might be warranted. Nevertheless, it is not to be doubted

40. Jördens, "Government, Taxation and Law," 59.
41. For an informative discussion of these procedures, see Llewelyn, "Tax Collection and the τελῶναι of the New Testament," 47–76. Jördens, "Government, taxation," 59.
42. Llewelyn, "Flight from Personal Obligations."
43. Victor, *Colonial Education*, 2.
44. See Morley, *Roman Empire*, 59, and esp. pp. 102–27.

that education played a significant role in socializing the youth in ancient Alexandria as well as in other cities, and Philo provides evidence for the view that education also played a political role in Alexandria. However, scholars are not unanimous in assessing the specific political role that education played in that city at the time of Philo.

Considering the types of education relevant in Alexandria, however, there was rather little change or development in the Greek educational system from Alexander the Great to the first century CE, and when the Romans arrived on the scene they to a large extent took over the Greek system, or let it continue in cities like Alexandria.[45] In its initial phase, education was primarily private. Further, education was mainly a possibility for children of rich families, and thus a prerogative of elite members in the cities. However, those given the privilege of attending gymnasial education would also be more exposed to the cultural values that this education represented. Considering postcolonial perspectives, it is important to note that the Romans distinguished between two primary groups of people in Alexandria: Greek citizens and Egyptians. This distinction had socioeconomic consequences, as Egyptians had to pay much heavier taxes than the others. The place of Jews in this system has been hotly debated,[46] but the distinction seems to have played a major role in the riots of 38 and 41 CE. A central prerequisite of being a Greek citizen was the education given in gymnasia: only those having such education were able to obtain Greek citizenship.[47] Thus, one of the means of social mobility attractive to Jews was extended education. It is a common opinion in recent research that Jews in general did not have Greek citizenship, nor did they all receive education in the gymnasia, but that they had a *politeuma* of their own. However, the riots of 38 and 41 CE and the later *Letter of Claudius* clearly point to the efforts of at least some Jews to attain such education.[48] On the one hand, if Philo's passages

---

45. See Marrou, *History of Education*. But see now also some modifying comments in Koskenniemi, "Philo and Classical Education."

46. See Tcherikover et al., eds., *Corpus Papyrorum Judaicarum*, vol. 2, no. 153; Tcherikover, *Hellenistic Civilization*, 311–18; Tcherikover, "Decline of the Jewish Diaspora," 4–8; and Borgen, "Philo of Alexandria," 108–13.

47. Citizens of a Greek city who had the right to participate in the general assembly, to elect and be elected to public office, and who (had) received their education in philosophy and athletics in a gymnasion, were the only ones considered "Greek." Tcherikover, "Decline of the Jewish Diaspora," 4.

48. See Tcherikover et al., eds., *Corpus Papyrorum Judaicarum*, vol. 2, no. 153; Tcherikover, *Hellenistic Civilization*, 311–18; and Tcherikover, "Decline of the Jewish

discussing such education[49] are to be taken autobiographically,[50] they are at least witnesses to the fact that some received such education without becoming apostates. However, Philo is also keen to emphasize Jews' own educational institutions as gatherings in their synagogues (*Spec.* 2:62–63; *Praem.* 66). On the other hand, there are also some passages in Philo's works revealing that Greco-Roman gymnasial education could be misused, an abuse exemplified by receiving education for the sake of the opportunities it gave to acquire greater social mobility. In *Leg.* 3:164–167 he rebukes those "who pursued education from a desire of an office under our rulers" (*Leg.* 3:167):

> The day is a symbol of light, and the light of the soul is training (παιδεία). Many, then, have acquired the lights in the soul for night and darkness, not for day and light; all elementary lessons (τὰ προπαιδεύματα πάντα) for example, what is called school-learning (τὰ ἐγκύκλια λεγόμενα) and philosophy itself when pursued with no motive higher than parading their superiority, or from desire of an office under our rulers. But the man of worthy aims sets himself to acquire day for the sake of day, light for the sake of light, the beautiful for the sake of beautiful alone, not for the sake of something else.

Thus, Philo most probably also saw a danger of apostasy in acquiring such education, not least due to influences from the imperial colonial powers and the students' wish to assimilate and advance their position in the political life of the city.[51] This interpretation is further made plausible

---

Diaspora." For another view, see Kasher, *Jews in Hellenistic and Roman Egypt*, 233ff, 310ff; Borgen, "Philo of Alexandria," 111, sums up the general opinion thus: "It is probable that some Jews in Alexandria were content with the status quo under which they were permitted to live according to their own laws and customs as a separate *politeuma* of its own. Furthermore, it is certain that others coveted Greek citizenship for the sake of higher social and political prestige and of economic advantages." See also the discussion in Koskenniemi, "Philo and Classical Education."

49. See esp. *Congr.* 74–80.

50. Such an interpretation is rejected in Wolfson, *Philo* 1:81, who thinks they may not have been derived from personal experiences of the Greco-Roman gymnasia, but from comparable Jewish education. Mendelson, *Secular Education*, 26, however, gives voice to the common opinion when he says that "In the absence of compelling evidence to the contrary, then, we should accept Philo's first-person statements concerning his education as we would those of other classical authors." See also Mendelson, "Reappraisal of Wolfson's Method"; and Borgen, "Philo of Alexandria," 115–17.

51. See further on these issues: Borgen, *Bread from Heaven*, 123–27; Mendelson, *Secular Education*, 30–31. Philo here thus seems to confirm the view of Royce M. Victor, quoted above.

by *Vita Mosis* 1:31, in which Philo strongly rebukes those who "look down on their relations and friends and set at naught the laws under which they were born and bred, and subvert the ancestral customs to which no blame can justly attach, by adopting different modes of life, and, in their contentment with the present, lose all memory of the past" (cf. *Spec.* 2:18–19). Considering the context of this passage, we can see that these are those who strive for socioeconomic mobility. Wolfson characterizes them as those led to apostasy "by the vulgar delusion of social ambition."[52] These issues illustrate in very vivid and realistic ways the colonizing role gymnasial education could play in a city such as the colonized Alexandria.[53] It was not only a way of introducing Greek ideas and ideals supported by the Roman colonizers, but it was also a way of trying to uphold, stabilize, and thus promote social distinctions and differences in the city.

PHILO IN ALEXANDRIA

The focus of this volume is not on the work and thought of Philo at large. This book aims at a much lesser area, namely some aspects of the social world of Alexandria as described by Philo; that is, we will discuss and present how Philo perceived some social issues and institutions of his time and place. By social issues and institutions, we mean how we, relying on his works, can describe how he considered the Diaspora situation of his community. In Part 2 we will discuss how he considered e.g., the mysteries and mystery terminology as relevant for his descriptions of his Judaism; how he considered social institutions such as the clubs and associations of his city, and how to cope with their gatherings; how he as a Jew considered and evaluated magic and magicians, and so forth. All of these issues were important aspects of the city life of Alexandria at Philo's

---

52. See his vivid description in *Philo*, 1:77: "Wealth in the Alexandrian Jewish community was derived from the non-Jewish environment through contacts with heathens. Such contacts with heathens thus became financial assets, and financial assets naturally became marks of a delusive social distinction, and the delusion of social distinction, in turn, led to snobbishness, obsequiousness, self-effacement, aping, simulation, pretense, and ultimately to a begging for permission to join whatever one had to join to become a heathen. This, we imagine, was the progressive pilgrimage of certain Alexandrian Jews from a seat in the row of the synagogue to a place at the tail end of the mystery processions of the heathen." Feldman, "Orthodoxy," 227, seems to accept Wolfson's categorization, though emphasizing that we do not know many apostates by name.

53. See here Koskenniemi, "Philo and Classical Education," 112–21. See also Victor, *Colonial Education* for the situation in Judea in the second century BCE.

time, and we presume that understanding how he perceived these issues will help us to understand more about Philo himself, how he perceived what it was to live as a Jew in a pluralistic city like Alexandria, and how he, as a colonized Jew, was able to cope with the Roman colonizers and their culture. On a larger scale, it might also help us understand what issues early Christians had to cope with as the new faith made its way out into the Mediterranean world of the first century CE. However, this latter focus is outside the main goals of the present study.

Philo's Social Location

We know a few aspects of Philo's personal life.[54] However, our knowledge is fairly good compared to what we know about other individuals from approximately the same period. The dates of his birth and death, however, cannot be given with exactitude. Most probably, his lifetime spanned the period between 20–15 BCE and 45–50 CE, but we have no solid indicators to go by to be more exact. In other words, he was a contemporary of both Jesus of Nazareth and Paul the apostle. However, there is little reason to presume that Philo and Paul knew each other, or that either had knowledge of the writings now associated with the other. Paul does not mention Philo, nor does any serious scholar today suggest that Philo mentions the Christians in any of his writings.[55] This does not mean that there was no contact between the tendencies and traditions found in Philo's works and those of early Christian literature. On the contrary, several scholars have used Philo's writings to illuminate theological conceptions and traditions found in or mirrored in the writings of Christians, and to explain debates and conflicts witnessed in the New Testament.[56] Hence, in addition to being an interesting personage by himself and a representative of Diaspora Judaism and the social life of the Jews in the Diaspora, he can also shed rewarding light for students of the New Testament and early Christianity.[57]

---

54. See Schwartz, "Philo, His Family and His Times."

55. See Colson et al., eds. and trans., in *Philo*, vol. 9 (LCL), 106–8.

56. See, e.g., the studies represented by these volumes: Borgen, *Early Christianity and Hellenistic Judaism*; Borgen, *Gospel of John*. See now also the work of his student, Bekken: Bekken, *Lawsuit Motif*; and the review articles by Siegert, "Philo and the New Testament"; and Bekken, "Philo's Relevance."

57. Concerning the reception of Philo in the first three centuries CE, see Runia, *Philo in Early Christian Literature*, and several chapters in Friesen et al., eds, *Reception of Philo*.

Philo's Socioeconomic Location

Philo most probably belonged to a rich and influential family in Alexandria. He thus belonged to the elite segment of the Alexandrian Jewish community. His brother Alexander Lysimachus was an "alabarch," perhaps an officer concerned with the administration of collecting taxes and customs.[58] Josephus says that Alexander "surpassed all his fellow citizens both in ancestry and in wealth" (*Ant.* 20:100). Josephus also tells us that Alexander once lent a large amount of money to Agrippa, or, to be more correct, to Agrippa's wife, Cypros, because he did not trust Agrippa (*Ant.* 18:159). Alexander also disclosed his wealth and demonstrated his reverence for the temple in Jerusalem by clothing nine of its ten gates with gold and silver (*B.J.* 5:205). Alexander's position in Alexandria was also expressed in his close relationship with Claudius and his mother, Antonia. Gaius Caligula, however, had him thrown in jail, but Claudius released him when he became emperor (*Ant.* 19:276). One of Alexander's sons, Marcus Julius Alexander, married Berenice, the daughter of Agrippa (*Ant.* 19:277). However, another son is mentioned more often in our sources, namely, Tiberius Julius Alexander.[59] According to Josephus, Tiberius left Judaism (*Ant.* 20:100)[60] and had a great career in the service of the Romans. Circa 46-48 CE, he was procurator of Judea (*Ant.* 20:100; *B.J.* 2:220), and ca. 66-70 CE, he was a prefect of Egypt (cf. *B.J.* 2:309, 492-98). He also participated actively in the campaigns against Jerusalem in 66-70 CE (*B.J.* 5:45-46; 6:237).

Thus, Philo undoubtedly belonged to the elite segment of the Jewish Alexandrian community.[61] What we do not know is how he, as a grownup, continued to relate to his wealthy family and how this relationship influenced his view of and attitude toward the Roman-colonizing powers in Alexandria. Feldman has suggested that "it would seem *a priori*

---

58. See the comments in Josephus (Loeb Classical Library) to *Antinquities* 18:259.

59. On Tiberius, see Turner, "Tiberius Iulius Alexander"; concerning his father, see especially Evans, "Alexander the Alabarch."

60. This interpretation of Josephus's statement has, however, recently been contested: Schimanowski, "Die jüdische Integration,"; and Schimanowski, *Juden und Nichtjuden*, 135-39. However, Wilson, *Leaving the Fold*, 29-33, characterizes him as a defector, one who left his Judaism. Similar interpretations in Sandelin, "Jews and Alien Practices," 15-20.

61. See also the summary in Seland, *Establishment Violence*, 82-93; Borgen, *Philo of Alexandria, An Exegete*, 14-26; and especially Schwartz, "Philo, His Family and His Times." Schimanowski seems to presuppose that Philo even had Roman citizenship: Schimanowski, *Juden und Nichtjuden*, 121-23.

unlikely that P(hilo) should be anti-Roman when his family was so close to the Romans."[62] This may not be easy to prove, and we should remind ourselves that many families include members who choose patterns of life and opinions that differ from the family's main currents of thought, not least when it comes to politics. Hence, I do not consider it impossible for Philo to have lived and thought somewhat outside of the ideals of his wealthy Roman-serving family.

Philo must, however, for at least some period, have had close contact with his nephew Tiberius. It is generally accepted in recent research that Tiberius figures directly or indirectly as a debater with his uncle in two of Philo's writings.[63] In *De Providentia*, they discuss whether the world is governed by the providence of God, an issue that Tiberius doubts. In *De Animalibus*[64] the topic set up for discussion is "Whether Animals have Reason."

To be rich at this time and in this world also implied power, and power meant influence. However, we do not know precisely how and where Philo fits into these structures; he might have been a solitary scholar caring little for the turmoil of both social and political life, or he might have been an active politician for many years. Many details will probably remain hidden in darkness. However, we might presume that he lived relatively close to influential people in the city and participated in some of their 'influence.' Hence, he may be characterized as an 'influencer' in his time and social settings. His extensive literary production corroborates this view.

Philo's Sociocultural Location

The Jewish community members in Alexandria were probably situated along various stages of the social ladder regarding wealth. Still, few belonged to elite groups holding positions in political or religious institutions outside of their own *politeuma* structures. I once suggested that the Jewish communities in the Diaspora, in some respects, represented a community type called the 'pariah community.'[65] Now, I don't think this

---

62. See Feldman, "Scholarship on Philo and Josephus (1937–1959)," 285. I owe this reference to Nikiprowetzky, *Le Commentaire*, 218.

63. Borgen, "Philo of Alexandria," 249–50; Colson et al., eds. and trans., *Philo*, vol. 9 (LCL), 447–53.

64. See Terian, "Critical Introduction."

65. Seland, *Establishment Violence*, 89–93.

is a pertinent description, not least because of the negative connotations often associated with the term 'pariah.' The Jews of Alexandria, however, represented a minority, although they might have constituted a considerable part of the population in cities such as Alexandria. The presence of Jews in several parts of the Roman world antedated that Empire by centuries; hence, during our period, they had long been a part of the economic and social system of the Diaspora. Nevertheless, in the Letter of Claudius to the Alexandrians (41 CE) he stated that the Jews were living in a city "not their own."[66] Hence, Roman authorities did not consider them indigenous to their host country. Philo relates that in Alexandria, there were five quarters, named after the first letters of the alphabet: "Two of these are called Jewish because most of the Jews inhabit them" (*Flacc.* 55). We also know that most Jews in Rome lived in a particular sector of the city (cf. *Legat.* 155). However, these did not make up ghettos, as Jews also resided in other parts of the city. In some cities, many Jews gathered according to professional activities, as was usual in preindustrial cities.

Furthermore, and very important for our focus, the Jews had a sociopolitical organization, a *politeuma*, acknowledged by the Roman authorities. It was an institution with its own constitution and administration, and through this they could perform certain in-group functions, and probably also some of a judicial character. However, these were limited, as the Jews lacked the right to impose capital punishment, even though the Torah prescribes such measures in several cases.[67] The existence of such a *politeuma* is a view that is denied or questioned by some scholars today,[68] but it still has several followers and strong support.[69] However, in the agonistic culture of the first-century Mediterranean world, the character of their Jewish community as a minority community

---

66. For the text of this letter, see Bell, ed., *Jews and Christians in Egypt*; and Tcherikover et al., eds., *Corpus Papyrorum Judaicarum*, vol. 2, no. 153.

67. That the Jews did not have the rights of capital punishment is hardly to be doubted. See the brief discussion in Seland, *Establishment Violence*, 17-42.

68. See Feldman, *Jew and Gentile*, 92; Mélèze-Modrzejewski, "How to Be a Greek," 77-78; Pearce, "Jerusalem as 'Mother-City'"; Barclay, *Jews in the Mediterranean Diaspora*, 43, note 73; 64-65. Harland takes it in many cases to be a term for association, not a 'public' institution as argued by Smallwood (see next footnote); see Harland, *Dynamics of Identity*, 41-42.

69. Smallwood, *Jews Under Roman Rule*, 225-27; Kasher, *Jews in Hellenistic and Roman Egypt*, 233-61; Borgen, "Judaism"; Schwartz, "Philo, His Family and His Times" 16-17; Harker, *Loyalty and Dissidence*, 212-20; McGlynn, "Politeuma."

and the limitations of their jurisdiction are important for understanding Philo's social-cultural location and many parts of his works.

Philo's attitudes toward several parts of Alexandria's Greco-Roman cultural institutions seem to have been relatively open and investigative. According to some sayings in his writings, he knew through personal experience various forms of cultural activities in the city. He wrote about wrestling competitions and boxing contents (*Prob.* 26), horse races (cf. Eusebius, *Praep. ev.* 7:14, 58 [Hypothetica]), and it is evident that Philo frequented the theater and attended concerts (*Ebr.* 177; *Prob.* 141), and even participated in symposia and club gatherings (*Leg.* 3:155–56).[70] Hence he moved freely in the upper-class social and leisure activities of his time.

Philo's Educational Location

His view of encyclical education illustrates Philo's attitude toward Greco-Roman culture and its encyclia paideia.[71] It seems to be Philo's view that these institutions represent an issue of "adiaphora"; they are in and by themselves neither only good nor bad (cf. *Congr.* 35; *Fug.* 212–213). But they are, according to Philo, only preliminary to the study of the real and genuine philosophy represented by the Law, i.e., by Judaism.

Several sayings in his works suggest that Philo himself had undergone encyclical education (*Congr.* 74–76). However, it is unclear in what setting he received such an education.[72] Wolfson[73] believes that Jews had such educational institutions of their own but surmises that Philo's sayings are perhaps not related to actual education. Kasher[74] argues that Jews did not at all want to receive Greco-Roman education of the encyclia, since such participation would represent apostasy. The disagreement in recent research on this question is due to the case that the education of the encyclia was necessary to obtain citizenship rights, and it is not entirely clear if Jews enjoyed these rights at the time of Philo. Presupposing

---

70. See Borgen, "'Yes,' 'No,' 'How Far?,'" 27; Seland, "Philo and the Clubs," 124.

71. Kasher, "Jewish Attitude"; Mendelson, *Secular Education*; Kasher, "Jews in Hellenistic and Roman Egypt."

72. Sterling, "'Thus Are Israel,'" 17, note 79, says that "Given Philo's ability to write sophisticated Greek, his firsthand knowledge of Greek literature, and his philosophical knowledge, I am certain that he received his education in the gymnasium."

73. Wolfson, *Philo* 1:79–81.

74. Kasher, "Jews in Hellenistic and Roman Egypt."

that such education, however, was accessible to some Jews, at least to the rich, and due to the fairly good knowledge of these institutions evidenced in the writings of Philo, it is the opinion of many scholars today that he received his education in a Greco-Roman cultural setting, i.e., in a gymnasium.[75] Hence, it is no surprise that Philo's writings demonstrate that he had a pretty good knowledge of Greco-Roman culture, not least of the various philosophers and their ideas. The influence from the works of Plato and from Pythagoreans and Stoics is especially prominent in his works. His quotations of and allusions to various philosophers are numerous.[76]

Philo's Professional Location

In *Ant.* 18:259 Josephus comments on the Alexandrian delegation that was sent to Rome to intercede for the Jews with the Emperor Gaius Caligula. Josephus here presents Philo as "a man held in the highest honor, brother of Alexander the alabarch, and no novice in philosophy." It is also evident from Philo's writings that he held official positions in the city, and the story of the delegation to Rome is described in his *De Legatione*. However, it is not clear what kind of office he held and for how long. Goodenough[77] emphasized "that his duties were of a judicial character" but admitted that "this cannot be demonstrated." The autobiographical section of *Spec.* 3:1–5 has been interpreted as indicating that Philo first lived a relatively long period of his life when he was primarily concerned with his philosophy and writing. He was later drawn reluctantly into the political life and work of the Jewish community in Alexandria. This is a possible interpretation, but it is difficult to say anything more explicit about when Philo had to engage in the political affairs of his city (contra Goodenough). *Spec.* 3:1–5 might be seen primarily as an exhale of frustration over his political work compared to the activity as a philosopher, a

---

75. See e.g., Schwartz, "Philo, His Family and His Times" 18. Hadas-Lebel is, however, more reluctant. She states, on the basis of the observation that even some Greeks did not attend the gymnasium, but had private teachers, that "we have to concede, however, almost total uncertainty about Philo's education. What we can assume is that he benefitted from reputable teachers and worked through the syllabus that was available to him with obvious enthusiasm." Hadas-Lebel, *Philo of Alexandria*, 55. See also the cautious comments in Koskenniemi, "Philo and Classical Education."

76. Wolfson, *Philo* 1:93, lists twenty-three philosophers he finds cited in the works of Philo. See also Sterling, "'Jewish Philosophy.'"

77. Goodenough, "Philo and Public Life."

task he took much more delight in (cf. *Spec.* 2:44). We will have to return to this issue in the next chapter.

Scholars taking their point of departure in the literary activities of Philo have suggested that he must have had a thorough education, and some suggest that he might have also been a teacher himself. Gregory E. Sterling has set forth an interesting hypothesis about Philo's scholarly activities: "I suggest that Philo had a private school in his home or personally owned structure for advanced students which were similar to schools of higher education run by individuals throughout the Greco-Roman world."[78] The evidence for this is undoubtedly circumstantial, but Sterling provides several plausible arguments for this view. First, he points to the plausibility that Philo worked within an exegetical tradition. His references to other exegetes, whether literalists or allegorists, may indicate this.[79] Second, Philo probably worked with sources of some kind (cf. *Mos.* 1:4); third, we have some extant works that Philo probably knew (by Aristobulus, Pseudo-Aristeas, and Ezekiel the Tragedian); hence, he was working within a tradition that also continued after him.

Sterling also works with other indicators in Philo's texts, including his descriptions of the Therapeutae and the nature of several of his works, especially his two books on *Questions and Answers* and his commentaries.[80] Hence, it is possible that Philo functioned as a teacher, working in a setting comparable to those we know from other teachers during approximately the same time. Such a context would represent an appropriate setting for many of his works, especially his allegorical commentaries.

Philo's View of Israel among the Peoples

Philo had a very high view of Israel and its role in the world. The unique status of the Jewish population is frequently characterized in terms of honor, with particular emphasis on their distinctiveness as an ethnic group compared to other peoples. Hence, according to Philo, the Jewish nation is "a nation dearest of all to God" (*Abr.* 98). They are "the best of races" (*Congr.* 51) and are "preferred and chosen" by God (*Conf.* 56; *Migr.* 60). In this last passage Philo uses Deut 7:7, where God's election is grounded in his love alone. In *Spec.* 4.181, however, it is grounded in

---

78. Sterling, "School of the Sacred Laws," 150; Sterling, "School of Moses."
79. See Hay, "Philo's References"; Shroyer, "Alexandrian Jewish Literalists."
80. Sterling, "School of the Sacred Laws," 154–60.

the "precious signs of righteousness and virtue shown by the founders of the race."[81] The Jews, further, are "God's portion" (*Spec.* 4:159, 179-180; *Legat.* 3; *Post.* 89, 93; cf. Deut 32:7-9). They stand in a special relation with God, and this distinctiveness is related to their Law: "they are living under exceptional laws" (cf. *Spec.* 4:179; *Ios.* 42; *Conf.* 141). The Law is here described as marking them out in relation to the other nations, and as constituting their special relation to God. The Law is the special prerogative of Israel, as Israel is the special portion of God, set apart for him alone.[82] The Jews thus constitute a singularity in the world.

Philo's conception of the people of Israel is thus also firmly grounded in their God-given Law: it is the observance of the Law that constitutes the Jews as the people of God and that thereby functions as the element qualifying who is to be regarded as kinsfolk (συγγενεῖς), e.g., *Spec.* 3:155 (see also 4:159 and 1:317):

> Those whom we call our kinsfolk (συγγενεῖς) or within the circle of kinsmen our friends are turned into aliens by their misconduct when they go astray: for agreement to practice justice and every virtue makes a closer kinship (συγγένεια) than that of blood, and he who abandons this enters his name in the list not only of strangers and foreigners but of mortal enemies.

Accordingly, although kinship by blood is important, there is a kind of kinship ranked above that of blood: the one based on observance of the Law and thus on the honoring of God, "which is the indissoluble bond of all the affection which makes us one" (*Spec.* 1:52, cf. 1:317).[83] Thus proselytes also belong to this συγγένεια as they are "incomers" who have come to "the clear vision of truth and the worship of the one and truly existing God" (*Virt.* 102, cf. 179). In a somewhat exaggerated manner Philo can say that "Moses himself was the best of all lawgivers in all countries" (*Mos.* 2:12). A few sections later he says that "not only Jews but almost every other people, particularly those which take more account of virtue, have so far grown in holiness as to value and honor our laws" (*Mos.* 2:17). At the same time, however, he cherishes the eschatological hope that when Israel prospers, "each nation would abandon its peculiar

---

81. See here *Praem.* 166, where the patriarchs are said to be supplicants for the Jews.

82. See Philo's use of Exod 19:5 where he presents the prophetic and priestly aspects of the people; see especially Abr. 56, 98.

83. For a brief overview of the meaning of nomos/law in Philo, see Reinhartz, "The Meaning of Nomos," 337-45.

ways, and, throwing overboard their ancestral customs, turn to honoring our laws alone" (*Mos.* 2:44).[84]

Israel as a 'nation' is also destined to be a special nation with special roles in the world; e.g., it is "a nation to be destined above all others to offer prayers for ever on behalf of the human race that it may be delivered from evil and participate in what is good" (*Mos.* 1:149),[85] and Moses is described as "legislator of the Jews" and as "the interpreter of the Holy Laws" (*Mos.* 1:1). Hence, according to Philo, "Moses himself was the best of all lawgivers in all countries, better in fact than any that have ever risen among either the Greeks or the barbarians, and that his laws are most excellent and truly come from God, since they omit nothing that is needful" (*Mos.* 2:12).

But Philo also describes himself as a 'cosmopolites,' and the Law of Israel is described as in accord with the natural Law of the world. To Philo, the Torah is not only the particular Law of the Jews; it is also in accord with the natural law of the world. Here, Jewish particularism seems to be rising to a higher level of a particular kind of universalism. The patriarchs can be described as living laws (*Abr.* 5:276); even before the Torah had been given, the patriarchs were living in accordance with the law because they were living according to nature, the originals and living laws. And the Torah as containing written and particular laws constituted copies of the unwritten laws (*Abr.* 5):

> for in these men, we have laws endowed with life and reason, and Moses extolled them for two reasons. First he wished to shew that the enacted ordinances are not inconsistent with nature; and secondly that those who wish to live in accordance with the laws as they stand have no difficult task, seeing that the first generations before any of the particular statutes was set in writing followed the unwritten law with perfect ease, so that one might properly say that the enacted laws are nothing else than memorials of the life of ancients, preserving to a later generation their actual words and deeds.

---

84. For a review of the possible extent of eschatology in Philo's works, see the various views of these scholars: De Savignac, "Le Messianisme"; Fischer, *Eschatologie und Jenseitserwartung*, 184–213; Hect, "Philo and Messiah"; Borgen, "'There Shall Come Forth a Man.'"

85. See Seland, "Forbønn hos Filo"; and Borgen, "Two Philonic Prayers."

According to Sidney Sowers,[86] by stating that the patriarchs bore in their souls the law on which the Torah is based, Philo sought to provide support and legitimation for the Torah within the context of contemporary Hellenism. The Torah is thus not only the particular law of the Jews, but it is in harmony with the law of nature (*Mos.* 2:48). While there has been some debate concerning whether Philo was the first to frame the concept of natural law in Greek, it appears now more probable that he was drawing on Stoic ideas.[87] But in his sphere of thought, this realization gave the law of the Jews—the Torah—its universal importance. Hence, when tempted by Potiphar's wife, Joseph says, "We children of the Hebrews follow laws and customs which are especially our own" (*Ios.* 42), but there is no contradiction; these laws were to be considered identical to the laws of nature. Philo could hardly have given a stronger expression of the importance of the Jewish people and their Torah in the world.

Philo thus has a very high view of Israel's role and place in the world, a view that influenced his view of how he considered the apostates among his people[88] and how he considered the Romans as colonizers.

Summary and Outlook

The Jewish population had a significant historical presence in Alexandria, one of the three largest cities in the Roman Empire. Philo's family belonged to the affluent elite in the city: His brother Alexander was among the wealthiest individuals in the municipality, and one of his sons later in the first century attained the position of prefect of Egypt. However, the nature of Philo's relationships with his family members remains unclear to contemporary scholars. Due to his scholarly inclinations and literary pursuits, he may have been somewhat isolated within the family. Yet, he ultimately assumed a political role by leading a Jewish delegation to Rome circa 38–41 CE. Nevertheless, his extensive literary output suggests that he devoted much of his life to scholarly activities.

Egypt was a Roman province from 31 BCE. Consequently, Alexandria was subject to Roman law, which influenced numerous aspects of life. Roman taxation was substantial, as was the cultural impact of

---

86. Sowers, *Hermeneutics*, 45.

87. See Koester, "ΝΟΜΟΣ ΦΥΣΕΩΣ." Contra Koester, see Horsley, "Law of Nature." See also Winston, "Philo's Ethical Theory," especially 381–86; Najman, "Law of Nature"; and the articles in this volume: Runia et al., *Laws Stamped*.

88. On Philo's views of the apostates, see Seland, *Establishment Violence*, 103–81.

Roman fiscal policies, education, and values. The Jewish population in Alexandria was, nonetheless, considerable. Philo likely developed and operated within a predominantly Jewish milieu in Alexandria, maintaining a high regard for Jewish culture and perspectives on the role of Jews in the world.

The subsequent chapter will provide a more extensive examination of Philo's works, and will offer pertinent reading strategies in order to understand them.

3

Philo's Writings

Reimagining Relevant Reading Strategies

> "I tell the story of Moses as I have learned it,
> both from the wonderful monuments of his wisdom
> which he has left behind him,
> and from some of the elders of the nation;
> for I always interwove what I was told
> with what I read...."
>
> *Vita Mosis* 1:4

INTRODUCTION

THIS CHAPTER WILL INITIALLY address the genres, intended readership, and chronology of Philo's writings. As most dates and characterizations pertaining to Philo's life and works are subject to extensive scholarly debate, the perspectives concerning these issues remain open to discussion, and one can scarcely assert a generally accepted consensus concerning all aspects of his life. Additionally, diverse viewpoints exist regarding the appropriate reading strategies to be employed when examining his works.

ON THE GENRES, DATES, AND INTENDED READERS OF PHILO'S WRITINGS

Philo's literary output is substantial. Approximately forty of his works remain extant; however, indications within several of these texts, as well as observations by certain early church fathers, suggest that his corpus must have encompassed at least twenty additional titles. Philo's oeuvre extends beyond the exegetical commentaries on the Pentateuch, that is, on the Law of Moses, the Jewish constitution. It also encompasses philosophical treatises and apologetic works and addresses contemporary political issues.[1] Philo was likely not an isolated scholar confined to his office, composing theoretical expositions of ancient scriptures; rather he was an individual who most probably engaged deeply in the philosophical, political, and religious life and circumstances of his Jewish community in Alexandria. Consequently, he was presumably active as an educator and participant in the synagogue(s). Furthermore, he was likely a significant proponent of his interpretations of Judaism among both his fellow Jews and neighboring non-Jews.[2] Accordingly, in his works, he focuses on both the intramural and intermural aspects of Jewish life in Alexandria.

The Question of Genres

Scholarly discourse has addressed the classification and genre determinations of Philo's works. The present analysis employs the contemporary categorization of his oeuvre that is widely accepted in current academic circles.[3] According to this perspective, the works of Philo can be categorized as follows: the majority of his writings can be classified into two primary groups, designated as the allegorical commentaries[4] and the

---

1. For a more comprehensive presentation of Philo's works, see Borgen, *Philo of Alexandria, An Exegete*. I also draw on my earlier presentation in Seland, *Establishment Violence*, 75–82. See also the more general introductions by Goodenough (*Introduction*); Sandmel (*Philo of Alexandria*); Schenck (*Brief Guide*); Seland, ed. (*Reading Philo*); and now above all Niehoff, *Philo of Alexandria*.

2. See also Borgen ("Philo of Alexandria," 151), who states that "Philo's intention is to conquer the surrounding culture ideologically by claiming that whatever good there is has its source in Scripture and thus belonged to the Jewish nation and its heritage. In this way Philo represents the dynamic and offensive movement of the Jews who infiltrated the environment of the Alexandrian citizens around the gymnasium."

3. See Borgen, "Philo of Alexandria," 117–18.

4. I.e., QG, QE, Leg., Cher., Sacr., Det., Post., Gig., Quod., Agr., Plant., Ebr., Sobr., Conf. Migr. Heres. Congr. Fug. Mit. Somn. One might also have QG and QE as a subcategory here.

Exposition of the Law of Moses.⁵ Then there are some works that Peder Borgen, for example, characterizes as works that apply pentateuchal principles to contemporary issues and events;⁶ others are categorized as primarily philosophical,⁷ historical, or apologetic writings.⁸ The efficacy of Borgen's categorization lies in its recognition that Philo was primarily an exegete and expositor of the Scriptures and that when he applied pentateuchal principles to various issues in other books, he presupposed the exegetical methodology he had developed in his expository works. However, a limitation inherent in this categorization is that it may inadequately convey the diversity of the genres concerned.

The allegorical commentaries consist of eighteen titles and twenty-one books. These texts commence with a biblical passage from within the range of Gen 2:1—41:24 and contain exegetical commentary on various issues present in or associated with these passages. Some of the expositions are notably complex, and contemporary readers approaching these works for the first time may encounter significant challenges in comprehending Philo's writings. Samuel Sandmel has characterized the potential experiences of a novice reader as follows: "An earnest reader may find his attention waning and, in all sincerity, ennui can begin to manifest." This, Sandmel further postulates, "is especially the case when Philo weaves into his exposition new citations from Scripture and turns to expound these, however far afield doing so may take him."⁹ Nevertheless, readers who invest time in engaging with these works will find them elucidating and illustrative of Philo's intellectual milieu.

An additional challenge inherent in trying to characterize the writings of Philo is the difficulty in formulating genre classifications that align with labels Philo would have recognized as acceptable. This issue pertains to the distinction between *emic* and *etic* descriptions today. This is illustrated by the label for the (mostly) nonallegorical expositions of Philo, the group of treatises usually called the Exposition,¹⁰ which comprises *De Opificio Mundi*, *De Abrahamo*, (plus two lost works possibly

---

5. That is, *Opif., Abr., Ios., Decal., Spec., Virt., Praem.* The *Vita Mosis* is also placed in this group by several, if not by most, scholars. See esp. Goodenough, "Philo's Exposition"; Delling, "Wunder -Allegori-Mythos," 74. Sterling, "Philo of Alexandria's *Life of Moses*."

6. I.e., *Hypot., Vita, Cont., Quod., Aet., Prov. Anim.*

7. These are *Anim., Prob., Aet., Prov.*

8. That is, *In Flaccum* and *De Legatione*, and *Contempl.* and *Hypoth.*

9. Sandmel, *Philo of Alexandria*, 79.

10. 'The Exposition' as a comprehensive label is a completely modern label.

titled *On Isaac* and *On Jacob*), *De Josepho, De Decalogo, De Specialibus Legibus* 1–3, *De Virtutibus, De Praemiis et Poenis*, and most probably *De vita Mosis* 1–2—these last-mentioned works functioning as a companion piece, perhaps even as a kind of introduction.[11] Philo himself comments on the contents of these works in *Praem* 1–3 as dealing with the creation of the world, with history, and with legislation.

However, concerning the genre of Philo's works, some[12] have pointed out that a similar method to that used by Philo in the Exposition may be found in the Biblical Antiquities of Pseudo-Philo, the Genesis Apocryphon, and the book of Jubilees. Some scholars have termed these works "rewritten Bible" or "narrative midrash" (German: *erzählender Midrasch*).[13]

The numerous paraphrases, omissions, and additions that characterize the use of Torah texts in *De Specialibus Legibus* suggest that this work may be compared with works just mentioned, such as the book of Jubilees and Pseudo-Philo's Biblical Antiquities. However, it is important to note that this comparison pertains to the literary nature of *De Specialibus Legibus*—and in terms of content, the narrative midrashim may indeed contain substantial material of both a haggadic and a halakhic nature. Philo himself, in fact, explicitly states at least once that his works are not merely a recapitulation of the Old Testament stories and laws but that commentary is incorporated: Regarding the narrative of Moses, he asserts that he will "tell the story of Moses as I have learned it, both from the sacred books . . . and from some of the elders of the nation; for I always interwove what I was told with what I read" (*Vita Mosis* 1:4).

However, the characterization of 'rewritten Bible' or 'rewritten Scripture' has also been revived without closely associating it with 'midrash.' If one interprets the label as signifying that an author, based on certain 'biblical' text(s)—whether smaller or larger units—reworks these not only by retelling them but by rewriting, rephrasing, paraphrasing, or omitting elements, and adding other aspects, thus producing some 'new' (re)written texts, then the label might be considered functional as an emic label. In Philo's works, one finds both orally and textually transmitted

---

11. On *De vita Mosis* as belonging to the Expositio, see Goodenough, "Philo's Exposition"; and now Sterling, "Philo of Alexandria's *Life of Moses*," which argues that it is an introduction to the Exposition of the Law. See now also Hunt, ed. and trans., *De vita Mosis* I.

12. E.g., Borgen, "Philo of Alexandria," 234; see also Nickelsburg, "Bible Rewritten."

13. See Vermes, *Scripture and Tradition in Judaism*; Weimar, "Formen Frühjüdischer Literatur."

traditions, encompassing stories and laws, as well as expositions taught by other exegetes and the results of his own textual analysis.[14] An examination of his extensive body of work today indicates that he likely had access to a substantial library, potentially encompassing both private and public collections. However, this observation does not imply that the Exposition should be categorized as 'rewritten scripture.' *De vita Mosis*, along with *De Abrahamo* and *De Josepho*, more appropriately belong to the genre of biography, as Philo himself asserts ("I purpose to write the life of Moses . . . ." *Mos.* 1:1).[15] However, these works also contain several sections that draw upon biblical passages through retelling and rephrasing and thus can be characterized as 'rewritten scripture' within a biographical context.[16]

In the context of examining Philo and ancient biographies, Sean Adams, in his eminent work on *Greek Genres and Jewish Authors*, specifically addresses *Vita Mosis*, *On Abraham*, and *On Joseph*.[17] He strongly argues that one should not consider Philo as working only within a single genre but in a plurality of genres, even within one and the same book: "Philo likely modelled his Exposition on a work that participated in multiple genres,"[18] namely the works of Moses (cf. *Praem* 1). Hence, Adams concludes:[19]

> The specific genre divisions of the Pentateuch (i.e., cosmological, historical, and legal) are likely the literary models for Philo in his Exposition, with the lives of the patriarchs fulfilling the historical aspect. Overall, the fact that Philo unapologetically presents the Pentateuch as having multiple genres implies that

---

14. Here see Hay, "Philo's References"; and Hay, "Philo's View of Himself."

15. James R. Royse calls it "an encomiastic biography of the Jewish legislator." See Royse, "Works of Philo," 34, but also as "an apologetic and historical work." See pp. 34, 47, and 50–51. See also Borgen, "Philo of Alexandria," 235: "Thus the book was written to tell the Gentile readers about the supreme lawgiver whose laws they are to accept and honor. It was also to strengthen the Jews for their universal role." "Philo has added features which resemble a Greek *bios*, a biographical novel." See further on these issues Damgaard, *Recasting Moses*, 1–21, 49–87.

16. Maren Niehoff ("Philo and Plutarch," 383) calls Philo a "biographer in a Midrashic or exegetical mode, who felt the same freedom as other ancient interpreters of Scripture."

17. Adams, *Greek Genres and Jewish Authors*, 277–92.

18. Adams, *Greek Genres and Jewish Authors*, 290. In *Pream.* 1, Philo states that "The oracles delivered through the prophet Moses are of three kinds. The first deals with the creation of the world, the second with history, and the third with legislation."

19. Adams, *Greek Genres and Jewish Authors*, 290.

he had a theory of genre that was sufficiently flexible to allow for internal differentiation within a series and even within a work (e.g., Genesis).

Considering the variety of genres used by Philo, and the many viewpoints offered in recent research, this conclusion can hardly be bettered.

The works of Philo that are most relevant to understanding his perspectives on the Roman Empire in the years from approximately 38 CE are, indeed, *In Flaccum* and *De Legatione*. These texts are generally categorized as historical works, albeit with evident and unconcealed additional agendas. Unfortunately, these are the only works that can be dated with a reasonable degree of certainty (see below).

The Dates and Addressees of the Allegorical Commentaries

There is not much dissension in recent research regarding the addressees of Philo's allegorical commentaries. These works appear to presuppose a readership possessing a sophisticated knowledge of Scripture and philosophy.[20] Consequently, they are predominantly regarded as compositions intended for insiders, potentially for his students in Alexandria. Specifically, they are considered works written during Philo's earlier years when he resided in Alexandria prior to the critical period of 38–41 CE, and most likely authored for fellow Jews who were either initiated into or in the process of being initiated into his teachings.[21] Ellen Birnbaum's characterizations of the Jewish audience of intended readers for the allegorical commentaries are convincing: "Jews like himself who were well educated in Scripture and Jewish tradition, on the one hand; and Greek school subjects and philosophy, on the other."[22]

---

20. Birnbaum, *Place of Judaism*, 18–19.

21. Goodenough argued that the *Allegorical Commentaries* were written for the Jews, for the insiders, hence not for beginners. See Goodenough, *Introduction*, 47–48. With some variations in emphasis, this is still a much-preferred view. See also Niehoff, *Philo of Alexandria*. 173–244.

22. Birnbaum, "Leader with Vision," 68. See also Sterling in Runia, ed. and trans., *On the Creation*, xii: "for advanced students or other exegetes in the Jewish community."

The Dates and Addressees of the Historical Writings: *In Flaccum* and *De Legatione*

As previously noted, there is currently no general scholarly consensus regarding the precise dates of any of Philo's writings. However, the treatises most pertinent to the present topic of politics are the two historical works, namely *In Flaccum* and *De Legatione ad Gaium*. These are the only texts that can be dated with certainty in terms of the terminus a quo, that is, the earliest possible date they must have been composed. Given that these treatises recount historical events from 38–41 CE, they must have been written after this period. It is possible that *De Animalibus* was composed during the same time frame.[23] The possible terminus ad quem, however, is next to impossible to state, as we do not even know the date of his death. Many, probably most scholars, date them to the forties or early fifties CE.[24]

The dating of Philo's works is highly complicated and fraught with difficulties influenced by one's understanding of his life and work. If he were active in political functions and offices during most of his adult life it is not only possible but rather plausible that his work as an author and expositor of the Scriptures must have taken place during a rather long period.[25] John Dillon has set forth the interesting but hardly provable suggestion that "at a certain stage of his education he experienced a kind of conversion, a rediscovery of his own culture and traditions." This "conversion" did not lead him to abolish the Greek culture, but to "an application of it to the Jews' sacred books, particularly the Pentateuch, the books of Moses."[26] The first part of Dillon's suggestion can scarcely be proved or disproved as there is next to nothing in terms of evidential material in Philo's works for such a 'conversion experience.' The last part is, however,

---

23. We cannot place all his philosophical writings in his earlier period and the exegetical works in his later one. If *De Animalibus*, however, belongs to his later years it shows that his philosophical interest was very intact at that time. On the other hand, it is scarcely reasonable to place all his writings in his later years, as Terian has suggested. See Terian, "Critical Introduction."

24. See e.g., van der Horst, *Philo's "Flaccus,"* 4, who dates *In Flaccum* to 40 or 41 as the most probable date.

25. In recent years Maren R. Niehoff has been a prolific scholar arguing that the whole of the *Exposition* (and probably some other works too) are to be dated after 38 CE, several possibly even written in Rome. I will return to her view below, as it is very important for the present study: see Niehoff, "Josephus and Philo"; Niehoff, "Philo's Exposition in a Roman Context"; Niehoff, *Philo of Alexandria*.

26. Dillon, *Middle Platonists*, 141.

more to the point. But it is, after all, probably a more suitable description of Philo's attitude to the Empire to say that his point of departure was his understanding of Judaism, and that he tried to apply and interpret his Judaism for his contemporaries in the context of the Roman colonizing Empire as a teacher, philosopher, and politician.[27]

Concerning the addressees of *In Flaccum*, Goodenough argues that it was written for a Gentile audience after the death of Gaius, and possibly for the new prefect in Alexandria.[28] *De Legatione*, on the other hand, he surmises was written after the accession of Claudius, and as a presentation to just that emperor.[29] In contemporary scholarship, the prevailing consensus appears to be that these significant political works of Philo were composed for both Jewish and Gentile audiences, potentially including Roman authorities. Consequently, they represent and present Philo as engaging in a form of discourse from within the Empire.

Maren R. Niehoff is convinced that *In Flaccum* and *De Legatione* are primarily written for Jews. She does not find that they contain "features characteristic of an apologetic work addressed to the new emperor."[30] On a more positive note, she observes that the opening in *Legat.* 3 is particularly suitable for Jewish readers rather than others, and that this observation is corroborated by several additional features in *Legatio*.[31]

---

27. A few scholars have suggested that it is rather futile to search for an exact location in time and space for Philo's intended readers. Maybe Philo's works should be read and interpreted without presupposing a specific intended audience. In 1986, David Runia (*Exegesis and Theology*, 192) suggested that maybe he rather wrote, in fact, for himself: "Philo is writing his long series of treatises in the first place for himself. They are material record of his quest to fathom the depths of wisdom contained in scripture, a quest of which he was prepared to share with others. The question of Philo's projected audience needs to be borne in mind, but it is not, in my view, going to play a decisive role when we confront the question of how we should read Philo." It must be added that Runia was here primarily thinking of the allegorical writings. In the same year, David M. Hay ("Philo's View of Himself," 52) wrote that "it seems likely that Philo wrote his treatises for an 'open-ended' readership, one not limited to Alexandria and, perhaps, not limited to his own time.... Perhaps Philo deliberately avoided inserting any very particular description of intended readers in his treatises because he expected, or at least hoped for, a wide and continuing audience." Such viewpoints are, however, not voiced by many today, if by any.

28. Goodenough, *Politics*, 15–16.

29. Goodenough, *Politics*, 19.

30. Niehoff, *Philo of Alexandria*, 40.

31. See especially Niehoff, *Philo of Alexandria*, 40–44.

The Dates and Addressees of the Exposition

Concerning the quest for the addressees of the Exposition, one will find that the answers to this question can be assembled in three groups: written for Jews, written for Gentiles,[32] or for both Jews and Gentiles.[33] The last-mentioned group might be further divided into two subgroups according to which group Philo considered as his primary readers: Gentiles or Jews. Nevertheless, challenges persist in situating Philo's works temporally and spatially. There is a paucity of concrete evidence within his writings for who Philo's primary readers are. Consequently, many assessments of the writing chronology for separate works within the Exposition and of its potential recipients rely often on the present-day reader's (broad) interpretations of the intended audience from indications in the texts, or from the conjectures of present-day scholars about the probable readership based on today's perspectives. To some degree, one may construct inherent or implied[34] readers and postulate who the intended readers were. But doing so entails a problematic leap of argumentation and understanding. One should distinguish more clearly between the implied and intended readers.

For the Jews: The view that the *Expositio* was written primarily for the Jews, but that Philo also took account of the possibility that his works could be used in a presentation of Judaism to interested Gentiles[35] was most popular some years ago.[36] Erwin R. Goodenough's student, Samuel Sandmel, is one of the strongest advocates for this position. Sandmel states that the writings of the Exposition are defensive and apologetic, sometimes even indignant, and he is of the opinion that the Exposition was

---

32. Goodenough, "Philo's Exposition," 117; Goodenough, *Introduction*, 30ff.

33. Koester, *Introduction to the New Testament*, 1, 273ff.; Borgen, "Philo of Alexandria," 118. Birnbaum, *Place of Judaism*, 20: "Jews and non-Jews—whether hostile or friendly—who know little about Jewish beliefs and practices." See Birnbaum, "Leader with Vision," 68.

34. I use 'implied' here with the literary meaning of the readers inherent in the texts, that is as a textual construct. Alas, not a few scholars use 'implied readers' in the meaning of the 'intended readers.'

35. This seems also to be the solution preferred in Morris, "Jewish Philosopher Philo."

36. See Massebieau, "Classement." Massebieau refers to τοῦ ἡμετέρου ἔθνους in *Decal.* 1 as indicating Jewish readers; see also *Spec.* 1:153 and 1:314. See also Sandmel, "Philo Judaeus," 11. See Sandmel, *Judaism and Christian Beginnings*, 465, note 47: "for Jews on the fringe of Judaism, to deter them from impending apostasy" (Tcherikover et al., eds., *Corpus Papyrorum Judaicarum*, vol. 1, no. 78).

written for "a Jewish audience, those who seemed ignorant of their Jewish heritage and inclined to or on the verge of apostasy: the Exposition was an effort to retain these Jews for Judaism."[37] Victor Tcherikover concurred with the efforts to identify the Jews as the intended recipients and agreed that the text was not intended for advanced Jewish readers. Instead, it was designed as a more simplified exposition that would be comprehensible to a less erudite Jewish audience. Consequently, it was composed with the objective of disseminating the practical aspects of Moses's teachings for everyday application.[38] Some scholars contend that Philo's utilization of Gentile philosophical concepts and literary genres does not necessarily indicate that he wrote primarily for Gentile readers but rather reflects his own education and the philosophical traditions he applied. Others posit that it is implausible to assume that the *Expositio* was composed with Gentiles as the sole intended audience. There are indeed extant apologetic works that were evidently written for a Gentile readership, such as *Contra Apion* by Josephus and Philo's *In Flaccum*, *De Legatione*, and *Hypothetica* (*Apologia pro Ioudaeis*). However, these texts differ significantly from the Exposition, which addresses specific Jewish laws.

For the Gentiles: Goodenough was one of the most prominent advocates in the interwar period for the perspective that the Exposition was composed for a Gentile audience.[39] The author's arguments clearly demonstrate the close relationship between the question of addressees and that of purpose. This perspective is also intricately connected to the author's view of Jewish jurisprudence in relation to Roman jurisdiction.[40] He demonstrates less certainty regarding the date of Philo's works compared to the identification of the addressees. In recent years, a significant number of scholars—potentially a majority—have come to view the Exposition as being written for both Jewish and Gentile audiences, as

---

37. Sandmel, "Philo Judaeus."

38. Tcherikover et al., *Corpus Papyrorum Judaicarum*, vol. 1, no. 78.

39. See Goodenough, "Philo's *Exposition*"; Goodenough, *Jurisprudence*; Goodenough, *Politics*; Goodenough, *Introduction*, 35. In opposition to Massebieau, he points to *Spec*. 2:79 and 3:29 as indicating that Gentile readers were in Philo's mind.

40. See this description: "One large part of the Exposition, namely De Specialibus Legibus, which is a great analysis of the Jewish Law to show how it is in practical harmony with the Gentile jurisprudence of contemporary Egypt, seems to me wholly pointless as designed for Jews. But such an argument would be highly significant for Gentiles—who had a great interest in the Jewish religion but retained the point of view toward legal administration set for them by the Roman prefect and iuridicus." Goodenough, "Philo's Exposition," 117. See also Goodenough, *Jurisprudence*.

exemplified by the works of Sandmel, Borgen, and Birnbaum, among others.[41] Furthermore, Albert C. Geljon and David T. Runia have emphasized that we, in fact, have only two fixed points to work with in dating Philo's works. The first is *Spec.* 3, where Philo speaks biographically of his times of political troubles. Many scholars—perhaps the majority—read this as referring to the troubles in Alexandria in 37–38 CE. The other "fixed point" is *Legat.* 1, where he describes these troubles and states that he was by then already an old man (ἡμεῖς οἱ γέροντες). "If we make the plausible assumption that all the treatises of the Exposition were written in the same period, Philo must have written the work during the last ten to fifteen years of his life."[42] The probable corollary of this is that the allegorical commentaries must have been written earlier than the Exposition. "But all this is all a matter of conjecture,"[43] they conclude somewhat resignedly. In the subsequent paragraphs, this discussion of addresses and dates will conclude with a more detailed examination of Maren R. Niehoff's perspective, which offers a more optimistic approach to arriving at a plausible view.

EXCURSUS I: *The View of Maren R. Niehoff*

Maren R. Niehoff is undoubtedly one of the more prolific scholars within the field of Philo studies in recent years. In addition to authoring several monographs,[44] she has published a flow of articles, many directly related to how to understand Philo of Alexandria in his relation to Rome. Most interesting and relevant for our focus here is her biography of Philo.[45]

---

41. Sandmel characterized the intended readers as "friendly Gentiles or uninformed Jews on the threshold of apostasy." And he can surmise that "yet it is just as likely that he is appealing to half-assimilated Jews, arguing that since outsiders could have so high a regard of Judaism, there is reason for half-assimilated Jews to do the same." Sandmel, *Philo of Alexandria*, 47 and 52. Borgen agrees with Goodenough that the *Exposition* was written for Gentiles, but states that Goodenough overlooks, however, that it was at the same time "written for Jews to strengthen them for their universal role." Borgen, "Philo of Alexandria," 118. Birnbaum basically agrees with this position. Birnbaum, "Leader with Vision," 68; Birnbaum, *Place of Judaism*, 20. Birnbaum and Dillon, eds. and trans., *On the Life of Abraham*, 26–29: "for a range of different readers and with multiple purposes" (p. 29).

42. Geljon and Runia, eds. and trans., *On Cultivation*, 5.

43. Geljon and Runia, eds. and trans. *On Cultivation*, 5.

44. Niehoff, *Figure of Joseph*; Niehoff, *Philo on Jewish Identity*; Niehoff, *Jewish Exegesis*.

45. Niehoff, *Philo of Alexandria*. See also the following articles of hers: Niehoff, "Philo's Exposition in a Roman Context"; Niehoff, "Josephus and Philo"; Niehoff, "Einführung

Here, she sets forth her view of Philo's life, his works, and his views on various topics, including that of politics, which is very relevant here. Very early in the introductory sections of her biography, she presents the following thesis-like statement concerning how to understand Philo and his work:[46]

> We rather have to understand Philo's intentions in each series of writings and ask for which purpose he used that particular literary format. Who was his implied[47] audience in each case, and what may have been the circumstances of his writing? Following these questions and adapting a comparative method, we can draw conclusions from the different texts about the cultural milieu in which each of them emerged. In each case I point to a close connection between literary genre, cultural context, and choice of philosophy.

Moreover, the author posits that Philo's intellectual development was influenced by his change in occupation and geographical location, specifically his relocation from Alexandria to Rome (and potentially his subsequent return to Alexandria).[48] Of significant importance is the consideration of his diverse interlocutors in the various locations:

> Given that Philo stayed in Rome for at least three years (38–41 C. E.), I argue that his journey was a crucial experience, not only politically, but also intellectually. It had an immediate effect upon his choice of literary genre, Jewish identity, and philosophical orientation. Philo refashioned himself, constructing a new identity and offering new interpretations of his tradition.

Concerning Philo's writings, Niehoff argues that his main allegorical work, *the Allegorical Commentary*, was written in Alexandria before 38 CE, hence representing his earliest works.[49] It represents Philo the

---

in die Schrift (MigrAbr)"; Niehoff, "Ist Philon ein typischer Vertreter des Diasporajudentums?"; and Niehoff, "Philon als Biograph."

46. This and the following quotation are taken from Niehoff, *Philo of Alexandria*, 3.

47. As I understand this expression, Niehoff does not use 'implied audience' or 'implied reader' in the literary sense as denoting the audience or reader inherent in the texts, but more in the sense of 'the audience or reader intended by the author.'

48. She is very vague, however, concerning whether Philo ever returned to Alexandria. At least she finds it probable that he stayed in Rome between 38 and 41 CE and possibly even longer: "Philo stayed in Rome at least until early 41 CE, when Gaius was assassinated, and most probably much longer in order to continue the negotiations with his successor, Claudius." Niehoff, "Josephus and Philo," 135.

49. See Niehoff, *Jewish Exegesis*.

Alexandrian, living and working in Alexandria, being a Jewish Platonist.[50] The historical treatises in the *Embassy to Gaius* (*De Legatione ad Gaium*, abbreviated *Legat.*) and *Against Flaccus* (*In Flaccum*, abbr. *Flacc.*) were written when he served as the leader of a Jewish embassy in Rome, and the so-called Exposition and his philosophical treatises were written partly when in Rome 38–41 CE and partly after that period.[51] During his sojourn in Rome, he established closer connections with the Roman Stoics and incorporated more of their philosophical principles. This perspective has several implications for her interpretation and delineation of Philo's biographical account: "He sets out as a systematic Bible commentator in Alexandria, discussing Scripture with his Jewish colleagues and offering transcendent Platonic insights resonating with Alexandrian discourses."[52] However, Philo's life changed dramatically when he stayed in Rome; it became "a turning point in his life, drawing him out of his contemplative mode in Alexandria into Roman politics and discourses."[53] During his sojourn in Rome, he encountered novel literary genres and Roman philosophical perspectives and experienced a significant interaction with Roman culture. Niehoff appears to interpret this interaction as predominantly favorable. She argues that "a prominent part of the Exposition belongs to the genre of historiography"; his works in the Exposition "gravitate toward the Stoic positions," and he addresses readers who are unfamiliar with the basics of Judaism and the Jewish Scriptures.[54]

Furthermore, she describes Philo's stay in Rome as having lasted for several years, not only in 38–41 but even longer, possibly for several years. Hence, it comes only as a corollary that she also considers the Exposition to have been written in Rome. She also argues that Philo adopted a pro-Roman attitude as he wrote about both Augustus and Tiberius as exemplary Roman emperors who respected Jewish privileges throughout the empire (*Legat.* 143–161).[55] Both Philo and Josephus emerge[56]

---

50. Niehoff, "Philo's Role as a Platonist in Alexandria."

51. Niehoff, "Philo's Exposition in a Roman Context"; Niehoff, "Josephus and Philo," 135–36. In Niehoff, "Einführung in die Schrift (MigrAbr)," 7–9, she argues that all of his writings, except the *Allegorical Commentaries*, were written in Rome ca. 40–49.

52. Niehoff, *Philo of Alexandria*, 10. Niehoff, *Jewish Exegesis*.

53. Niehoff, *Philo of Alexandria*, 11.

54. Niehoff, *Philo of Alexandria*, 7–8.

55. For a very different view, see Delling, "Philons Enkomium auf Augustus."

56. Niehoff, "Josephus and Philo," 140.

as upper-class Jews, who trust the Roman administration, while criticizing those countrymen, usually of lower social status, who have taken up weapons against Rome. Both faced serious conflicts between Rome and the Jewish population of their home cities, trying to overcome them by a mediating position. Both moreover believed that divine providence proved their interpretation of contemporary politics to be the right one.

The present study will subsequently challenge these perspectives, particularly regarding the interpretation and assessment of Philo's view of culture and politics, proposing that Niehoff presents the political situation in a more favorable light than Philo's actual portrayal. It is my working hypothesis that the political circumstances of Rome and its relationship with the Jewish population contributed to a radicalization of Philo's perspective on the Roman colonizing empire.[57]

It follows, therefore, that Niehoff not only posits the Exposition as having been composed in Rome but also contends that the intended audience of the Exposition comprised readers lacking prior familiarity with the Jewish Scriptures. Furthermore, she proposes that the work should be regarded as a historiographical piece influenced by and tailored for a Roman readership.[58]

Her view of the time of writing the Exposition has been accepted by several.[59] Her perspectives on the influence of Stoic philosophy on Philo's later works have garnered some scholarly support, although there exist more critical or cautious viewpoints and interpretations within the academic community.[60] Consequently, her biography of Philo and her other related studies constitute noteworthy contributions to the discourse surrounding Philo and his social and ideological milieu.

---

57. It is telling that when she sums up her view of what Philo's stay in Rome meant to him, politics or his view of Rome is hardly mentioned. See Niehoff, *Philo of Alexandria*, 11 and 14. It's conspicuous to me that she focuses that one-sidedly on his intellectual development even though she admits that Philo "never mentions contact with Roman intellectuals, not even with his late contemporary Seneca," who had partly grown up in Alexandria, and spoke fluent Greek. See further on this also Koskenniemi, "Philo and Rome."

58. Niehoff, "Philo's Exposition in a Roman Context," 1–7.

59. Lanzinger, exempla gratia, describes the *Exposition* as "ein literarisches begleitprojekt zu seiner politischen Agenda . . . , die ebenfalls darauf abzielt, die Angelegenheiten der Juden in ein positives Licht zu rücken." Lanzinger, "Einführung in die Schrift," 8.

60. See Hunt, ed. and trans., *De vita Mosis* 1.8–16, who leaves the context of the composition and intended audience open.

One of the scholars who has published a more comprehensive evaluation and criticism of Niehoff's biography of Philo is the Finnish scholar Erkki Koskenniemi.[61] He identifies and examines three specific areas that he contends are the most problematic aspects of Niehoff's comprehensive interpretation of Philo's biography: the duration of Philo's sojourn in Rome, her interpretation of the chronological order of Philo's works, and Niehoff's proposition regarding a discernible evolution in Philo's philosophical thought.

Regarding the extension of Philo's sojourn in Rome, it is, furthermore, argued here that Niehoff's assessment is excessively optimistic concerning both the precise timing of his arrival in Rome and the duration of his stay there.[62] Koskenniemi argues that Philo might have arrived in that city as late as winter 39–40 and possibly did not participate in the second embassy. Hence, he may have stayed there less than two years. While this may sound speculative, the data we have does not support a firm conclusion but is open to several readings.[63]

Moreover, Koskenniemi indicates that Philo was of advanced age upon his arrival in Rome (cf. *Legat.* 1). He further contends that Niehoff tends to overstate the impact of Rome on Philo: "Rome was not a superb cultural centre that could easily impress a learned man educated in Alexandria"—Alexandria was not a peripheral location.[64] Therefore, it is not evident that Philo would have altered his primary lines of thought during his sojourn in Rome. This consideration is also significant when examining the shift in philosophical preferences proposed by Niehoff, specifically that Philo transitioned from Platonic to Stoic patterns in his thinking. Niehoff presupposes a particular sequence of Philo's works and identifies a distinct progression from Platonic to Stoic patterns. However, if the chronology of Philo's works remains uncertain, the evolution of his thoughts is similarly indeterminate.

Lastly, Koskenniemi examines Niehoff's perspective on the plausible evolution of Philo's philosophical inclination from Platonism to Stoicism.[65]

---

61. Koskenniemi, "Philo and Rome."

62. Koskenniemi, "Philo and Rome," 116–20.

63. "It is not out of the question that Philo stayed several years in Rome and wrote many of his treaties there. However, this claim does not seem to be supported by sources, and none of his treatises can be located in Rome with certainty." Koskenniemi, "Philo and Rome," 119.

64. Koskenniemi, "Philo and Rome," 120.

65. Koskenniemi, "Philo and Rome," 126–37.

This issue is also closely related to the question of how and where Philo acquired knowledge of Greek philosophical thought. While Niehoff posits that Philo was significantly influenced by Stoicism in Rome, Koskenniemi contends that Stoicism was well-established in Alexandria as well, and that Stoicism was neither novel to Philo nor were its influences substantially more pronounced in Rome compared to Alexandria: "A great deal of Stoic philosophy had become common property well before Philo's time; unsurprisingly, the Stoics are present everywhere in his works, both pro and contra."[66] Furthermore, Koskenniemi especially attacks her view that Philo was influenced by the Sophists, especially what have been called "the Second Sophistic."[67] He asserts that the term "Second Sophistic" lacks a clear definition historically and presently. Furthermore, he contends that all representatives of the Second Sophists existed in the post-Philo era, and that most scholars have, until recently, been hesitant to characterize them as a cohesive movement. Consequently, he advises caution when employing "the second Sophistic" as a broad term, and suggests that if used in a narrow sense, "the phenomenon postdates Philo."[68]

RELEVANT READING STRATEGIES

As further background for better understanding the issues to be dealt with later, I will here give a brief review of some of the more central works and their specific reading strategies in vogue concerning Philo and politics by focusing on the relevant works by Sterling Tracy, E. R. Goodenough, Samuel Sandmel, Ray Barraclough, Maren R. Niehoff, and Katell Berthelot. Others might have been added, but I consider these (some of) the most important ones for the present study.[69]

Philo on Rome and Politics

In his study, published as far back as 1933, Sterling Tracy dealt with Philo's attitudes toward the Roman principate by primarily focusing on

---

66. Koskenniemi, "Philo and Rome," 133. On Koskenniemi's view of Philo's relation to the various philosophies, see Koskenniemi, *Greek Writers and Philosophers*.

67. See Koskenniemi, "Philo and Rome," 134–37. In addition to his book on *Greek Writers and Philosophers*, see here also Koskenniemi, "Philo and the Sophists."

68. Koskenniemi, "Philo and Rome," 135, 137.

69. Here I quote extensively—with only a few changes—from my former presentation in *Reading Philo*: See Seland, "Philo as a Citizen," 51–55.

his late historical works, such as *In Flaccum* and *De Legatione ad Gaium*. Tracy here claims it is important to distinguish Philo's separate roles—first as a member and leader of the Jewish πολίτευμα in Alexandria, next as a member of the larger Jewish Diaspora community, next as a resident of Alexandria, and finally as a subject of the Roman emperor (pp. 9–21). Tracy does not question the existence of such Jewish πολίτευματα in Alexandria and argues that the executive powers within the community lie with a special γερουσία (p. 9–10): "Certainly it was all-powerful in the time of Philo" (p. 13), and Tracy considers Philo to have been a member and leader of this Jewish *politeuma* (p. 14). Concerning Philo's place as a Jew in Alexandria, Tracy does not consider him a Greek or Roman citizen but interprets the statements in Philo's work on citizenship (e.g., *Flacc.* 53, 172) to be concerned with membership in the Jewish *politeuma* (pp. 16–19). Regarding *In Flaccum* and *De Legatione*, Tracy argues that the general political aim of Philo in these works is clear: "Both are undisguised attacks on Roman policy. Both advance the idea that a peculiar sanctity hedges about the Jewish people, that no Roman emperor can harm them with impunity" (p. 23).

In the last chapter of his relatively brief study, Tracy sharpens Philo's negative posture toward the Roman imperial system thus: "Political allusions in his philosophical works antedating the *In Flaccum* and *De Legatione* indicate that he had long recognized the fundamental incompatibility of the Roman imperial system and the polity of the Jewish people" (p. 48). Here Tracy points to an understanding and reading of Philo's writings that a few years later would be further developed by E. R. Goodenough, namely, that Philo's works include both direct statements concerning the Roman administration and indirect criticisms of Roman practices and institutions.[70] Tracy further notes that Philo nowhere outside *De Legatione* and *In Flaccum* has any words of praise for the emperor or Roman rule as such, and he finds that several aspects of Philo's descriptions of Moses's leadership are presented in terms that indicate its superiority to Roman rule. Furthermore, he argues that in describing and dissecting the practical politician in *De Josepho*, Philo had in mind the current prefect of Egypt (p. 53). Hence, when Philo does praise Roman rule or rulers, it should be read as primarily indicating apologetic purposes.[71]

---

70. See e.g., *Spec.* 2:90–95; 3:157–168 concerning Roman tax collection.

71. Tracy, *Philo Judaeus and the Roman Principate*, 51. This view is compatible with the view of Delling, "Philons Enkomium auf Augustus."

Erwin R. Goodenough's book *The Politics of Philo*, published in 1938,[72] remains probably still the most comprehensive study of these aspects in Philo's works. A central thesis in Goodenough's reading strategy is that Philo is to be read as an opponent of the Romans, and that he wrote against the Romans both openly and in coded form. He argues that Philo was at the same time both a privileged citizen and an alien in Alexandria. He belonged to the elite segments of the Jewish communities in the city, but at the same time, he was an outsider, not having access to the same privileges as Roman citizens. Furthermore, Philo was not an admirer of the Roman authorities: "he loved the Romans no more than the skipper of a tiny boat loves the hurricane."[73] In such circumstances, Goodenough argues, any opponent of the Romans had to be careful in what he said about the Roman authorities; if he was to mention them at all, he might have to do it cryptically or rhetorically (cf. *Somn.* 2:82–91).[74] Hence, Goodenough suggests that Philo is to be read as dealing with politics in three ways: directly, primarily in his *In Flaccum* and *De Legatione*; in his allegorical work on dreams, in code, as in *De Somniis* (especially *Somn.* 1:219–225 [Joseph?]; 2:61–64 [vainglory]; 78–91 [Joseph?] and 2:116–133). Then, in the Exposition, he comments on politics through innuendo, that is, through negative, indirect allusion. This latter method is to be detected in *De Josepho*, a treatise that Goodenough argued was written primarily for Gentiles,[75] and one in which Joseph is read and described in light of the Roman prefect in Egypt during Philo's time.[76]

Concerning the addressees of *In Flaccum*, Goodenough reads it as written for a Gentile audience after the death of Gaius, and possibly for the new prefect in Alexandria.[77] *De Legatione*, on the other hand, he surmises was written after the accession of Claudius and as a presentation to just that emperor.[78] Be that as it may, it seems obvious to most readers that these important political works of Philo should be read as written for both Jews and Gentiles, possibly even including the Roman authorities. Goodenough also finds some messianism in Philo's works, but it is

---

72. Goodenough, "Philo and Public Life," 77–79; Goodenough, *Politics*.

73. Goodenough, *Politics*, 7.

74. Goodenough, *Politics*, 4–6.

75. See especially Goodenough, *Introduction*, 61–62.

76. See Goodenough, *Politics*, 21–41; Goodenough, *Introduction*, 61.

77. Goodenough, *Politics*, 10–11; Goodenough, *Introduction*, 59; van der Horst, *Philo's "Flaccus,"* 15–16.

78. Goodenough, *Politics*, 19.

described in such a veiled way that "what he does say shows that there was much more thought of it than he dares to write."[79] Many scholars are of the opinion that Goodenough overstates his case,[80] but the issue of hidden agendas in Philo's writing style has also gained some support. We will have to deal more with his views on how to read Philo below.

Samuel Sandmel, once a student of Goodenough, has a brief chapter on Philo's political theory in his introductory book on Philo.[81] Considering Philo as a citizen and practical politician, he agrees to a large extent with Goodenough. Sandmel notes the somewhat surprising silence in Philo's works about the state of affairs in Judea, and also the almost complete absence of any allusion to David as a king or to his dynasty. This indicates to Sandmel that "Philo is concerned more with the situation of the Jewish community in Alexandria as part of a unique *politeuma* than with the Judean situation and experience."[82] To a large degree he also supports Goodenough's view that Philo criticized the Roman Empire in a veiled way in describing the ideal constitution by drawing on the Scriptures.[83] For instance, Philo's description of Joseph in an allegorical commentary is "a veiled description of a wicked Roman official."[84] Thus by allegory and by describing the constitution of the Jews as ideal, Philo can indicate Roman shortcomings.

A 1984 study by *Ray Barraclough* is probably one of the best and most comprehensive—after Goodenough—in dealing with various sides of Philo's politics on both the theoretical and practical levels.[85] Here Barraclough focuses both on Philo and the Roman world, and on Philo's theory of rule. He is critical of several of Goodenough's readings concerning the addressees of Philo's political writings and about Roman rule. Barraclough considers *De Legatione* to have been written for a wider Gentile audience, perhaps even for some with considerable political power, but also for those among the Jews who were "wavering in their faith that their God was still

---

79. Goodenough, *Politics*, 115.

80. See e.g., Barraclough, "Philo's Politics," 448–49.

81. Sandmel, *Philo of Alexandria*. See also Sandmel, "Philo Judaeus: An Introduction to the Man, His Writings, and His Significance."

82. Sandmel, *Philo of Alexandria*, 103.

83. "In his allusions to Roman rule, Philo had to be guarded in what he wrote, lest Romans learned of it and regard his views, as well as him, as subversive." Sandmel, *Philo of Alexandria*, 103.

84. Sandmel, *Philo of Alexandria*, 103.

85. Barraclough, "Philo's Politics."

sovereign over the affairs of mankind."[86] *In Flaccum*, moreover, was, by Barracloughs estimation, probably written for the new prefect as well as for Claudius himself. Barraclough does not agree with Goodenough, however, that Philo failed to appreciate the benefits of Roman rule. The Roman order was much more in accord with the conditions Philo considered most desirable in a state than Goodenough's interpretations of him allow.[87]

Goodenough's views have not won general acceptance. Yet some minor studies are more positive about his presentations of Philo as a politician critical of the Roman Empire, but even these studies do not back up all of Goodenough's claims about Philo as a politician.[88] David M. Hay, for example, discusses Philo's politics and exegesis in the treatises called *On Dreams*, and he finds that Philo offers both overt political criticism (*Somn.* 1:219–225; 2:78–91; 2:115–133) and some political views in allegorical forms (*Somn.* 2:42–64; 2:283–299). Hence he concludes that "part of Philo's purpose in *De Somniis* was to present answers to some of the political problems which he and his fellow Jews were facing."[89] Furthermore, the Danish scholar *Per Bilde*, investigating *In Flaccum* and *De Legatione*, concludes that he finds a "threatening tone" in these works, and that Goodenough is right to interpret them as hidden warnings to the Roman elite: If the traditionally positive view of imperial politics were to become a negative view, such a change would call forth an armed Jewish resistance that would represent severe difficulties for the Empire.[90]

Another interesting scholar to be briefly mentioned here is *Katell Berthelot*. In one of her recent articles dealing with Philo's view of the Roman Empire, she[91] argues that Philo's perception of the Roman Empire

86. Barraclough, "Philo's Politics," 450–51.

87. Barraclough, "Philo's Politics," 452, 472.

88. See also Seland, "'Colony' and 'Metropolis,'" 20. See Chapter 6 below.

89. Hay, "Politics and Exegesis," 438.

90. Commenting on *In Flaccum* and *Legatio*, he states that "these menacing features in the two writings, which most scholars do not pay attention to, cannot and should not be explained away. I therefore share Goodenough's interpretation that they are Philo's barely disguised warnings to the Roman élite: If the traditionally positive Roman policy towards the Jewish population is changed to negative, as it happened under the Emperor Caligula, there is a real risk that such a change will provoke armed Jewish resistance of an extent that will cause serious problems to Rome." Bilde, "Philo as a Polemist," 112. Reprinted in Bilde, *Collected Studies on Philo and Josephus*, 207–24. See also Birnbaum on *In Flaccum*: "Philo . . . may also wish to sound a warning to Gentiles to stop their maltreatment of his people." Birnbaum, *Place of Judaism*, 21.

91. Berthelot, "Philo's Perception of the Roman Empire." See also Berthelot, *Jews and Their Roman Rivals*.

was less positive than has generally been argued. She presents her views by carrying out an analysis of Philo's discourse about *pronoia*, *tychè* and the *translatio empirii*, and corroborates some of Goodenough's views. Philo's view, she argues, is apparent in his rejection of the idea that Rome would last forever due to divine providence.[92] Philo, she states, expected that the Empire would fade away, but Israel would blossom as no other nation ever had:[93] "Philo expected all empires—even the Roman Empire—to decline at some point in the course of history, and Israel to rise."[94] Hence, Philo's perception of Rome is less positive than has often been argued. Berthelot does not, however, deal more explicitly with Philo's role in practical politics in her study.

In her more recent book (2021), Berthelot deals with *Jews and Their Roman Rivals*. In that title she reveals part of her thesis, namely, that "the Roman empire represented a qualitatively different challenge than those Israel had previously encountered," a challenge that consisted of two factors distinguishing Rome from earlier challenges: "the first lies in the paradoxical similarities between Roman and Jewish self-definitions; the second in Rome's policy toward the Jews from the reign of Vespasian to that of Hadrian, which could be interpreted as an attempt to eradicate the Jewish cult and replace Jerusalem with Rome."[95] Berthelot draws a lot on Philo, and it might be argued that these two tendencies were evolving even earlier than at the time of Vespasian.

EXCURSUS II: *Allegory and Politics in Philo's Works*

Peder Borgen ends his survey of Philo studies from World War II to the 1980s[96] by suggesting that further investigations should consider how Philo attempts to make the allegorical method serve his Jewish aims. This challenge is not new, and studies and opinions on the topic are many and variegated. The topic has been taken up in a specific way in recent years by David Dawson, Jonathan Dyck, and Ellen Birnbaum, who focus separately on how Philo's allegories might work as vehicles to spread his cultural and sociopolitical ideas and aims.

---

92. Berthelot, "Philo's Perception of the Roman Empire," 177–84.
93. See especially Berthelot, "Philo's Perception of the Roman Empire," 184–87.
94. Berthelot, "Philo's Perception of the Roman Empire," 185.
95. Berthelot, *Jews and Their Roman Rivals*, 3.
96. Borgen, "Philo of Alexandria," 128–32.

In describing his own heuristic view on allegory (1992), *David Dawson*[97] sketches three ways in which allegorical interpretations might work. First, it might work as socially endorsing and supportive. If, for example, the literal sense of a text is 'culturally shocking,' an allegorical, nonliteral reading might neutralize the culturally deviant meanings of the literal text.[98] On the other hand, "if the readily apparent sense of the text is the culturally endorsed literal sense, an allegorical reading might provide a revolutionary challenge to prevailing cultural norms."[99] And then, thirdly, Dawson proposes another way that allegorical readings can revise culture, used sometimes by allegorical readers who are proponents of scripturallly based religions. This happens when allegory is used to enable scripture itself to absorb and reinterpret culture: "Rather than simply subverting pre-allegorical, literal readings, allegorical readings of this third sort bring meaning previously unrelated to scripture into a new and really revisionary relationship with scripture as read in the pre-allegorical, literal manner."[100]

Coming to Philo, then, Dawson elaborates on how he sees Philo and some other Hellenistic Jewish writers make sense of the world with the help of allegorical interpretations:[101]

> How can the world, in all its Greek character, be the same world so adequately described in Jewish Scripture? How, for instance, in its scientific reality can it be a world that is properly understood in terms of the Jewish Passover? Hellenistic Jews do not respond to such questions with the simple claim that truth is to be found in both Greek texts and Scripture. Their claim is much bolder, and from a classical point of view thoroughly presumptuous. Jewish interpretative subordination is in fact a hermeneutical usurpation in which classical writers are demoted to the status of mosaic epigones, condemned merely to echo his original and sublime insights. Authentic Greek culture is actually Jewish. Aristeas, Aristobulus, and other now-forgotten Ptolemaic Jews bequeathed this reading of Scripture as a revisionary interpretation of Greek culture to Philo, who developed it on an even grander scale.

---

97. Dawson, *Allegorical Readers and Cultural Revision*, 73–126.
98. Dawson, *Allegorical Readers and Cultural Revision*, 10.
99. Dawson, *Allegorical Readers and Cultural Revision*, 10.
100. Dawson, *Allegorical Readers and Cultural Revision*, 10.
101. Dawson, *Allegorical Readers and Cultural Revision*, 82.

Hence Philo here stands on the shoulders of some of his predecessors. Philo, however, develops this procedure further. Sometimes Philo might subordinate his Hellenistic heritage to Scripture by having Scripture directly proclaim Hellenistic philosophical wisdom. Accordingly, Philo might emphasize that Moses is prior to the Hellenistic writers and surpasses them in wisdom (*Mos.* 1:21):[102]

> Because Moses came before the classical authors, his rewriting paradoxically becomes original writing, and the classical writers become his weak imitators. Philo's allegorical readings seldom contradict competing classical sources. Instead, whatever of value they contain has been anticipated by the author of the master text of the Pentateuch.

This is what Dawson calls Philo's *reinscription*, a reading through which the intellectual and cultural wisdom of his society originally came from Moses and had been written first by Moses. Hence some of Philo's allegories can be read as an usurpation or subverting of the Hellenistic values and ideas in favor of his Judaism. In many ways this is close to how Borgen argues for his view that Philo was a "conqueror, on the verge of being conquered," though Borgen does not associate his view of Philo so closely with Philo's allegorical interpretations.[103]

In his 2002 work with its subtitle *The Politics of Allegorical Interpretation*, Jonathan Dyck[104] sets out to discover what Philo's work might say about the formation, maintenance, and transformation of Jewish cultural identity in the Diaspora. Dyck disagrees very clearly with Dawson, finding that the main problem with Dawson's view is that it does not do justice to what Philo does when he interprets Scripture allegorically, and Dyck disagrees with the characterization of Philo's procedures as 'subversive.' Instead of 'subversive,' Dyck prefers the label 'subordinate,'[105] and he blames Dawson for having overlooked that Philo privileges the allegorical over the literal. Dyck introduces a distinction—to me a somewhat strange one in this context—between what Philo thought he was doing and what he actually did do; that is, Dyck thinks that Dawson does not adequately distinguish between intention and social consequences

---

102. Dawson, *Allegorical Readers and Cultural Revision*, 112.
103. On Borgen's view, see esp. Borgen, *Philo of Alexandria, An Exegete*, 140–57.
104. Dyck, "Philo, Alexandria and Empire."
105. Dyck, "Philo, Alexandria and Empire," 166.

in Philo.[106] In investigating Philo's relation to the literalists and the allegorists, Dyck comes to the conclusion that Philo belittles the literalists and sides with the allegorists. Dyck's conclusion thus runs like this:

> It is my view that, far from revising (let alone subverting) Greek culture and imperial rule, Philo was endorsing it. Not necessarily in a conscious way but rather by participating in a discursive tradition that sought to recast Judaism in a form appropriate to its imperial and cosmopolitan environment. Philo represents a form of Judaism which had come to terms with a high degree of socio-cultural and political assimilation and acculturation. Furthermore it accommodated Judaism to the dominant culture via practices such as allegorical interpretation without abandoning its distinctive traditions and practices.[107]

Ellen Birnbaum (2003), for her part, does not fully agree with either Dawson or Dyck but steers a middle course.[108] One the one hand, she asserts that the subordination of Greek wisdom to Jewish Scripture was certainly one way Jews could claim superiority. On the other hand, allegorical interpretations might also promote other views, such as a universalist one or a neutral one. However, in line with views stated earlier,[109] she restates that in (some of) Philo's allegorical interpretations, Israel loses its ethnic features, and Philo's interpretations seem to "allow for the possibility that *all* who are virtuous and wise may stand in special relation to God" (see *Post.* 91–92).[110] In this way, according to Birnbaum, Philo is here seen to give new meaning to some particular Jewish marks of identity, and to transcend ethnic and political definitions in favor of other distinctions related to intellectual and spiritual qualities. According to Birnbaum, Israel does not encompass only ethnic Jews but also includes those who are able to see God, whether Gentiles or Jews.

In the end, however, by way of conclusion, it is clear that some Philonic allegorical interpretations can express a sense of superiority, but not in all cases. Allegorical interpretations may also reflect social and political realities, but "it is difficult to ascertain decisively whether correlations are

---

106. To me that is a much more far-ranging distinction than what Dawson and Dyck in fact deals satisfactorily with in their studies in view here.

107. Dyck, "Philo, Alexandria and Empire," 174.

108. See Birnbaum, "Allegorical Interpretation," 307–29. See also her "Philo on the Greeks," 37–58.

109. Birnbaum, *Place of Judaism*.

110. Birnbaum, "Allegorical Interpretation," 319.

actual or merely possible."[111] A more thorough assessment, however, has to draw on more than just Philo's allegorical interpretations.

Every reader of Philo's work will not have to read many pages before discovering some of Philo's allegories. And his allegorical interpretations are not to be found only in his so-called allegorical commentaries, but are present in most of his other works too. Philo is an allegorist, but he is also a literalist (*Migr.* 89–93):

> There are some who, regarding laws in their literal sense in the light of symbols of matters belonging to the intellect, are overpunctilious about the latter, while treating the former with easy-going neglect. Such men I for my part should blame for handling the matter in too easy and off-hand a manner: they ought to give careful attention to both aims, to a more full and exact investigation of what is not seen to be stewards without reproach . . . These men are taught by the sacred word to have thought for good repute, and to let go nothing that is part of the customs fixed by divinely empowered men greater that those of our time.

Then Philo gives some examples of what might be at stake here:

> It is quite true that the Seventh Day is meant to teach the power of the Unoriginate and the non-action of created beings. But let us not for this reason abrogate the laws laid down for its observance, and light fires or till the ground . . .
>
> It is also true that the Feast is a symbol of the gladness of the soul, but we should not for this reason turn our backs on the general gatherings of the year's seasons.
>
> It is true that circumcision does indeed portray the excision of pleasure and all passions . . . but let us not on this account repeal the law laid down for circumcising . . .
>
> Nay we should look on all these outward observances as resembling the body, and their inner meanings as resembling the soul. It follows that, exactly as we have to take thought for the body, because it is the abode of the soul, so we must pay heed to the letter of the laws.

There has been a significant and voluminous discussion about the understanding of these passages, and the understanding of how Philo did cope with allegorical possibilities or—as he would probably say—their necessity for understanding how to live in the world, observing the Torah.

---

111. Birnbaum, "Allegorical Interpretation," 329.

We will also see in the next chapter how some of Philo's more political statements have been formulated, and how they are to be read—that is, how to understand what may be hidden in his statements and descriptions. Indeed Philo talked about how to cope with Roman rule and rulers in sayings that need decoding to be understood.

SUMMARY AND OUTLOOK

Philo of Alexandria was a prolific author: approximately forty of his works remain extant, and according to commentaries from certain church fathers, his oeuvre may have encompassed at least twenty additional titles. Moreover, the possibility exists that further works remain undiscovered. Additionally, his known corpus comprises expository exegetical works on the Torah, philosophical treatises, apologetic works, and historical works addressing contemporary events.

In the preceding pages, it has been argued that what is referred to as Philo's allegorical commentaries are likely his earliest works, composed in Alexandria prior to 38 CE. Following the events of 38–41 CE, he authored his historical works *In Flaccum* and *De Legatione ad Gaium*. These were followed by his comprehensive works on the *Special Laws*, today designated as the Exposition, encompassing ten works; additionally, some philosophical works exist. Beyond the diverse perspectives regarding the chronology of his work, there has been extensive scholarly discourse concerning Philo's allegories, as well as on the characterization of the genres of his works, a debate that persists in current academic circles.

Maren R. Niehoff, a prominent scholar residing and working in Israel, has produced what is arguably the most comprehensive investigation in recent years of Philo's life and work, a study she appropriately designates *An Intellectual Biography*. In the present work I follow her assertions in situating the Exposition in the period after the Alexandrian pogrom and Philo's sojourn in Rome (38/39/41 CE).

In the next chapter, I will deal briefly with Philo as a politician, especially focusing on his attitudes toward the Roman Empire.

4

Philo and Practical Politics

Reimagining Philo the Politician

> "There was a time when I had leisure for philosophy and for the contemplation of the universe and its contents . . . But, as it proved, my steps were dogged by the deadliest of mischiefs, the hater of good, envy, . . . and [it] ceased not to pull me down with violence till it had plunged me in the ocean of civil cares . . ."
>
> SPEC. 3:1–3

INTRODUCTION

ACCORDING TO E. R. Goodenough, Philo employed 'coded' language to caution his readers against the Romans, partially to critique them. In recent scholarship, there has been discourse regarding whether Paul the apostle utilized 'coded' language in his epistles as well. One may particularly note the works of Harrison and Heilig, who incorporate a similar interpretation in their analyses of specific sections of Philo's *De Somniis*. A more thorough examination of these Philonic texts will subsequently be conducted.

It may be considered somewhat anachronistic to devote such extensive attention to Goodenough's perspectives, as demonstrated in the preceding chapters and subsequent pages. Nevertheless, examining certain aspects of his exegesis of Philo, without necessarily endorsing all components thereof, may prove valuable. Regardless of individual opinions, Goodenough remains a preeminent figure among earlier Philo scholars, and his interpretations of Philo may still offer substantive insights. His work is significant for comprehending the research history pertaining to Philo, and he should continue to be regarded as a valuable discussion partner on various issues related to understanding Philo's works.

The significance of more recent studies of Paul and his perspectives on the Roman Empire may be considered less pertinent in the current context. Nevertheless, there are some parallels between studies of Paul and studies of Philo when it comes to historical context and methodology. On the one hand, there is ongoing discourse about the merit of searching for 'coded' messages in Paul's writings; the methodologies employed have been subjected to substantial critique, but they have also found acceptance in some quarters.[1] Concurrently, Paul and Philo are two distinct individuals engaged in divergent forms of work within different contexts. The most salient issues representing differences between Paul and Philo can be delineated as follows: Paul was a 'Christian' Jew, adhering to the belief in Jesus of Nazareth as the Messiah, composing epistles to his coreligionists in various communities in the Diaspora. He did not belong to the elite strata of society, and he maintained a somewhat strained relationship with Jewish synagogues. Moreover, he held no political offices or responsibilities in Jewish or Roman contexts but was regarded with suspicion by certain Roman and Jewish authorities. Conversely, Philo belonged to an affluent and influential family involved in politics at multiple levels. He did not compose epistles but rather books of an expository nature, as well as historical and philosophical works intended for both Jewish and non-Jewish audiences and was most likely active as an instructor in the synagogue(s) of Alexandria. Additionally, he was politically engaged both in his hometown and in Rome.

Several aspects differentiate Philo from Paul, and there are also multiple features that make it more appropriate to investigate issues of politics in Philo than in Paul. Moreover, various aspects of Philo's biography remain ambiguous. Despite Philo's membership in a wealthy and presumably influential family, limited information is available regarding his familial relations. Based on *Spec.* 3, it appears that from early on he

---

1. See for instance, Kim, *Paul and the New Perspective*; Barclay, "Why the Roman Empire Was Insignificant to Paul"; McKnight and Modica, eds., *Jesus Is Lord, Caesar Isnot*. The literature from both sides is impossible to present, or even name, here.

chose a divergent lifestyle from that of his family members, withdrawing from political activities and dedicating himself to philosophy and Torah studies. Additionally, certain passages indicate his disdain for urban life and for the perspectives and interests of the general populace. Daniel R. Schwartz interprets such statements as "aristocratic prejudice" and "snobbish remarks of a wealthy pensioner, tucked away in his study in one of the family's residences."[2] At the same time, Goodenough goes to the other extreme, considering Philo a person with extensive judicial experience and competence.[3] Both perspectives may be overstating their claims based on insufficient evidence. Although Philo may have spent several years in scholarly seclusion, he subsequently traveled to Rome, potentially as the leader of a delegation to the emperor (cf. *Ant.* 18:259), to negotiate the conditions of the Jews in Alexandria. However, what were his personal views regarding the Romans, the emperor, and the empire? While it is not possible to ascertain Philo's innermost thoughts and emotions, several of his statements have been cited to elucidate his sentiments about Roman authority. However, some of these statements are expressed in ambiguous terms; some are even interpreted by certain scholars as 'coded' messages, conveying significant negativity towards the colonizing Roman Empire and its rulers. Such 'coded' messages would be particularly relevant in a postcolonial context where caution was necessary, especially for an individual like Philo with political affiliations and ambitions. Consequently, it is imperative to examine some aspects of Philo's biography more closely before addressing the significant and problematic events of 38–41 CE and then proceeding to present some cultural criticisms of Philo in Part 2.

---

2. Schwartz, "Philo, His Family and His Times." See his colorful descriptions on page 14: "Given the illustrious ties of Philo's brother and nephews, it seems that while we might imagine Philo as the retiring, studious and respected resident of an upstairs suite of Alexander's palatial home in Alexandria or of some nearby residence, we should also imagine him as emerging from his chambers now and then, as the opportunity arose, to share in the visits of wealthy businessmen, Roman officials, and members of the Herodian family."

This imaginative description might also be turned around and lead one to ask if Philo possibly was living further away from his family both locally, economically and culturally. But that would all be just speculation. We don't know.

3. Goodenough, "Philo and Public Life," 77–79; Goodenough, *Jurisprudence*.

FROM PHILOSOPHER TO POLITICIAN: THE AUTOBIOGRAPHICAL VALUE OF *SPEC.* 3:1–6

There are few autobiographical remarks in the works of Philo.[4] One of the most extensive passages concerns his relationship to political life in Alexandria. In his two works *In Flaccum* and *De Legatio* we can observe Philo as a practicing politician, dealing with the Romans. We can also find several politically colored statements in some of his other works, for his politics are rooted in his wider ideology.[5] Nevertheless, the duration of Philo's direct involvement in politics remains uncertain, as evidenced by the following passage, which indicates that his engagement in political endeavors was neither continuous nor preferred, but rather imposed upon him. The passage presents interpretative challenges; therefore, it merits quotation in extenso:[6]

> There was a time when I had leisure for philosophy and for the contemplation of the universe and its contents, when I made its spirit my own in all its beauty and loveliness and true blessedness, when my constant companions were divine themes and verities, wherein I rejoiced with a joy that never cloyed or sated. I had no base or abject thoughts nor grovelled in search of reputation or of the wealth or bodily comforts, but seemed always to be borne aloft into the heights with a soul possessed by some God-sent inspiration, a fellow-traveller with the sun and moon and the whole heaven and universe. Ah then I gazed down from the upper air, and straining the mind's eye beheld, as from some commanding peak, the multitudinous worldwide spectacles of earthly things, and blessed my lot in that I had escaped by main force from the plagues of mortal life. But, as it proved, my steps were dogged by the deadliest of mischiefs, the hater of the good, envy, which suddenly set upon me and ceased not to pull me down with violence till it had plunged me in the ocean of civil cares, in which I am swept away, unable even to raise my head above the water. Yet amid my groans I hold my own, for, planted in my soul from my earliest days I keep the yearning for culture which ever has pity and compassion for me, lifts me up

---

4. I here draw upon and elaborate on my description in Seland, "Philo as a Citizen," 60–63.

5. See here, e.g., the study of Borgen (*Philo of Alexandria, an Exegete*, 158–93), who has characterized *In Flaccum* and *De Legatione* as works applying the principles of the Torah.

6. The translation used here is the Loeb Classical Library (LCL) edition: Colson et al., eds. and trans., *Philo*, vol. 7.

and relieves my pain. To this I owe it that sometimes I raise my head and with the soul's eyes—dimly indeed because the mist of extraneous affairs has clouded their clear vision—I yet make shift to look around me in my desire to inhale a breath of life pure and unmixed with evil. And if unexpectedly I obtain a spell of fine weather and a calm from civil turmoils, I get me wings and ride the waves and almost tread the lower air, wafted by the breezes of knowledge which often urges me to come to spend my days with her, a truant as it were from merciless masters in the shape not only of men but of affairs, which pour in upon me like a torrent from different sides. Yet it is well for me to give thanks to God even for this, that though submerged I am not sucked down into the depths, but can also open the soul's eyes, which in my despair of comforting hope I thought had now lost their sight, and am irradiated by the light of wisdom, and am not given over to lifelong darkness. So behold me daring, not only to read the sacred messages of Moses, but also in my love of knowledge to peer into each of them and unfold and reveal what is not known to the multitude. (*Spec.* 3:1–6)

Philo appears to assert or imply at least three points in this passage. First, there existed a period during which he could dedicate himself entirely to his esteemed theological and philosophical studies: "There was a time when I had leisure for philosophy and for the contemplation of the universe and its contents" (3:1). This era is characterized as the zenith of his life, a time when he "rejoiced with a joy that never cloyed or sated." He does not, however, specify at which stage of his life this period occurred or its duration. Peder Borgen has interpreted this section of *De specialibus legibus* as depicting a "Heavenly Ascent of Philo," that is, "his own inspired ascent in a way similar to the description of the ascent found in *Op. Mund.* 70."[7] In another article, Borgen compares the text of Philo to similar texts in the Revelation of John and repeats his view of Philo's 'report' as a report of ascent and descent: "In this passage, *Spec.* 3:1–6, Philo has a report on his own ascents as he experienced them in two different situations. In one situation he felt himself to be at a distance from earthly troubles, *Spec.* 3:1–2. In the other, he was deeply involved in the cares and troubles of the Jewish *politeia*, 3:3–6a."[8]

---

7. Borgen, "Heavenly Ascent in Philo."
8. Borgen, "Autobiographical Ascent Reports," 314. Reprinted in Borgen, "Autobiographical Ascent Reports: Philo and John the Seer," (2021), 249–60.

Second, Philo experienced a phenomenon described in terms that present significant interpretative challenges: an event occurred that "ceased not to pull me down with violence till it had plunged me in the ocean of civil cares, in which I am swept away, unable to raise my head above the water." This description likely serves as a means of informing or reminding the readers that Philo had been engaged in scholarly pursuits for a considerable period before being compelled to involve himself in political matters and activities. "As it stands, the passage is a cry against his having had to abandon a life of contemplation in order to devote himself to political matters."[9]

Third, the situation depicted in this text is likely composed in consideration of subsequent events, reflecting the author's circumstances at the time of writing—he is engaged in public service. Periodically, he manages to allocate time away from his official responsibilities to engage in more philosophical pursuits: "if unexpectedly I obtain a spell of fine weather and a calm from civil turmoils, I get me wings and ride the waves and almost tread the lower air, wafted by the breezes of knowledge which often urges me to come to spend my days with her, a truant as it were from merciless masters in the shape not only of men but of affairs, which pour in upon me like a torrent from different sides" (*Spec.* 3:5). During these intervals, he is able to conduct research and provide instruction, to "unfold and reveal what is not known to the multitude" (*Spec.* 3:6).

The principal aspects of Goodenough's interpretation of this period may be considered plausible: "What the passage indicates is that Philo spent a period in his youth as a recluse (presumably with the Therapeutae), but perceived that his people required his presence to such an extent that he returned to them, and subsequently found solace during his leisure hours by composing works on the mystical message of the Scriptures, while dedicating his primary career to public service."[10] However, several questions remain unresolved: Specifically, at what point did Philo find it necessary to depart from his contemplative lifestyle, what were the underlying reasons for this departure, and what subsequent occupation did he pursue? These inquiries have yet to receive definitive and uncontested responses from scholarly research.

A contemporary interpretation of the circumstances that compelled Philo to suspend his contemplative and literary pursuits reads *Spec.* 3:1–6

---

9. Goodenough, *Politics*, 66.

10. Goodenough, *Politics*, 68. His reference to Philo staying with the Therapeutae is, however, more dubious.

as alluding to the pogrom in Alexandria in 38 CE, and Philo's subsequent journey to Rome in 38/39 CE as a member (potentially the leader) of the delegation to Emperor Gaius Caligula. The purpose of this delegation was to negotiate the status of Jews in Alexandria in the aftermath of the pogrom. This perspective has garnered increased acceptance in recent scholarly discourse.[11] Peder Borgen, too, considers this scenario and seems to vacillate between acceepting and rejecting it in his book *Philo of Alexandria, an Exegete for His Time*. Finally, he comes down on the side of rejecting it.[12] Scholars who reject this proposal do so because if the events of 38 CE were indeed the contextual background for *Spec.* 3:1–6, then works such as *Spec.* 3, *On the Virtues*, and *On Rewards and Punishments* must be dated later.[13] But once this new dating is made plausible—as by Maren R. Niehoff, for example—then the view that *Spec.* 3 relates to the troubles of 38–41 becomes both possible and plausible.[14]

The last question related to the understanding of *Spec.* 3 is what kind of work Philo might have had as the basis for the problems behind this text. Goodenough contends that "there can be no doubt that Philo actually spent the major part of his life in some public office."[15] Later in the same article, he surmises that "his duties were of a judicial character, in which he had to administer Jewish Law in harmony with the Hellenistic law of Alexandria, though this cannot be demonstrated."[16] In his work called *The Jurisprudence of the Jewish Courts in Egypt*, Goodenough

---

11. Morris, "Jewish Philosopher Philo," 844; Niehoff, *Philo of Alexandria*, 7–8.

12. See Borgen, *Philo of Alexandria, An Exegete*, 171–75 and 181. In his study Borgen, "Autobiographical Ascent Reports" (reprinted in Borgen, *Illuminations*), he says that it does not "without doubt" prove that it refers to the pogrom. But he admits that if Philo refers to earlier events, they probably were preludes to the events of 38–41 CE. We know, however, very little about such 'preludes.'

13. As for others arguing that Spec. 3:1–6 is written after the events of 38–40 CE, see e.g., Mach, "Choices for Changing Frontiers," 319–33. See also Kraft, who is arguing for a late date for Philo's descriptions of Joseph: Kraft, "Tiberius Julius Alexander and the Crisis in Alexandria According to Josephus," 175–84. See now also the view of Kaiser, *Philo von Alexandrien. Denkender Glaube—Eine Einführung*, 30–40. Kaiser seems to present *In Flaccum, De Legatione* as belonging to a "Zwischenperiode," followed by a third phase in which he locates *Abr., Ios., De vita Mosis, Decal., Spec.* 1–4., *Virt.* and *Praem.*

14. Morris, "The Jewish Philosopher Philo," 844. See also Cover, "Israel Scriptures," 171, who states that "Philo penned this series after his failed leadership efforts in the embassy to the Roman emperor Gaius Caligula."

15. Goodenough, "Philo and Public Life," 77.

16. Goodenough, "Philo and Public Life," 79.

suggests that Philo was "a practical political administrator of some kind during much of his life,"[17] but he admits this suggestion is a guess.

The majority of scholars have not adhered to Goodenough's relatively precise definition of Philo's profession; nevertheless, they would likely concur that Philo must have held a position of public responsibility to be elected as a representative delegate of the Alexandrian Jews to the emperor in Rome in 38–41 CE. It is evident, however, that by becoming a member of that delegation to Rome, Philo entered the political sphere, regardless of his prior occupations.

To conclude, while there is still some discussion about what period of life *Spec.* 3 refers to, I agree with Niehoff[18] and several others[19] that it most probably refers to the troubles in Alexandria in 38 CE, which led to Philo's appointment as the leader of the Jewish embassy to Rome. No other known occurrences in Philo's life appear to align more closely with the description provided in *Spec.* 3:1–6.

NONDATABLE (AND CODED?) DESCRIPTIONS OF CRUCIAL EPISODES WITH THE ROMANS

The majority of texts interpreted as alluding to perceived or actual events, and which are presumed to be presented in 'coded' forms by Philo, are challenging to date. Some may be more appropriately considered as references to archetypal situations rather than to specific, datable occurrences. Conversely, concrete and datable situations may also serve as exemplars. Subsequent sections will address several such instances.[20]

---

17. Goodenough, *Jurisprudence*, 9.

18. Niehoff, *Philo of Alexandria*, 7–8; Niehoff, "Philo's Exposition"; see also Niehoff *Jewish Exegesis*, 169–85. Runia seems to accept this view in Runia, "Philon von Alexandria," col. 608.

19. See Bloch on *De vita Mosis* (Bloch, "Alexandria in Pharaonic Egypt," esp. pp. 71 and 76), and Schaller on the *Expositio* (Schaller, "Philon von Alexandreia und das 'Heilige Land,'" 13–27).

20. For a somewhat broader description of "Tension and Influence" in Philo's world and time, see Borgen, *Philo of Alexandria, An Exegete*, 158–75.

Warnings to Avoid Roman Officers and Beasts in the Streets: *De Somniis* 2:78–92

In *De Somniis* 2:78–92, there is an extended passage that certain scholars have identified as indicating Philo's acute awareness of the consequences of provoking or antagonizing Roman authorities in Alexandria. Furthermore, these scholars suggest that Philo cautioned his readers to exercise prudence in their behavior and to impose self-restraint:

> 83 Surely then they are all lunatics and madmen who take pains to display untimely frankness (παρρησίαν ἄκαιρον), and sometimes dare to oppose kings and tyrants in words and deeds. They do not perceive that not only like cattle are their necks under the yoke, but that the harness extends to their whole bodies and souls, their wives and children and parents, and the wide circle of friends and kinsfolk united to them by fellowship of feeling, and that the driver can with perfect ease spur drive on or pull back, and mete out any treatment small or great just as he pleases.
>
> 84. And therefore they are branded and scourged and mutilated and undergo a combination of all the sufferings which merciless cruelty can inflict short of death, and finally are led away to death itself.
>
> 85 These are the rewards of untimely free-speaking (ἀκαίρου παρρησίας), which in the eyes of sensible judges is not free-speaking at all; rather they are the guerdons of silliness and frenzy and incurable brainsickness....
>
> 91 Again, do not we too, when we are spending time in the market-place, make a practice of standing out of the path of our rulers and also of beasts of carriage, though our motive in the two cases is entirely different? With the rulers it is done to shew them honour, with the animals from fear and to save us from suffering serious injury from them.
>
> 92 And if ever occasions permit it is good to subdue the violence of enemies by attack, but if they do not permit the safe course is to keep quiet, and if we wish to gain any help from them the fitting course is to soften and tame them.

The text likely does not address specific events, but rather generalizes about the relevant attitudes of the colonized population towards the colonizers in urban settings, particularly during encounters in city streets. Given the narrow nature of streets in preindustrial cities, Philo's descriptions become vivid and conceivable even in contemporary times.

Goodenough writes about this passage that "The Jews could hardly have mistaken Philo's meaning," and he adds: "The propitiating attitude he was advising was the only one a sensible Jew or other non-Roman subject in the Empire could take under the existing circumstances. But he loved the Romans no more than the skipper of a tiny boat loves a hurricane."[21] This way of hinting at the power of the Roman colonizers and their ways of representing a threat to their subjects has been labeled "coded language" or "hidden transcripts."[22] Harrison finds this perception plausible and valuable: "Given the political vulnerability of the Jews under Tiberius, Caligula, and Claudius, Philo's advice is particularly pointed as he explains the symbolism behind this imagery (2:92): '. . . it is good thing to attack our enemies and put down their power; but when we have no such opportunity, it is better to be quiet; but if we wish to find perfect safety as far as they are concerned, it is advantageous to caress them.'"[23]

However, the question arises as to whether Philo is indeed referring to the Romans in this context. Alternative interpretations of Philo's words about the authorities in question have been proposed. Ray Barraclough has posited that Philo is "referring more generally to relationships with Gentile power-groups," and he contends that it is the Alexandrian Greeks, rather than the Romans, who are the subject of this discourse.[24] However, Christoph Heilig's criticism of this perspective appears to be justified when he identifies that in the preceding context (*Somn.* 2.78–79), Philo explicitly refers to rulers.[25] Consequently, a reference to the Romans and the political situation in Alexandria remains the most plausible interpretation.

Maybe David Hay's conclusion should be accepted but with some qualifications. He says that "there can be little doubt that Philo is effectively teaching his readers that in general even tyrannical rulers should be

---

21. Goodenough, *Politics*, 6–7. See Borgen, "Philo of Alexandria," 111.

22. See the brief review of research in Harrison, *Paul and the Imperial Authorities*, 28–33, and 300–308.

23. Harrison, *Paul and the Imperial Authorities*, 305. Harrison quotes here from Yonge, trans., *Works of Philo*. The translation of the Loeb Edition is given above. See Yoder, *Representatives of Roman Rule*, 96: "It seems likely that Philo is criticizing Jews whose open criticism and defiance of those on power could lead to suspicion being cast on the whole Judean ἔθνος. Instead, Philo recommends the use of 'blandishment and honeyed words' (τιθασείαις καὶ μελίγμασι, 2:89)."

24. Barraclough, "Philo's Politics," 536. See also Oertelt, *Herrscherideal und Herrschaftskritik*, 239–41.

25. Heilig, *Hidden Criticism?* 12.

submitted to and obeyed, lest they exercise overwhelming power to injure Jews and their loved ones."[26] Therefore, in general, Philo cautions his readers to exercise patience, maintain distance, and refrain from provoking the Romans: Avoid their presence, and they will disregard you.

Efforts to Abolish the Sabbath: *Somniis* 2.123–132

In *Somniis* 2.123–132, Philo presents "one of the ruling class" who wanted to do away with the law concerning the Sabbath. Philo does not identify this ruler, and consequently, the details of the event remain unspecified. Therefore, both issues are subjects of considerable scholarly debate. The relevant text follows:

> 123. Not long ago I knew one of the ruling class who when he had Egypt in his charge and under his authority purposed to disturb our ancestral customs and especially to do away with the law of the Seventh Day which we regard with most reverence and awe. He tried to compel men to do service to him on it and perform other actions which contravene our established customs, thinking that if he could destroy the ancestral rule of the Sabbath it would lead the way to irregularity in all other matters, and a general backsliding.

However, upon observing that individuals did not comply with or acquiesce to his plans, but instead became more fervent in their adherence to the Torah, he presented arguments in favor of his proposal, asserting that he possessed the authority to subjugate the Jews (*Somn.* 2:125–129). Philo, in contrast, argued against the ruler, stating:

> 130. What shall we say of one who says or even merely thinks these things? Shall we not call him an evil thing hitherto unknown: a creature of a strange land or rather one from beyond the ocean and the universe—he who dared to liken to the All-blessed his all-miserable self?

There have been some discussions as to the identity of this ruler. Colson[27] mentioned that some have suggested that the ruler was, in fact,

---

26. Hay, "Politics and Exegesis," 434. See Yoder, *Representatives of Roman Rule*, 96: "Philo advocates caution (εὐλάβεια, 2:82) and discourages 'untimely frankness' (παρρησία ἄκαιρος, 2:83. 85), reminding his reader that these rulers have the power to punish not only the speakers but also their families and their entire people."

27. See Colson et al., eds. and trans., *Philo* 5:609; and *Filón de Alexandría, Sobre los Sueños; Sobre José*, 155, note 272. Goodenough, *Politics*, 29, too argues against this date

Flaccus, but Colson also refutes this considering what is said about Flaccus in *In Flaccum*. He suggests that it may be an allusion to Flaccus' predecessors, Iberus or Vitrasius Pollio, but without any further arguments for his suggestion. The most radical interpretation of this event is probably the one presented by Robert A. Kraft. In several articles published in Festschriften, the author has posited that Philo's reference in *De Somniis* 2:123–132 to a specific ruler governing Egypt who had decided to abolish the sacred law concerning the Sabbath might allude to Tiberius Alexander, Philo's nephew. Tiberius Alexander served as governor of Egypt in the 60s CE. If this hypothesis is correct, then it would suggest that multiple works by Philo belonging to the allegorical commentaries were composed significantly later than previously assumed, and consequently, Philo's lifespan may have extended into the 60s CE. However, the author's propositions have not generated substantial scholarly discourse, potentially due to their radical nature, the inherent challenges in dating Philo's life, and the implications of a later dating for *De Somniis*.

Another effort to date this event is carried out by Michael F. Mach.[28] He points out that the episode is located almost at the end of *De Somniis* 2, and he adds: "Indeed, it has been observed that the allegorical exploration of the biblical text in *de somniis* is much more outspokenly political, facing political problems and even persecution of Jews, offering advice to the members of the community as well as repeating the definition of Israel through behavior instead of ethnic origin."[29] And he surmises, "Does the surprising end of *de somniis* mean that we have to see at least this part of the allegorical commentary as Philo's latest work?"[30] This suggestion, like Kraft's mentioned above, has not led to substantial discussion. The lack of scholarly engagement is likely attributable to the radical dating of *De Somniis* and other works by Philo, a position that, in the present author's assessment, appears justified.

According to Philo's text, the prefect's efforts were unsuccessful despite his employing both threats and arguments. No additional information regarding such attempts to abolish the Sabbath is available in other Egyptian sources.

---

and identity of the ruler involved as that would presume a late dating of *De Somniis*.

28. Mach, "Choices for Changing Frontiers."
29. Mach here refers to Hay, "Politics and Exegesis."
30. Mach, "Choices for Changing Frontiers," 327.

The Tax Collector of *Spec.* 3.159–168

The broader context of this text pertains to Philo's examination of the seventh commandment (οὐ φονεύσεις—*Spec.* 3:83–209). Following an analysis of various cases of homicide involving diverse individuals and circumstances, Philo addresses the possibility of an innocent individual suffering capital punishment as a substitute for a criminal. The specific and somewhat unusual case addressed in 3:159–168, particularly in the initial portion of that section, concerns the authorities imposing punishment on the relatives of an individual who failed to fulfill his tax obligations (3:159–166, cf. Deut 24:10–16). Philo asserts that this situation had occurred within the Jewish community, presumably in recent times (ταχθεὶς παρ' ἡμῖν).[31] Philo states the case thus:

> An example was given a little time ago in our own district by a person who was appointed to serve as a collector of taxes. When some of his debtors whose default was clearly due to poverty took flight in fear of the fatal consequences of his vengeance, he carried off by force their womenfolk and children and parents and their other relatives and beat and subjected them to every kind of outrage and contumely in order to make them either tell him the whereabouts of the fugitive or discharge his debt themselves. As they could do neither the first for want of knowledge, nor the second because they were penniless as the fugitive, he continued this treatment until while wringing their bodies with racks and instruments of torture he finally dispatched them by newly invented methods of execution.

Given the ambiguity surrounding Philo's reference to "a little time ago," it is not possible to ascertain the precise date of the tax collector's actions. Philo employs this anecdote as an illustrative example of the potential treatment individuals might receive, or had previously experienced, from a tax collector. It is noteworthy that the tax collector in question was not necessarily of Roman origin, but rather an individual employed in the service of the Roman colonial administration.[32] However, according to Philo, the inappropriate conduct of the colonizers served to highlight the superiority of the Jewish Torah: "So then our legislator took these things into consideration and observing the errors current among other nations regarded them with aversion as ruinous to the ideal

---

31. Borgen, *Philo of Alexandria, An Exegete*, 173–74.
32. On the role of tax collectors in the Roman world, see Llewelyn, "Tax Collection."

commonwealth" (*Spec.* 3:167). Nevertheless, the Jewish population had to exercise caution to avoid provoking the Roman authorities, whose actions were often unpredictable.

The aforementioned three cases may be more accurately characterized as typical situations of life and work in Alexandria rather than 'coded messages.' They represent circumstances that would be relatively familiar among Jewish inhabitants of Alexandria, but they likely also indicate and describe the precarious existence of the colonized in relation to the colonizing authorities of Alexandria.

Nevertheless, the incident that most significantly demonstrated the power of the colonizers was the event commonly referred to as the pogrom of 38 CE and the subsequent negotiations between the Jews and the representatives of the Empire in Rome.

On the Pogrom of 38 CE

A concise overview of the primary events of this pogrom has been provided in the Introduction to the present study; however, it is pertinent to delineate some of its salient features here. In summary, during the period of 38–41 CE, a significant event occurred in Alexandria that irrevocably altered the circumstances of the Jewish population in that city. The principal sources for this historical incident are predominantly Philo, followed by Josephus. Philo was an eyewitness to these events and was also involved in political endeavors on behalf of the Jewish community to address the ensuing issues. He served as a member—potentially also the leader—of an embassy dispatched from Alexandria to Rome to negotiate with the emperor.[33] The story of what happened during these years—the how to sequence and describe the events—has been researched and retold repeatedly and has been an object of comprehensive and critical scholarly examination.[34]

Central to this narrative is the pogrom in Alexandria in 38 CE. The pogrom resulted from a confluence of political events and circumstances both imperially in Rome and locally in Alexandria, involving the Roman prefect and local Jewish rights. The scope of this discussion precludes an examination of the historical questions pertaining to the

---

33. Josephus, *Ant.* 18:259. See also Seland, "Philo as a Citizen," 63–72.

34. See e.g., Pucci Ben Zeev, "New Perspectives"; Atkinson, "Ethnic Cleansing"; Bremmer, "First Pogrom?"; Gambetti, "Attack."

chronology of the specific events,[35] and the way Philo describes these issues in light of his symbolic and theological universe.[36] However, this analysis offers some preliminary observations and commentary on their relevance for understanding Philo's life and his perspective on the Roman Empire.

According to Philo, the riots of 38 CE were attributed to multiple factors. One of the most significant was the political inefficacy of the incumbent governor, Flaccus. Following the demise of his patron, Emperor Tiberius, Flaccus experienced a period of political impotence. The interim before the reestablishment of the local governor's authority was exploited by certain adversaries, resulting in verbal and physical aggression against the Jewish population. The ascension of Gaius Caligula to the imperial throne exacerbated the conditions in Alexandria. The initial assaults rapidly escalated into severe civil unrest: Jewish synagogues were subjected to attacks, desecration, or arson (*Legat.* 133–134), and the governor was compelled to issue a proclamation designating the Jews as "foreigners and aliens" (*Flacc.* 54) in Alexandria. This was subsequently followed by the expulsion of the Jewish population from various districts of the city, confining them to a single area, which was consequently transformed into a ghetto, "the first known ghetto in the world."[37] As the anti-Jewish riots progressed, their severity intensified: Residences were plundered, numerous individuals evacuated the city to coastal areas (*Legat.* 124), and many were publicly exposed and subjected to various forms of dishonor. Some individuals experienced physical assault, mob violence, flagellation, and forcible dragging through marketplaces; others were immolated or crucified (*Legat.* 130–134; *Flacc.* 65–72). Ultimately, the unrest appears to have culminated in an attack by Flaccus on the central institution of the Jewish community, their senate or 'gerousia,' i.e., their council of elders. The members were subjected to flagellation, with some succumbing to the ordeal, in a manner perceived as utterly humiliating to the Jewish population (*Flacc.* 75–85). Philo himself characterizes this as "the height of harshness"; the elders were not subjected to the customary method of flagellation befitting their status, but rather they were treated in the same manner as the native Egyptians; that is, "they were treated

---

35. See Smallwood, *Jews Under Roman Rule*, 235–42; and esp. van der Horst, *Philo's "Flaccus,"* 18–38. Gambetti, *Alexandrian Riots*, 137–93.

36. On these aspects, see e.g., Borgen, *Philo of Alexandria, An Exegete*, 176–93.

37. Smallwood, *Jews Under Roman Rule*, 45.

like Egyptians of the meanest rank and guilty of the greatest iniquities" (*Flacc.* 80).

Philo was directly involved in political affairs during this tumultuous period, as he was likely an eyewitness to the events in Alexandria and one of the participants in—according to Josephus, the leader of—a delegation to Emperor Caligula in Rome. According to Niehoff, this "journey was a crucial experience, not only politically, but also intellectually." She even goes as far as to say that "Philo refashioned himself, constructing a new identity and offering a new interpretation of his tradition."[38] But in the end, I find that she is paying less attention to the possible changes in Philo's political views and more attention to his philosophy. So I focus on Philo's view of the colonizing power, the Roman Empire.

PHILO, THE JEWISH DELEGATION, AND THE EMPEROR

Philo's objectives in journeying to Rome were to present the Jewish situation in Alexandria to the emperor, anticipating that he would function as an impartial arbiter and resolve their concerns.[39] Contrary to expectations, rather than assuming the role of an impartial judge, the emperor, to Philo's considerable astonishment, confronted them as an accuser (*Legat.* 350). Furthermore, according to Philo, they were unable to engage the emperor in a discussion regarding the situation in Alexandria; instead, he admonished them for their refusal to acknowledge his divinity and for their reluctance to offer sacrifices to him; they opted only to sacrifice on his behalf (*Legat.* 352–367).

Philo reports that they initially received a brief audience with the emperor, who pledged to consider their case more thoroughly later. However, several months elapsed before the second hearing occurred. In the interim, Gaius ordered the installation of his statue in the Jerusalem temple, an event Philo addresses extensively in *Legat.* 184–198, 207–348 (see below). When the second meeting eventually transpired, the emperor received them in a garden, conversing with them while inspecting the arrangements and a house therein. The entire scenario demonstrated to Philo that Gaius exhibited minimal interest in their case: "In a derisive manner, he inquired: 'Are you the god-haters who do not

---

38. Niehoff, *Philo of Alexandria*, 7.
39. Here I draw upon my sketch in Seland, "Philo as a Citizen," 66–67.

acknowledge me as a god, a deity recognized among all other nations but not to be named by you?'" (353). The opposing delegation seized this opportunity to disparage the Jews. The Jews protested, but as they all proceeded through the garden, the emperor continued his inspection of a house, posing some questions but providing limited time to hear their responses. He concluded the meeting by declaring, "They appear to me to be individuals who are unfortunate rather than malevolent, and foolish in their refusal to accept that I possess the nature of a god" (366). In his narrative, Philo states twice that he and his fellow envoys were extremely apprehensive due to the emperor's words and reluctance to grant them a proper hearing (Legat. 357. 366).

The delegation to Rome thus failed completely to achieve positive results. Neither Philo nor Josephus indicate any further decision reached by the emperor in this matter. And Philo ends his *De Legatione* somewhat abruptly: "So now I have told in a summary way the cause of the enmity which Gaius had for the whole nation of the Jews, but now I must also describe the palinode" (373). We have no further knowledge of what the 'palinode' contained if it was ever written.

In describing her interest and methodology applied when researching and describing Philo's travel to and stay in Rome, Niehoff says that she "propose[s] to appreciate Philo's historical treatises in a more comprehensive fashion, namely, as literary texts that express his views on a wide range of topics. Events themselves are not my main concern, but Philo's interpretation of them. I ask how Philo uses events in the text to promote certain views and agendas."[40] I must admit that I find such a procedure to be in danger of being somewhat reductionistic; in avoiding questions about the historicity of the events themselves she emphasizes what she calls Philo's interpretations of them. But she does not consider to what degree the historical events as such influenced Philo's interpretations of them. I would emphasize that the events influenced both his interpretations and use of them, but I question how she can so easily overlook the fact that the events are to a large degree influenced by the colonizing powers', that is Rome's, handling of both the issues raised (i.e., Alexandria) and the emperor's treatment of the delegation. Philo seems shocked over the emperor's treatment of them, and of his treatments of the Jews as he tried to erect a statue of himself in the temple in Jerusalem,

---

40. Niehoff, *Philo of Alexandria*, 4–5.

and such events most probably enhanced Philo's impression of the colonizing superpower, Rome.

The Emperor Caligula's Effort to Erect a Statue in Jerusalem

According to *Flacc.* 41–43, images were installed in the synagogues in Alexandria during the pogrom, thereby desecrating the synagogues as such, and this became a primary impetus for the Jews to present the Alexandrian situation to the emperor. However, while Philo and the delegation were awaiting a hearing in Rome, they were informed that the emperor now intended to have a large statue of himself erected in the inner sanctuary of the Jerusalem temple (*Legat.* 184–348; see also Josephus: *Ant.* 18.261–310; *B.J.* 2.184–203).[41]

The main parts of this story can be given thus: While Philo and the other envoys (*Legat.* 184–186) were waiting for the emperor to grant them an audience, a messenger arrived, telling them that "Gaius has ordered a colossal statue to be set up within the inner sanctuary dedicated to himself under the name of Zeus" (*Legat.* 188). In the ensuing discussion, it became clear to them all that if such a plan was carried out, it would represent a desecration of the temple that would make it unfit for any Jewish use in the times to come, and Philo expressed his fears that it was "to be feared that the overthrow of the temple will be accompanied by an order for the annihilation of our common name and nation from the man who deals in revolution on so great a scale" (*Legat.* 194). In correspondence to the governor of Syria, Petronius, Emperor Gaius issued directives to implement his plans. However, Petronius recognized that such actions would likely provoke the Jewish population, potentially leading to unrest both within and beyond Judea. Conversely, failure to execute the emperor's plans would jeopardize Petronius's own life. Consequently, the ensuing negotiations with the Jewish community prompted Petronius to attempt to delay the implementation of the emperor's directives (207–253). The emperor's plans were subsequently communicated to King Agrippa (261–275), an announcement that rendered the king unconscious for several days. Upon regaining consciousness, he resolved to compose a letter to the emperor, which is extensively

---

41. For the historical and theological issues, see e.g., Smallwood, *Philonis Alexandrini Legatio Ad Gaium*; and Bilde, "Der Konflikt zwischen," 225–245 + 259–62.

documented by Philo in *Legat.* 276-329!⁴² The letter is significant as it likely contains more perspectives from Philo than from Agrippa; nevertheless, according to Philo, Agrippa consented to the text, and it was subsequently delivered to the emperor. Initially, the emperor acquiesced to Agrippa's proposal; however, he later reversed his decision (*Legat.* 334-337), issuing a new directive to have set up a statue of himself in the temple (*Legat.* 337-348). Nonetheless, Gaius was assassinated before the order could be executed, thus halting the work on the statue.

The extensive and detailed account of this event in Philo's book *De Legatione* indicates the significance he attributed to it; few narratives in his recounting of the Roman colonizers' interactions with the Jews are presented with such length and detail. While the incident was undoubtedly of grave importance, Philo's account presents challenges when evaluated as a historical source. Nevertheless, Philo's version is revealing and informative about his own perspectives on the matter. It must be acknowledged, however, that the historical questions concerning the actual events remain unresolved. The focus of this analysis, therefore, is on how Philo conceptualized and thus interpreted these events—and on how he wanted his readers to understand them.

Claudius's Letter to Alexandria

Shortly after these events, Gaius Caligula was assassinated, and his uncle Claudius ascended to the position of emperor. Claudius addressed the situation in Alexandria through an edict, preserved by Josephus (*Ant.* 19:280-285), and a letter—not mentioned by either Josephus or Philo—but preserved on a papyrus.⁴³ The majority of scholars consider the letter to be authentic; however, the edict is subject to more extensive discussion and critical evaluation. The two documents present significant challenges in reconciliation, and this analysis aligns with the perspective that the

---

42. Josephus has a somewhat different story here. He says that Agrippa arranged a banquet, inviting the emperor, and Gaius was so impressed that he offered Agrippa any boon he liked. Hence, when Agrippa asked the Emperor to give up his plans concerning the statue in Jerusalem, his wish was granted. Mary Smallwood comments thus on this: "It is difficult to reconcile these two stories.... If a choice is to be made between Philo and Josephus, the former's prosaic version seems preferable to Josephus' story with its fairy-tale ring." Smallwood, *Philonis Alexandrini Legatio Ad Gaium*, 291.

43. For the text of this, see Bell, ed., *Jews and Christians in Egypt*; or Tcherikover et al., *Corpus Papyrorum Judaicarum*, vol. 2, no. 153.

letter on papyrus is the most reliable evidence of Claudius's approach to addressing the situation in Alexandria.[44]

According to this text, the Alexandrians were instructed not to disturb the Jews who had long resided in Alexandria, and to permit them to adhere to their own religious practices. The Jews, conversely, were directed not to engage in activities beyond those they had previously been afforded, to refrain from sending dual delegations in the future, and to abstain from intruding into the gymnasium. Moreover, they were characterized as inhabitants of a city not their own and were prohibited from inviting immigrants from other regions of Egypt or from Syria.

The full implications of Claudius's regulations are not entirely evident, as no other sources mention them, not even Philo. Nonetheles, according to the letter, the social conditions of the Jews in Alexandria did not improve. If Jews sought Greek citizenship in the city, they were unsuccessful in obtaining it. Furthermore, they were prohibited from attempting to gain access to the gymnasiums, which provided the education crucial for citizenship, and they were warned against inviting immigrants from Syria. Additionally, Alexandria was characterized as a city that did not belong to them (ἐν ἀλλωτρίᾳ πόλει).[45] Consequently, their social circumstances likely worsened compared to their situation before 38 CE. The Empire had decreed: the Jews were to remain subjugated and colonized.

However, further inquiry into the influence of Claudius's letter on Philo's perception of Rome, the colonizing power, reveals a significant limitation: the absence of any direct reference to this correspondence in Philo's works. Assuming the authenticity of the letter, it likely represented a considerable impediment to the aspirations of Alexandrian Jews seeking improved social status and opportunities. Moreover, it presumably constituted a substantial setback for Philo in his political endeavors to secure greater recognition for the Jewish community in Alexandria.

---

44. For a brief discussion of these two texts, see Schäfer, *Judeophobia*, 145–52. For the most recent and probably also the most extensive discussion of these issues, see Gambetti, *Alexandrian Riots*, esp. pp. 220–38.

45. The Greek text of the Letter is given in Bell, ed., *Jews and Christians in Egypt*, 23–26.

IN RETROSPECT, AND PROSPECTS: PHILO AND ROME

This chapter proposes that there is a need for research examining Philo of Alexandria and his descriptions of aspects of and issues pertaining to the Roman Empire from multiple perspectives in and with various models of postcolonial studies. As an initial contribution to this field, the author published an article in 2010 analyzing Philo's concepts of 'metropolis' and 'apoikia' in relation to the postcolonial categories of 'mimicry' and 'hybridity'.[46] That article is adopted and partly reprinted below in the next chapter, and this volume as a whole expands on that work.

In order to understand Philo's role and social position vis-a-vis the Roman colonizers, aspects of the Roman imperial presence in Alexandria as well as relevant social locations of Philo were briefly presented (Chapter 2, above).

Philo's works may be characterized in various ways, and the dates of his compositions are subject to scholarly debate with diverse proposed chronologies. Moreover, there exist multiple interpretative approaches for comprehending Philo's works, as elucidated in the previous chapter (Chapter 3).

This chapter (the final for Part 1) examines some of Philo's descriptions of interactions with Roman authorities and their political dynamics, as well as Philo's approach to addressing these dynamics in his works.

In Part 1 overall, an emphasis has been placed on the categories 'mimicry' and 'hybridity'. The application of these categories extends beyond a primarily political focus, related to the empire as a political entity, to encompass cultural issues, examining how Philo perceived and conceptualized these elements. This analytical approach is addressed explicitly in Part 2, below.

This research is primarily motivated by the hypothesis that Philo's attitudes towards the Roman Empire were significantly influenced, even altered by the conflicts of the 30s and 40s CE. It is posited that insufficient attention has been given to the upheavals of 38–41 CE as a critical and transformative period in Philo's life, with substantial implications for his living and writing under the Empire. The fact that his most politically oriented works, *In Flaccum* and *De Legatione*, were composed after the deaths of Flaccus and Gaius Caligula is not coincidental. In examining

---

46. See Seland, "'Colony' and 'Metropolis.'" The main gist of that article will be used in Chapter 5 below.

Philo's altered circumstances during and after 38–41 CE—as he observed the Roman treatment of Jews in Alexandria and during his sojourn in Rome circa 38/39–42 CE—Philo began to express more overt criticism of the Roman colonizers in his writings. Nevertheless, a negative disposition towards the Romans is also discernible in several of his other works.

Philo's literary endeavors likely spanned several years, potentially extending over a period of three to four decades. Hence, Maren R. Niehoff suggests that "We . . . have to face the possibility of significant intellectual development throughout Philo's long and rich career."[47] Further on in her book, she argues that Philo's stay in Rome influenced his "choice of literary genre, Jewish identity, and philosophical orientation."[48]

We should hardly doubt the impact on Philo of his experiences in Rome. From Niehoff's biography of Philo, one gets the impression that Philo was primarily influenced in his "choice of literary genre, Jewish identity and philosophical orientation." However, in this volume I suggest that a greater emphasis on a progression in political perspective on the Roman colonizers is relevant to understanding Philo, and that a comparable evolution is evident in his approach to various cultural aspects in Alexandria.

---

47. Niehoff, *Philo of Alexandria*, 3.
48. Niehoff, *Philo of Alexandria*, 3.

PART 2

Four Exemplary Cases

5

Reimagining Philo on the Diaspora, Metropolis, and Apoikia
A Case of Political Mimicry

> "For so populous are the Jews that no one country can hold them, and therefore they settle in very many of the most prosperous countries in Europe and Asia . . . , and while they hold the Holy City where stands the sacred Temple of the most high God to be their *mother city* (μητρόπολις), yet those which are theirs by inheritance from their fathers, grandfathers and ancestors even farther back, are in each case accounted by them to be their fatherland (πατρίδας νομίσοντες) in which they were born and reared, while to some of them they have come at the time of their foundation as immigrants (i.e., colonists) (ἦλθον ἀποικίαν στειλάμενοι) to the satisfaction of the founders."
>
> *FLACC.* 46

INTRODUCTION[1]

THE ROMAN EMPIRE WAS present everywhere in Philo's world. It was heard, seen, and coped with every day of his life: at home, in the synagogue and in the streets; in business, law, and politics. From the presence of the Roman prefect and his administration in Alexandria to the many statues and temples in the city, the Roman Empire was inescapable.[2] F. F. Segovia, who is one of those who have extensively employed postcolonial perspectives in biblical interpretation, has characterized the reality of empire, that is, imperialism and colonialism, as "an omnipresent, inescapable, and overwhelming reality."[3]

In fact, whether living in Eretz Israel or in the Diaspora, one lived in and under the Roman Empire. In the present study, we focus on how this life was in the diaspora, that is, in the western diaspora, or to be even more precise, in the Diaspora of Egypt and Alexandria in particular. How did Jewish individuals evaluate their diaspora situation? Was it considered a favorable living condition? Was it perceived as a temporary circumstance, with the expectation of returning to Eretz Israel? Was it regarded as a calamity? Was it even interpreted as a form of punishment? It is evident that multiple perspectives exist among scholars attempting to characterize the first-century CE Jewish diaspora. The primary focus of this inquiry, however, will be, How did Philo conceptualize his diaspora experience? What terminology did he employ? Does an analysis of these terms through the lens of mimicry provide any additional insights? Prior to addressing these questions, a brief examination of the various viewpoints found in relevant scholarly literature on Philo and the Jewish western Diaspora will be presented.

Philo resided in Alexandria, Egypt. His homeland, the land of Israel, was under Roman occupation, as were Egypt and the majority of the regions surrounding the Mediterranean Sea, extending even beyond these boundaries. Rome was the dominant imperial power of his era, and its influence permeated every aspect of his existence. Furthermore, as a

---

1. This is a revised (i.e., in some sections abbreviated, in others expanded) version of Seland, "'Colony' and 'Metropolis.'"

2. Moxnes, "'He Saw the City Was Full of Idols.'"

3. See Segovia, *Decolonizing Biblical Studies*, 125; see further Carter concerning the New Testament: "The Roman Empire provides the ever-present political, economic, societal, and religious framework and context for the New Testament's claims, language, structures, personnel and scenes." Carter, *Roman Empire*, 1. This world was also the world of Philo.

resident of Alexandria, Philo belonged to a minority group within that city. The precise size of this group remains uncertain; most demographic figures from this period are largely speculative. Some scholars posit that the Jewish population may have constituted 10–15 percent of the Empire's total population.[4] Philo himself (*Flacc.* 43) posited that there were one million Jews in Egypt, which is undoubtedly an overestimation, as the total population of Alexandria during this period is now generally estimated to have been approximately half a million.

Philo articulates the sentiments and circumstances associated with the Diaspora experience through his description of the Jewish population's situation in Alexandria in the following manner (*Flacc.* 46; cf. *Legat.* 281):

> For so populous are the Jews that no one country can hold them, and therefore they settle in very many of the most prosperous countries in Europe and Asia. . . , and while they hold the Holy City where stands the sacred Temple of the most high God to be their *mother city* (μητρόπολις), yet those which are theirs by inheritance from their fathers, grandfathers and ancestors even farther back, are in each case accounted by them to be their fatherland (πατρίδας νομίσοντες) in which they were born and reared, while to some of them they have come at the time of their foundation as immigrants (i.e., colonists) (ἦλθον ἀποικίαν στειλάμενοι) to the satisfaction of the founders.

This statement elucidates the sentiments of Philo the Diaspora Jew and demonstrates the dual identities and allegiances he experienced while residing abroad in the Diaspora. Imperialism manifests itself in various areas and ways, not solely in the domains typically considered relevant, such as the field of politics. Cultural imperialism is frequently experienced by colonized populations in areas including, but not limited to, language, attire, housing, education, philosophy, and religion. The impact of imperialism extends beyond the direct imposition of certain opinions and attitudes on a colonized people by the empire, encompassing numerous indirect manifestations as well. In the Roman Empire, cultural elements such as the use of the Latin language, and religious aspects, including polytheism, emperor worship, and educational systems, were crucial to the lives of Jews in Alexandria.

Concerning the addressees of *In Flaccum*, Goodenough argues that it was written for a Gentile audience after the death of Gaius, and

---

4. See some older calculations in Harnack, *Mission und Ausbreitung*, 6–13.

possibly for the new prefect in Alexandria.⁵ *Legatio*, on the other hand, he surmises was written after the accession of Claudius, and for a presentation to just that emperor.⁶ Nevertheless, it is evident to the majority of scholars that Philo's significant political works were composed for both Jewish and Gentile audiences, potentially including Roman authorities. Consequently, they represent and present Philo's writing in response to the Empire.

Many scholars are of the opinion that Goodenough overstates his case,⁷ but the issue of hidden agendas in Philo's ways of writing back has also gained some supporters. David M. Hay discusses Philo's politics and exegesis in his treatise *On Dreams*, and finds that Philo here offers both overt political allegory (*Somn.* 1:219-225; 2:78-91 and 2:115-133), and some allegory within allegory (*Somn.* 2:42-64; 2:283-299). Hence, he concludes that "part of Philo's purpose in De Somniis was to present answers to some of the political problems which he and his fellow Jews were facing."⁸ Furthermore, in investigating *In Flaccum* and *Legatio* the Danish scholar Per Bilde concludes that he finds a "threatening tone" in these works and that Goodenough is right to interpret them as hidden warnings to the Roman elite: If the traditional positive politics of the Romans were changed into negative politics, such a change would call forth an armed Jewish resistance that would represent severe difficulties for Rome.⁹

The issue or phenomenon labeled postcolonialism has been variously interpreted and applied. R. S. Sugirtharajah has pinpointed that postcolonialism is a methodological category and that it as a critical practice has two aspects attached to it: "First, to analyze the diverse strategies by which the colonizers constructed images of the colonized; and second, to study how the colonized themselves made use of and went

---

5. Goodenough, *Politics*, 10-11; van der Horst, *Philo's Flaccus: The First Pogrom*, 15-16.

6. Goodenough, *Politics*, 19.

7. See e.g., Barraclough, "Philo's Politics," 448-49.

8. Hay, "Politics and Exegesis," 438.

9. "I therefore share Goodenough's interpretation that they are Philo's barely disguised warnings to the Roman élite: If the traditionally positive Roman policy towards the Jewish population is changed to the negative, as it happened under the Emperor Caligula, there is a real risk that such a change will provoke armed Jewish resistance of an extent that will cause serious problems to Rome." Bilde, "Philo as a Polemist," 223. This is a reprint of his Danish study from 2007: Bilde, "Filon som polemiker og politisk apologet," 178. See also Birnbaum on *In Flaccum*: "Philo . . . may also wish to sound a warning to Gentiles to stop their maltreatment of his people." Birnbaum, *Place of Judaism*, 21. See further Harper, *Paul and Philo*.

beyond many of those strategies in order to articulate their identity, self-worth, and empowerment."[10] In the present chapter, my focus is on the latter; on how Philo was writing back from the empire, that is, how he conceptualized and wrote about various aspects of his social world, and to what degree one might detect a more or less anti-imperial (hidden or not) agenda in his descriptions.

DIASPORA, METROPOLIS, AND *APOIKIA* IN RECENT PHILONIC RESEARCH

Prior to examining the anti-imperial aspects of Philo's utilization of 'diaspora', 'colony', and 'metropolis', it is necessary to briefly review some positions in recent scholarship concerning these issues. This analysis focuses on the Western Diaspora, excluding the eastern component situated within the Parthian Empire, which lay beyond Roman borders. Due to their disparate geographical locations, these two segments experienced divergent developmental trajectories with respect to both their social characteristics and religious evolution.[11] The Western Diaspora comprised most of the areas around the Mediterranean Sea, with Egypt having one of the largest settlements.[12] No fixed figure of the totality of Jews living in this area is possible, but more people were probably living outside Eretz Israel than within its borders.[13] We know, however, that there were several ways for Diaspora Jews to stay in contact with Eretz Israel: Two of the most important were probably pilgrimage (*Spec.* 1:69–70;

---

10. Sugirtharajah, "Charting the Aftermath," 7.

11. Edrei and Mendels, "Split Jewish Diaspora," presents some viewpoints on these developments as seen from their Jewish points of view: The article proposes that a language divide and two systems of communication led to a serious gap between the western Jewish diaspora and the eastern one. Thus, the western, Greek-speaking Jews lost touch with the Halakhah and the Rabbis, a condition that had far-reaching consequences on Jewish history thereafter. The Rabbis paid a high price for keeping their Halakhah in oral form, losing in consequence half of their constituency. An oral law did not develop in the western diaspora, whereas the existing eastern one was not translated into Greek.

12. A lot of studies present overviews of the western diaspora; see e.g., Stern, "Jewish Diaspora"; Feldman, *Jew and Gentile*. See also the sources compiled in Feldman and Reinhold, eds, *Jewish Life and Thought*; and Williams, ed., *Jews Among the Greeks and Romans*.

13. For some suggestions, see Stern, "Jewish Diaspora"; and Marshall, "Jewish Dispersion," 237–39. But the figures are mostly just that: suggestions.

Acts 2:5-11) and taxes; others were envoys and letters.[14] All male Jews between the ages of twenty and fifty were supposed to pay the required half-shekel tax in support of the sacrifices performed at the temple; some also paid tithes as well (see Philo, *Legatio* 156-157, 216, 291, 311-16; *Spec.* 1:77-78; Josephus, *Ant.* 16:162-172; 18:312-313), and Jerusalem was the goal for many pilgrims.[15]

Another much-discussed question is whether we can say anything about how Diaspora Jews considered their living in the Diaspora. Was it considered just a temporary situation, while in fact, they ought to return to Eretz Israel? Was it considered a calamity, perhaps even a situation of punishment? It turns out that there are several views in vogue among scholars trying to describe the Jewish views of the Diaspora.

Looking at the 'Bible' of the Diaspora, the Septuagint (LXX), we find a variety of terminology concerning the Diaspora. But the dominating terms are Διασπορά, used 11 times, and ἀποικία, used 30 times. We will have to return to these terms. There are also several texts, signaling a negative view of the Diaspora (cf. e.g., Bar 2:13-14, 29; 3:8; Tob 14:4b; Sir 36:13, 16; Tob 13:5; 14:5; Pss. Sol. 11:1-4; 17:44; 4 Ezra 13:39-48; 2 Bar 78:7).[16] On the other hand, "Josephus (*Ant.* 4.114-116) interprets the Diaspora as a sign of God's fulfillment of the promises given to Abraham that his descendants will be more numerous than the sands by the sea or the stars in the sky, such that one land will not be able to hold them,"[17] and there are several texts in the LXX witnessing the hope that one day there will be a return from the Diaspora (e.g., Deut 30:4-5; Neh 1:9 = 2 Esd 11:9; Ps 146:2; Isa 49:6; Bar 4:36-37; 5:5-6, cf. the prayers of 2 Macc 1:27; Pss Sol 8:28). Our focus here, however, is primarily on how Philo considered the Diaspora; hence we proceed to present some scholars considering this question, and then we turn to the works of Philo himself.

An older study by *Karl Ludwig Schmidt* (1891-1956) has had a great influence on later studies, not least because it was published in the famous *Theologisches Wörterbuch zum Neuen Testament*, edited by Gerhard Kittel, and translated into English in 1964.[18] He emphasizes that there is no

---

14. For a review of these relations, see e.g., Safrai, "Relations"; and Trotter, "Going and Coming Home."
15. See Philo, *Spec.* 1:69, see further Safrai, "Relations," 191-204.
16. Here see van Unnik, *Das Selbstverständnis*, 89-166.
17. DeSilva, "Jews in the Diaspora," 278.
18. Schmidt, "διασπορά."

single Hebrew term corresponding to the use of the Greek term διασπορά in the LXX. Furthermore, Schmidt says that

> The Heb. term which corresponds to διασπορά is גּוֹלָה or גָּלוּת, the Aram. גָּלוּ, emphatic גָּלוּתָא. All three words occur in Heb. OT and Rabbinic writings, and in the pregnant sense of the process of "leading away," "deportation," or "exile," or of the state of those "led away," "deported" or "exiled," they find the following equivalents in the LXX: →αἰχμαλωσία (which is also used for שְׁבִי, cf. Eph. 4:8 == ψ 67:18), ἀποικία, ἀποικισμός, μετοικεσία, παροικία (πάροικος, παροικεῖν).[19]

And he poses the important question: How did it come about that the Grecian Jews gradually abandoned these pregnant expressions in favor of διασπορά? Schmidt himself answers this question along the lines that they did that to veil the stark severity of the Hebrew expressions because of the changed and bettered conditions of life in the Diaspora.[20] The translators of the LXX seem to have preferred the term ἀποικία as a translation for the Hebrew גלה or its derivates when denoting the 'exile' of the Jews. The term διασπορά thus becomes a positive term, designating a more positive view of life in the diaspora. When it comes to Philo, Schmidt knows only *Praem* 115, which he interprets as purely allegorical, representing a psychological use and interpretation of the term: "Thus the historical and eschatological fact of the diaspora is psychologized as διασπορὰ ψυχική ... The fact itself is thus lost to view."[21]

Some More Recent Views

Aryeh Kasher (1935–2011)[22] argues that Philo did not consider the Jews of Alexandria to be citizens of the Alexandrian polis, but to have a political entity of their own, a so-called *politeuma*. The existence of such a *politeuma* is a view that is denied by some scholars today,[23] but it both had and still has several followers and firm support.[24] Hence, according

19. Schmidt, "διασπορά," 99.

20. Schmidt, "διασπορά," 100. So also Hadas-Lebel, *Philo of Alexandria*, 31; and Lieber, "Between Motherland and Fatherland."

21. Schmidt, "διασπορά," 101.

22. Kasher, *Jews in Hellenistic and Roman Egypt*.

23. See Mélèze-Modrzejewski, "How to Be a Greek," 77–78; Pearce, "Jerusalem as 'Mother-City'"; Barclay, *Jews in the Mediterranean Diaspora*, 43, note 73; 64–65.

24. Smallwood, *Jews Under Roman Rule*, 225–27; Borgen, "Judaism"; Schwartz,

to Kasher's reading, Philo's descriptions of the Alexandrian struggle for rights is to be read as a struggle not for citizenship in the polis, but for the rights of their *politeuma*. Philo seems to have considered Alexandria as his city, because his co-nationals had lived there for generations. Furthermore, Philo stated that the Jews had settled in the cities of the Diaspora as immigrants, and their settlements were 'colonies' (*apoikiai*), having Jerusalem as their metropolis. According to Kasher, in using such terms, Philo was trying to describe the status of the Jews in terms familiar to Greek readers: "Consequently he presented them as ordinary immigrants who laid the foundation for a 'colony' which according to its organization and rights was an independent body."[25] Kasher also sees this substantiated by *Mos.* 2.232; *Flacc.* 46–47 and *Legat.* 281–282. Thus, from Philo's point of view, the Jewish "colony" deserved "equal status" with other "colonies"; cf. *Conf.* 77–78.[26] Kasher thus concludes: "Alexandria could be considered a 'homeland' only in the political sense, for it was a place in which a Jewish 'colony'—organized as a separate ethnic union with a recognized political and legal status (*politeuma*)—had been established. Jerusalem is their mother city, not Alexandria."[27]

A study by W. C. van Unnik (1910–1978, published posthumously in 1993)[28] is probably one of the most comprehensive book-length studies of the use of the term διασπορά in Greco-Roman times. As the title says, the focus of the work is the self-understanding of the Jewish diaspora in this period. He takes one of his points of departure in the work of Karl Ludwig Schmidt (see above), and argues that the Jews did not primarily have a positive understanding of their diasporic existence, but that they stuck to the 'negative' view of the diaspora as a place of "Unglück für das Volk" as it denoted the deportation, exile, and dispersion of people. Concerning the term διασπορά itself, van Unnik sticks to an understanding of its meaning as the destructive decomposition into individual parts, an understanding he claims to find in Epicurus, as evidenced by Plutarch,[29] hence meaning dispersion more than exile or deportation. Furthermore, he observes that διασπορά in the LXX is never a translation of the Hebrew word for exile; גולה or its derivates. Concerning his investigation of Philo's works, he says

"Philo, His Family and His Times," 16–17; Harker, *Loyalty and Dissidence*, 212–20.
  25. Kasher, *Jews in Hellenistic and Roman Egypt*, 236.
  26. Kasher, *Jews in Hellenistic and Roman Egypt*, 237.
  27. Kasher, *Jews in Hellenistic and Roman Egypt*, 238.
  28. Van Unnik, *Das Selbstverständnis*.
  29. Van Unnik, *Das Selbstverständnis*, 74–75.

that Philo never uses the noun διασπορά as signifying a geographical dispersion of the Jews in the world.³⁰ The verb διασπείρω is, however, well known to Philo, and is not a neutral term, but one loaded with 'Unheil' (*Conf.* 118; *Congr.* 56–57; *Plant.* 59–60, cf. *Praem.* 127–152).³¹ Hence, van Unnik is convinced that Philo knew the scheme of sin-exile-return. But why does he then skip the term διασπορά? He knows the term, as *Praem.* 115 demonstrates. But when Philo wants to describe the situation of the Jews in the Diaspora, he instead uses other terms and expressions, as he describes the Jewish settlements as colonies (ἀποικίαι); they have migrated because they are so populous. According to van Unnik, Philo here does not use ἀποικία in the same way as the LXX where it appears several times as a translation for the Hebrew גלה or its derivates, but in the Greek meaning as a term for colonization rather than deportation and exile.³² Hence Philo as an apologist of the Jews is here drawing a rather positive picture of the Diaspora. But the main impression given by Philo's texts as a whole is that the Diaspora is a negative phenomenon.³³

James M. Scott (1995, 1997) deals with the terms 'mother-city' and 'colony' in the context of investigating Philo's view on Israel's restoration.³⁴ In dealing with *Flacc.* 45–46 and *Legat.* 281–283, Scott emphasizes that Philo's view of the Diaspora as colonization is a positive view, even though the colonization as such is a result of overpopulation. The aspect of 'overpopulation' is a kind of Greek 'topos' in dealing with colonization, a view that was also in vogue in Egypt. But Philo also pinpoints that the Jewish Diaspora is a way of colonizing the whole world: "Philo wants to show that, contrary to Egyptian tradition, the nation of the Jews is not merely an Egyptian colony which settled 'between Arab and Syria.' Rather, the Jewish nation is the one that is colonizing the world (including Egypt!)

---

30. Van Unnik, *Das Selbstverständnis*, 128.

31. See Siegert, who reviews van Unnik's book in The Studia Philonica Annual 6 (1994), pp. 192–199. He thinks that for Philo, the diaspora is to be considered as a punishment. Furthermore, as Philo has so few references to 'diaspora', van Unnik should have investigated the term paroikia (and derivates) too. I don't think, however, that such an investigation would have yielded any other results. See here also Bitter, *Vreemdelingschap bij Philo*.

32. Van Unnik, *Das Selbstverständnis*, 136–37.

33. "Es ist jedoch meiner Meinung nach nicht möglich, Philon ohne weiteres zum Kronzeugen einer optimistischen, stolzen Betrachtung der Diaspora zu machen." Van Unnik, *Das Selbstverständnis*, 137.

34. Scott, "Philo and the Restoration"; Scott, "Exile and Self-Understanding."

and vying for supremacy."³⁵ Similarly concerning Jerusalem: as mother city, Jerusalem is thus the center not only of world Judaism, but of the whole world. However, at the same time, according to Scott, one must not forget that there is evidence that Philo also considered the Diaspora a negative situation to be overcome in the future. Scott points to the fact that when Philo speaks of the Jewish settlements as ἀποικίαι, one must recall that in the LXX, this term usually translates the Hebrew Galuth (גולה, גלות), which refers to the Babylonian exile.³⁶

Maren R. Niehoff³⁷ does not consider *Flacc.* and *Legat.* to have been written for the Romans at all; on the contrary, they were written for the Jews of Alexandria. Criticism had arisen over the failure of the delegation headed by Philo in Rome, and another delegation with other ideas of how to solve the problems had been established. Philo wrote for the educated upper classes who did not yet favor the more radical course of these other Jewish parties.³⁸ Furthermore, according to Niehoff, his emphasis on Jerusalem as a mother city was "not originally part of Philo's myth of origins."³⁹ The references in *Flacc.* and *Legat.* were a relatively late development. They were not used as an argument against the Romans, but as an argument to the Jews to see their local problems in a wider framework, namely, as related to the emperor's plans to erect a statue of himself in the temple. Hence, the arguments in *Flacc.* and *Legat.* formed a construction on the side of Philo to strengthen Alexandrian Jews in their attitudes to Jerusalem. Niehoff's exposition is thus very much in opposition to that of Goodenough: for her, *In Flaccum* and *Legatio* were not intended for a Roman audience, they did not contain hidden attacks on the Romans but were defending Philo's pro-Roman politics.⁴⁰

At the same time, however, Niehoff emphasizes that Philo's "construction of Jerusalem as Mother-city" implied further classical Greek features of colonization,⁴¹ and Roman dimensions. In fact, she can say that Philo "modeled the role of Jerusalem on the position of Rome in the Empire," and that loyalty to Jerusalem would provide Alexandrian Jews

---

35. Scott, "Philo and the Restoration," 557–58.

36. Scott, "Exile and Self-Understanding," 189–93; Scott, "Philo and the Restoration," 563.

37. Niehoff, *Philo on Jewish Identity*.

38. Niehoff, *Philo on Jewish Identity*, 42.

39. Niehoff, *Philo on Jewish Identity*, 37–38.

40. See especially Niehoff, *Philo on Jewish Identity*, 39–40.

41. Niehoff, *Philo on Jewish Identity*, 34–35.

with "the same kind of identity as Roman citizenship," an identity that would "transcend the boundaries of a specific state and create a sense of world-wide community."[42] Strangely enough, she does not see any anti-Roman issues in such a program.

Erich S. Gruen[43] seems to present Philo as generally very positive toward the Jewish Diaspora. According to Gruen, the designation ἀποικία presented the Jewish settlements as colonies, that is, as secondary and inferior to the original: "But the term, in customary Greek usage, lacked pejorative overtones. And, as employed by Jewish writers, its implications were, in fact, decidedly positive."[44] Hence, the ways Philo uses ἀποικία can even be described as having a ring of pride and accomplishment. This Gruen finds exemplified in *Flacc.* 46 and in *Legat.* 281–282, and he is of the opinion that such positive evaluations and characterization of the Diaspora in Philo "eradicates any idea of the 'doctrine of return'. Diaspora Jews, in Philo's formulation at least, held an intense attachment to the adopted lands of their ancestors."[45] At the same time, however, they were also in good relationships with Jerusalem. Paying taxes and carrying out tours of pilgrimage to Jerusalem were ways of expressing solidarity and respect. But they also signaled that a return was unnecessary.

Hence while van Unnik emphasizes that Philo had a negative view of the Diaspora, Scott may say that Philo had both positive and negative characterizations. Gruen, however, seems to land squarely on the positive side, even finding no room for a future return to the homeland. Whether Gruen also leaves out the idea of an eschatological return is somewhat unclear in his works cited here, at least.

Sarah Pearce has an important article on Jerusalem as 'Mother-City' in the writings of Philo of Alexandria.[46] She discusses this with both Kasher and Niehoff. In general, Pearce does not support the interpretation of the mother city in Philo as claiming the centrality of Jerusalem over and against other homelands for the Jews. Against Kasher, she argues that his arguments that the Jews of Alexandria did not want citizenship in Alexandria, but only the rights of their Alexandrian *politeuma* does not fit the evidence. The little evidence there is supports more a struggle for

42. Niehoff, *Philo on Jewish Identity*, 36–37.

43. Gruen, *Diaspora. Jews amidst Greeks and Romans*. See also Gruen, "Hellenistic Judaism," 77–132, and Gruen, "Judaism in the Diaspora," 77–96.

44. Gruen, *Diaspora*, 241; Gruen, "Judaism in the Diaspora," 79.

45. Gruen, *Diaspora*, 243.

46. Pearce, "Jerusalem as 'Mother-City.'"

citizenship. Furthermore, the evidence for a Jewish *politeuma* in Alexandria is meager. Neither does she find that Niehoff is correct in suggesting that the image of Jerusalem as mother city was constructed in order to enhance the loyalty of the Jews in Alexandria to Palestine and Jerusalem. The Greek colonies did not have those strong feelings of attachment to their mother city as seem to underlie such arguments.

On the other hand, Pearce argues, the image of the mother city does not focus so much on Jerusalem as such; rather the focus of the image is on the Jewish settlements in the diaspora as 'colonies.' And this perspective and emphasis Philo has found in the Greek Bible. The term 'mother-city' is not much used in the LXX, but Jerusalem is depicted as mother, and ἀποικία is much more frequent. Hence Pearce's great emphasis is that the Jewish Scriptures are the point of departure for Philo's references and source: "Philo's primary influence here is not Greek descriptions of colonization, but the language of the translators of the Greek Bible."[47] From this, it follows that within such a framework, 'colonies' go together with 'mother-cities': "The identification of the mother-city with Jerusalem is derived from Scripture since the Golah, or in Greek-Jewish terms the ἀποικία, derives from that city. It is primarily in Scripture that we should look for the origins of Philo's reference to Jerusalem as μητρόπολις: The starting point, however, for this conceptualization is in the designation of communities outside Judaea as ἀποικίαι."[48] Pearce finds no tension between the notion of Jerusalem as mother city and Alexandria as home. But some questions remain though; for instance, why do these two terms show up primarily in *In Flaccum* and in *De Legatione*, and what is the purpose of Philo of using them just in these works? Pearce finds no tension between the notion of Jerusalem here as mother city and Alexandria as home.

THE DIASPORA AS CONCEPTUALIZED AND UNDERSTOOD BY PHILO

The term διασπορά occurs only twice in the works of Philo, and then in a somewhat special sense as it does not primarily denote the Jewish Diaspora as such (*Conf.* 197; *Praem.* 115). The first is a quotation from Deut 30:4, coming after a quote from Gen 11:8 (cf. the verb διέσπειρεν used there).

---

47. Pearce, "Jerusalem as 'Mother-City,'" 33.
48. Pearce, "Jerusalem as 'Mother-City,'" 34.

> For when these are scattered, those who have been living in exile for many a day under the ban of folly's tyranny, shall receive their recall under a single proclamation, even the proclamation enacted and ratified by God, as the oracles shew, in which it is declared that "if thy dispersion (ἡ διασπορά σου) be from one end of heaven to the other he shall gather thee from thence (ἐκεῖθεν συνάξει σε)" (Deut xxx.4). Thus it is well-befitting to God to bring into full harmony the consonance of the virtues, but to dissipate and destroy the consonance of vices.

But Philo allegorizes it, using it as an expression of how God gathers the virtues but dissipates the vices: "So that it is proper that the harmony of the virtues should be arranged and cherished by God, and that he should dissolve and destroy wickedness; and confusion is a name most appropriate to wickedness, of which every foolish man is a visible proof." The other occurrence of the term διασπορά is in *Praem.* 115, here used in the fields of ethics too:

> For continual appearances of good models stamp impressions closely resembling themselves on all souls which are not utterly obdurate and intractable; (115) and I say this with reference to those who wish to imitate models of excellent and admirable beauty, that they may not despair of a change for the better, nor of an alteration and improvement from that *dispersion*, as it were (ὥσπερ ἐκ διασπορᾶς ψυχικῆς), of the soul which vice engenders, so that they may be able to effect a return to virtue and wisdom.

Here Philo does not primarily use this term as a label of the condition of exile, or as a characterization of life outside Palestine, but in the field of ethics. It is, however, quite obvious that he knows the other denotation of the term as his quote from Deut 30:4 demonstrates. Hence Philo is familiar with this use of the term 'diaspora.' And one should not draw the conclusion that Philo has need for this term only in allegories, thus neglecting its more literal meaning. Philo himself criticizes those who disregard the literal meanings in preference for the allegorical or symbolic use and meaning: "Why, we shall be ignoring the sanctity of the Temple and a thousand other things, if we are going to pay heed to nothing except what is shewn us by the inner meaning of things ... It follows that, exactly as we have to take thought for the body because it is the abode of the soul, so we must pay heed to the letters of the laws" (*Migr.* 92–93). Accordingly, Philo knows the meaning of the term διασπορά as a term for exile and dispersion, but he himself prefers other terms. This may seem somewhat strange as in the LXX διασπορά is used 12 times, and "in all the 12 passages concerned it is a technical term for the 'dispersion of the Jews among the Gentiles,' and *abstractam pro concreto* for 'the Jews as thus scattered.'"[49] Hence it is a fact that Philo did not follow up on the Septuagintal use of διασπορά though he knew its role in the Septuagint. That is probably because he is not so much concerned about the idea of life in Diaspora as an exile, as a deportation, and a punishment from God. As an individual belonging to a generation considerably removed from the period of deportation, and cognizant that numerous Jews in the Diaspora had relocated for various reasons, he minimizes the deportation aspect and accentuates the settlement dimension. Philo on his side, thus prefers the term ἀποικία, but seems not to have taken up quite the same usage of ἀποικία as that found in the LXX where it is often used as a term for the גלה. In Philo it does rather mean migration and settlement of colonies. But still, one might wonder if not some of the connotation of exile still remains, only that Philo has other preferences and focus in his works.

But even though that is so, Philo knew that the diaspora conditions of his people were temporary. One day there will be a return (*Praem* 162-166). Philo is a Diaspora Jew, but he has not forgotten the history of his people, nor the promises ahead.[50]

ἀποικία and μετρόπολις in the LXX and Philo's Works, Except *In Flaccum* and *Legatio*

Philo was an expositor of Scripture, and while *Flacc.* and *Legat.* are not expository works as such, they are nevertheless history interpreted in light of the ideology set forth in his other works, or as Peder Borgen has characterized them: "Writings in which Pentateuchal material is applied

---

49. Schmidt, "διασπορά," 99.

50. See van Unnik, *Selbstverständnis*, 127-37, and esp. 137: "Was überwiegt bei ihm: der Kosmopolitismus oder die Zukunftserwartung einer messianischen Zeit mit der Rückkehr? Mit Hilfe der Psychologie kann ich mir die Sache nur so verständlich machen, dass die Verbindung von Zerstreuung mit der konkreten Situation, in der er lebte 'verdrängt' hat; dass aber auch für ihn das Wort der Schrift und die Erwartung seines Volkes dann und dann uberwältigend war. Er versuchte die Diaspora-Theologie zu vergessen, aber sie war zu tief in der Schrift verwurzelt. Es ist jedoch meiner Meinung nach nicht moglich, Philon ohne weiteres zum Kronzeugen einer optimistischen, stolzen Betrachtung der Diaspora zu machen."

to socio-religious factors in the Jewish community."[51] Hence, by studying terms used by Philo, one should also draw upon his version of Scripture, the LXX.

Even if we suspend for a moment a reading of the two historical works of Philo, we will find that he uses these terms several times, and in several of his works. A quick overview will reveal that he can present expositions of several topics with the help of these terms. Two main meanings dominate in his works; the one is that of 'migration' as such; the other is that of 'being sent out as a colony.' In the latter group the verb στέλλω is important, as that is often used together with ἀποικία in other works, signifying the sending out of colonies.[52]

But here a further look at the LXX should be relevant, as he in general is deeply indebted to its ideas and language. The term ἀποικία is used thirty-one times in the LXX; most of these are in the book of Jeremiah and in Ezra. The first deals with the exile, and the Greek word ἀποικία is most often here used as a translation of the Hebrew גלה or its derivatives, denoting the 'exilic' period or conditions of the Jews.[53] In the book of Ezra, all eight occurrences deal with those having returned from the exile in Babylonia (cf. Neh 7:6). It is thus an important word for describing the Jewish exile, and is most often translated as 'exile' in modern translations.[54] It is not, however, used together with μητρόπολις.

In Philo's works, this is quite different. The noun ἀποικία, which in its various forms is used forty-three times by Philo, is never used in the same way as in the LXX, that is as a word for the Jewish 'exile.' But in Philo's works it is used in dealing with at least the following other four topics: when Abraham is leaving his home and home and going into Canaan, he is said to *migrate* to Canaan;[55] when the people of Israel travel from Egypt to Canaan, they too are described as migrating;[56] then, when Philo describes the proselytes, they too are described as having performed a

---

51. See Borgen, "Philo of Alexandria. A Critical," 117–18. See also his "Application of and Commitment to the Laws of Moses," 86–101.

52. Kiefer, *Exil und Diaspora*, 218.

53. Kiefer, *Exil und Diaspora*, 217–18.

54. This is what one would have expected concerning the Bibles, as modern Bibles are translated from the Hebrew text. But the translation 'exile' is also used in the most recent English translation of the LXX; see Pietersma and Wright, eds., *New English Translation of the Septuagint*.

55. See *Abr.* 66. 68. 72. 77. 85; Heres 98.

56. See *Mos.* 1:71, 163, 170, 195, 222, 233, 236, 239, 255, 256; *Cong.* 84; *Spec.* 2:146, 150, 158.

crossing over from one setting to another, from one country to another;⁵⁷ in both the former and this latter the pertinent translation is not exile or colony, but rather migration. And then we have Philo's descriptions of the souls coming into the bodies of men, staying there for a while and then returning. The wise men's souls descending are compared to colonies sent from heaven, but they are not described as such: *Conf.* 77–78 is interesting also for our reading of Philo's understanding of the more political connotations of these terms:

> All whom Moses calls wise are represented as sojourners (παροικοῦντες). Their souls are never colonists leaving heaven for a new home (στέλλονται μὲν ἀποικίαν οὐδέποτε τὴν ἐξ οὐρανοῦ). Their way is to visit earthly nature as men who travel abroad to see and learn. So when they have stayed awhile in their bodies, and beheld through them all that sense and mortality has to shew, they make their way back to the place from where they set out at the first. To them the heavenly region, where their citizenship lies, is their native land (πατρίδα μὲν τὸν οὐράνιον χῶρον ἐν ᾧ πολιτεύονται); the earthly region in which they became sojourners is a foreign country. For surely, when men found a colony, the land which receives them becomes their native land instead of the mother city (τοῖς μὲν γὰρ ἀποικίαν στειλαμένοις ἀντὶ τῆς μητροπόλεως ἡ ὑποδεξαμένη δήπου πατρίς,), but to the traveller abroad the land which sent him forth is still the mother to whom also he yearns for to return.

In this text Philo presents and preserves a difference between one who travels in order to visit and learn, and one who is sent out as a colonist: the latter has a more relaxed relation to his homeland, his mother city, and considers his new place of residence to be his homeland, his πατρίς. These are distinctions we also meet in *Flacc.* and in *Legat.* Hence, in the works of Philo, the idea is not that of exile, but the much more positive idea of migration and settlements or colonies.⁵⁸

The term μητρόπολις, on the other hand, is found only seven times in the LXX, but there is no specific Hebrew terms underlying its use. Furthermore, on several occasions, the use of μητρόπολις in the LXX has no equivalent in the Hebrew text, so it is to be considered an expansion or interpretation of that text (Josh 10:2; 15:13; 21:11; Esth 9:19; Isa 1:26).

---

57. See *Spec.* 4:178; *Virt.* 102, 219; *Praem.* 16–17.
58. See Hadas-Lebel, *Philo of Alexandria*, 31–40; Leonhardt-Balzer, "Diaspora Jewish Attitudes," 89–93.

In Josh 10:2, e.g., the Hebrew text says "like one of the royal cities" while the LXX has μητρόπολις. Hence, in several cases, a congruent translation might be 'capital city'. This is probably also the explanation for the fact that it is never used together with ἀποικία.

This term, μητρόπολις, is rare in the works of Philo too, as it is prevalent in only ten text segments, five of them belonging to *De Legatione*. The term is often lexicalized as 'capital city,' and this seems also to be the denotation of most of the cases in Philo: According to *Flacc.* 46, it would seem that Jerusalem is the capital city of the Jews because their holy temple is located there. However, this is nowhere explicitly stated by Philo but remains a probable inference (*Legat.* 203, 294, 305, 334). On other cities called 'mother-cities' meaning 'capital cities,' see *Somn.* 1.41. The Logos is described as the most excellent mother city (*Fug.* 94), and finally the soul has its mother city (*Somn.* 1.181). The most relevant passage for us is again *Conf.* 77–78 in which 'colony' and 'mother-city' are combined. Hence, we now turn to Philo's use of these terms in *In Flaccum* 46 and *Legatio* 281–282.

"Colony" and "Mother-City" in *In Flaccum* and *Legatio* as Cases of Mimicry and Hybridity

At this point, it might be pertinent to quote the relevant passages from Philo (*Flacc.* 46; *Legat.* 281–282; LCL trans.):

> For so populous are the Jews that no one country can hold them, and therefore they settle in very many of the most prosperous countries in Europe and Asia . . . , and while they hold the Holy City where stands the sacred Temple of the most high God to be their *mother city* (μητρόπολις), yet those which are theirs by inheritance from their fathers, grandfathers and ancestors even farther back, are in each case accounted by them to be their fatherland (πατρίδας νομίζοντες) in which they were born and reared, while to some of them they have come at the time of their foundation as immigrants [i.e., colonists] (ἦλθον ἀποικίαν στειλάμενοι) to the satisfaction of the founders. (*Flacc.* 46, italics added)

> As for the holy city, I must say what befits me to say. While she, as I have said, is my native city (ἐμὴ μέν ἐστι πατρίς) she is also the mother city (μητρόπολις) not of one country Judaea but of most of the others in virtue of the *colonies* (διὰ τὰς ἀποικίας) sent out at diverse times to the neighbouring lands Egypt, Phoenicia, the

> part of Syria called the Hollow and the rest as well as the lands lying far apart, ...
> And not only are the mainlands full of Jewish *colonies* (τῶν Ἰουδαϊκῶν ἀποικιῶν) but also the most highly esteemed of the islands Euboea, Cyprus, Crete... (*Legat.* 281–282, italics added)

The historical and literary contexts of these two works of Philo are similar, but not identical. In his *In Flaccum*, Philo has just talked about Flaccus's deteriorating rule vis-a-vis the Jews (1–24), which reaches a climax when Herod Agrippa arrives in the city, and the enemies of the Jews are erecting statues of the emperor in the synagogues (25–40). Then follows the critical passage of 45–53, in which Philo ponders the danger such riots would represent if they spread to other parts of the Empire where Jews are also to be found: "For so populous are the Jews that no one country can hold them" (46); the Jews are holding Jerusalem as their mother city, even though they have stayed in other parts of the empire for a long time.

The context of the text segment from *Legat.* is part of the story about what happened when Agrippa, upon visiting Rome, got to know that Emperor Gaius Caligula intended to erect a statue of himself in the Jerusalem temple. Agrippa fell immediately ill, and after recovering a bit, he wrote a letter (*Legat.* 276–329) to the emperor from which the quotation above is taken. His mentioning the Jewish settlements and labeling them 'colonies' emphasizes to the emperor their interrelationship with one another and with Jerusalem; further, Agrippa urges the emperor to grant peace to Jerusalem because it would also profit many other cities of his empire. Although this request is placed in the mouth of Agrippa, in what must be considered a fictive letter,[59] it certainly also represents the opinion of Philo.[60]

When reading *In Flaccum* and *De Legatione*, one should first of all keep in mind that we are here dealing with two works of quite a different nature compared to the rest of Philo's works. These are not expositions of some texts or aspects of the Pentateuchal Law but represent his way of writing in what we might call historical representations of central events in the life of Philo and his Alexandria, evaluated in light of Pentateuchal values. Furthermore, as there seems to be wide agreement that his expository works were written with both Jews and non-Jews in mind, and his

---

59. Kiefer, *Exil und Diaspora*, 405.

60. See here the convincing arguments made in Amir, *Die Hellenistische Gestalt*, 53, note 5.

allegorical works were more for his initiated Jewish readers,[61] these two historical works were most probably written not only for Jews but possibly even more for the non-Jewish authorities, including the successor of the prefect Flaccus in Alexandria and the Roman imperial authorities.[62] Hence, as we have suggested above, we read these works as Philo writing back from the Empire. Here we are meeting Philo as a Jewish politician and should read him as such.

Some scholars emphasize that Philo is here speaking as an apologist, and hence his expressions are exaggeratedly positive.[63] However, while Philo may be apologetic, his arguments would be worthless if there were not a strong core of truth in his statements. And speaking as an apologist-should not be viewed as exaggeratingly dishonest or flattering; to confuse apologetic with dishonest exaggeration or flattery would be to dishonor the intended readers and receivers of Philo's message.

Several scholars state that in using the terms ἀποίκια and μητρόπολις, Philo is using the language of the Septuagint, which again is influenced by ancient Greek colonization.[64] But these issues should not be overplayed. Pearce, on her side, argues that Philo evidently uses the terminology of the Septuagint, but not that of the Greek colonies.[65] It should probably not be denied, however, that in using the term ἀποικία, the LXX translators were to some extent influenced by the colonization processes they knew—that is, by Hellenistic customs and the Greek language, as this is a typical colonization term. In this way they probably also to some extent changed the view of the Diaspora situation, from deportation to emigration. Pearce's argument that Philo is influenced by the LXX but not by language and customs around Greek colonization fails to persuade. The combination of ἀποίκια and μητρόπολις is not found in the LXX but is a central combination in descriptions of Greek colonization. This fact points to some influence from colonization language. Hence Philo is probably influenced by language from the LXX; that book was, after all, his Holy Scriptures. But by his combination of these terms in *In Flaccum*

---

61. For a discussion concerning these issues, see e.g., Borgen, "Philo of Alexandria."
62. See here the discussion in Horst, *Philo's "Flaccus,"* 15–16.
63. E.g., Scott, "Philo and the Restoration," 558. For a more relevant view, see van Unnik, *Das Selbstverständnis*, 127–28.
64. Amir, *Die Hellenistische Gestalt*, 52–56; Mélèze-Modrzejewski, "How to Be a Greek," 72–80; Niehoff, *Philo on Jewish Identity*, 34–35.
65. Pearce, "Jerusalem as 'Mother-City,'" 33.

and *Legatio*, it also seems that he strengthens and emphasizes the colonial aspects of these terms.

Furthermore, some scholars have pointed to the possibility that there might be an anti-Egyptian function or even purpose here. Scott points to Diodorus Siculus (1.28—29.6), who states that the Egyptians claim that "a great number of colonies were scattered from Egypt over the whole inhabited world," which includes the nation of the Jews.[66] Scott surmises that Philo's positive view of the Diaspora as a worldwide colonization "is probably in part a response to this Egyptian tradition."[67] Hence, while Philo's mimicry here cannot be labeled as anti-imperial, some culture criticism might be involved.

Niehoff's position[68] that these two works of Philo are written only for Jews and not at all for Romans is a rare viewpoint. Furthermore, her assertion that Philo is constructing a novel way of thinking by establishing Jerusalem as the mother city is probably not tenable either, as Jerusalem had by his time been for ages the central city for Jews.

Yehoshua Amir, from his side,[69] seems to overplay the influence on Philo from Greek colonization. He states that Philo's expressions do not quite fit the political reality of his time: during Philo's era the colonies were not sent out from the cities but from and by the state ("vom römischen Imperium"). In addition to the terms ἀποίκια and μητρόπολις, another aspect taken as evidence for the influence of Greek colonization language on Philo is his argument that Jewish colonies were begun because the Jews were such a populous nation that no country alone could hold them (*Flacc.* 46). But this is a common emphasis in Philo's works, and Jörn Kiefer is probably right in reading it as an expression of God's promises to Abraham (Gen 12:2; *Congr.* 3; *Spec.* 1.7 etc):[70] "Die Ausbreitung der Diaspora ist für Philo letzlich also die Erfüllung biblischer Verheissung."

But there is another factor that has not been taken into consideration enough here, and that is the simple fact that Philo is writing neither in Hebrew nor in Latin *but in Greek*. Hence, when he wants to describe the Jewish Diaspora as a kind of colonization process, he has to use the Greek terminology. And the Greek terminology by definition represents

---

66. Scott, "Philo and the Restoration," 557–58; Scott, "Exile and Self-Understanding," 183–84. See also Gafni, *Land, Center and Diaspora*, 58, footnote 1.

67. Scott, "Exile and Self-Understanding," 183, footnote 29.

68. Niehoff, *Philo on Jewish Identity*, 42.

69. Amir, *Die Hellenistische Gestalt*, 53.

70. Kiefer, *Exil und Diaspora*, 407.

the language of Greek colonization. This is such a simple fact that it seems never to have been paid any attention. The consequences of this are that the pinpointing of Amir,[71] who states that Philo's descriptions do not match the social realities of colonization in his time, is rendered rather meaningless. Philo is here *mimicking* the colonization processes, both Roman and Greek. His Greek language should not lead us to consider Greek colonization as his social and conceptual background alone. Niehoff points unknowingly to this aspect of mimicry when she states that "Philo . . . implied an unmistakably Roman dimension in his notion of mother city. This is most visible in his emphasis on the universal distribution of the Jewish colonists."[72]

But she also points to some other aspects that function as Philo's mimicry of the Romans in his descriptions: Philo's association of the Jerusalem with the ends of the earth might be read as echoing the Roman identification of Urbs with Orbis; likewise, Philo's speaking in the *Legatio* of Jewish donations to Jerusalem might be read as such mimicry. Hence Philo thus "modelled the role of Jerusalem on the position of Rome in the Empire."[73] Niehoff does not, however, use the model of mimicry in describing these aspects. To her they rather represent Philo's descriptions of Jerusalem in order to make Jews consider Jerusalem as their primary city of identity.

However, her view of Philo's intended readership as being his fellow Jews only, instead of also finding readers among the Romans, is problematic,to say the least. Furthermore, she considers the views of Philo on ἀποίκια and μητρόπολις to be a late development in his thinking. But this is contradicted by his use of these concepts in *Conf.* 77-78 and *Mos.* 2:232. Philo's more extended uses of these terms in *In Flaccum* and *Legatio* are not evidence of a late development but of *an altered situation* and an *altered intended readership*. It is the political issues that are at stake in these two volumes that make Philo describe the Jewish settlements in the various cities and countries in these ways.

If we read Philo here as writing back from the Empire, we see a Philo who, in these ways, mimics the Roman Empire in his descriptions of the Jewish settlements by calling them ἀποικίαι and by describing Jerusalem as their μητρόπολις. Mimicry and hybridity are never representing complete identity, but similarities. Hence, all claims that Philo's use of

71. Amir, *Die Hellenistische Gestalt*, 53.
72. Niehoff, *Philo on Jewish Identity*, 36.
73. Niehoff, *Philo on Jewish Identity*, 36-37.

terms like ἀποικία and μητρόπολις is anachronistic or out of touch with the historical realities of his times, are off target both because he is writing in Greek, the lingua franca of his time, and *because of his mimicking purposes*. Furthermore, as mimicking does not denote identity, the result is often some sort of hybridity. Read in light of the Roman colonizing activities of his day, Philo's descriptions of the Jewish settlements as colonizing might very well look like a hybrid description to a Roman reader.

Hence, there is a kind of double message from Philo to his readers: First, in *In Flaccum* he writes that the tumult that had come against the Jews in Alexandria might spread to other cities in the Mediterranean world, because the Jews were to be found everywhere (*Flacc.* 46); second, in Legatio he warns that Jewish riots over the raising of an emperor statue in the Jewish metropolis might result in uproar all over the empire, for the Jews had their colonies everywhere. Hence, the warnings are clear enough, but Philo's underlying self-understanding is associated with his view of the Jewish settlements as kinds of colonies sent out from Jerusalem up through the decades and centuries. In this understanding of Jews' place in and effects upon the Roman Empire, Philo mimics both Greek and Roman colonization language. The Romans might smile at the hybridity involved in Philo's characterizations. But to Philo, they were real enough.

Finally, is it mere coincidence that the passages in which ἀποικία and μητρόπολις are joined and given the most explicit political coloring are to be found in Philo's most political writings, and in those works that are probably among his latest, written after the problematic years of 38–41 CE? By drawing upon our considerations at the end of the previous chapter, we might surmise that something happened to Philo's views of the Roman authorities, leading him to become more explicitly political and negative towards the empire. Hence, what we are dealing with here is the anti-imperial Philo writing back from the Empire—against the Empire.

CONCLUSIONS

The perspectives of postcolonial readings have been popular in literary studies for some time now, and are being increasingly used in biblical and classical studies. In the studies of Diaspora Judaism, however, and in studies of Philo of Alexandria in particular, they are virtually absent.

In the present study, we have tried to focus on some terms in the most political writings of Philo, the *In Flaccum*, and the *Legatio ad Gaium*.

These two books, which are probably not only the most political, but also among the latest of Philo's many works, are considered to have been written not only for a Jewish readership but also for non-Jews, possibly even for Roman persons of authority. So we are inclined to follow E. R. Goodenough's view of the intended readers. While I do not subscribe to all parts of his view of Philo as a politician, I concede that nevertheless in these two late works, we meet Philo the politician.

The terms rendered 'colony' (ἀποικία) and 'mother-city' (μητρόπολις) are found in several of Philo's works. Conceptually, these terms belong to Greek colonization language. Important for our understanding of Philo is that he could find these terms in his Greek translation of the Hebrew Scriptures, in what we have come to call the LXX. In these writings, however, they have more of a role in the semantic field of 'migration,' whereas in *In Flaccum* and *Legatio* they regain their meanings of 'mother-city' and 'colonies'/'colonizing'—given that Philo uses the related verb στέλλω in combination with ἀποικία.

From our reading of two passages in *In Flaccum* 46 and *Legatio* 281–282, we suggest that there are elements of mimicry and hybridity in Philo's use of these terms. Philo uses them to describe the Jewish Diaspora communities in the Roman Empire. As part of Philo's writing back from the Empire, they are important for his conceptualization; read in light of Roman colonizing activities they might very well have looked somewhat hybrid. But that is often the result of mimicry in a context of colonization. The colonized try to copy the colonizers, but the results, intended or not, are often mimicry resulting in hybridity.

6

Reimagining Philo and the Mysteries

A Case of Mimicry and Hybridity?

> "I myself was initiated under Moses the God-beloved into his greater mysteries, yet when I saw the prophet Jeremiah, and knew him to be not only himself enlightened, but a worthy minister of the holy secrets, I was not slow to become his disciple."
>
> CHER. 49

INTRODUCTION

THE LIFE OF PHILO of Alexandria is believed to have extended from approximately 20 BCE to approximately 50 CE. Throughout most of his lifetime, he resided in the cosmopolitan city of Alexandria, located in Egypt, where he was deeply immersed in his Jewish community and the diverse cultural settings of the city. Philo's interactions with society were complex and multifaceted, and therefore various angles must be considered when analyzing both his life and work.

Philo's attitude toward the Greco-Roman world of his time has been characterized by Peder Borgen as the attitude of "a conqueror, on the verge of being conquered." The main issue inherent in Borgen's formulation is that it was Philo's intention "to conquer the surrounding culture ideologically by claiming that whatever good there is has its source in Scripture and thus belonged to the Jewish nation and its heritage."[1]

This procedure may be characterized using several categories; however, a postcolonial scholar might inquire whether this approach closely resembles mimicry and whether the resultant outcome could potentially be classified as hybridity. In other words, do certain modified forms emerge from mimicked elements, resulting in a product that is analogous to yet distinct from the original? Consequently, one might consider whether Philo can be interpreted as attempting to transcend his circumstances by adopting and adapting specific aspects of the Greco-Roman world to persist as a colonized Jew.[2]

Therefore, this study too will adopt a postcolonial perspective in examining Philo and his utilization of language commonly referred to as "mystery language." This approach elucidates how Philo employed linguistic elements and categorizations to engage with the Greco-Roman culture in Alexandria.

GREEK MYSTERY CULTS: SOME CENTRAL ISSUES

Several mystery cults existed in the Greco-Roman world during the first century CE. Among the most prominent were the Eleusinian mysteries, the mysteries of Isis and Osiris, and the Mithraic mysteries. Additional cults that could have been included and described here are the Dionysiac and Cybele cults. However, this discussion will primarily focus on some central aspects of the Demeter mysteries in Eleusis, particularly because numerous scholars suggest that these were most significant for the development of mystery cults at large,[3] and because many also suggest that Philo's use of mystery terms is influenced by terminology related to the Eleusinian cult.[4]

---

1. Borgen, "Philo of Alexandria," 150–54, here cited from 151.

2. See Seland, "'Colony' and 'Metropolis' in Philo," 13–36.

3. Bowden, *Mystery Cults in the Ancient World*, 26–48: see p. 26: "The Eleusinian Mysteries were the most revered of all ancient mystery cults."

4. My description draws especially upon the works of Burkert, Mylonas, and Bowden. See Burkert, *Ancient Mystery Cults*; Mylonas, *Eleusis and the Eleusinian Mysteries*. See also Østby, "Eleusis"; Bremmer, *Initiation into the Mysteries*; and Bowden, *Mystery Cults in the Ancient World*, 26–48.

The term 'mystery' comes from the Greek verb μύω, which means *to shut, to close*; in the context of the Greek mysteries, this aspect has been interpreted both as *to shut one's mouth* (that is, to keep a secret by not telling anyone about the mysteries) and also *to shut one's eyes*, in order to open them when the holy things are to be disclosed.[5] In the passive forms, the verb μύω is translated as *to be initiated*. Several mystery terms are then derived from this verb: those who are initiated into a μυστήριον are called μύστης, and one of the functionaries is called a μυσταγωγός.

George E. Mylonas describes several Eleusinian mystery functionaries.[6] The hierophant (ἱεροφάντης) had a high-priestly role at Eleusis, one of the most important mystery cults in ancient Greece. Only he could show the initiates the holy things (*epopteia*), and he alone could enter the *Anaktoron*, the holiest of the holy rooms in the complex, also called the *telesterion* (τελεστήριον), and he, "with the other members of his gens, was the interpreter of the unwritten, ancestral laws that governed the celebration ... In general, he was in charge of the Sanctuary and was responsible for the celebration."[7] Some of the *hierophantides* were his chief assistants. Another important figure was the mystagogos (μυσταγωγός), who introduced those who were to be initiated. In addition, there were several other functionaries, such as the torchbearer (*dadouchos*; δᾳδοῦχος), the herald (*hierokeryx*; ἱεροκήρυξ), and other priestly persons.

The Eleusinian mysteries encompassed multiple stages or degrees of initiation; however, the precise number and nature of these stages remain unclear in contemporary scholarship. George E. Mylonas states that there were probably only three stages: "the preliminary initiation into the Lesser Mysteries, the initiation proper into the Greater Mysteries, known as the *telete* (τελετή), and the *epopteia* (ἐποπτεια), or highest degree of initiation."[8] However, the significance of these rites remains unclear.[9] Philo demonstrates an awareness of the distinction between the greater and lesser mysteries (*Leg.* 3:100; *Cher.* 49; *Sacr.* 33) and employs several conventional terms associated with the mysteries, albeit not with all. These issues will be revisited subsequently.

---

5. Meyer, "Mystery Religions"; Bremmer, *Initiation into the Mysteries*, 5–11.
6. Mylonas, *Eleusis and the Eleusinian Mysteries*, 229–37.
7. Mylonas, *Eleusis and the Eleusinian Mysteries*, 230.
8. Mylonas, *Eleusis and the Eleusinian Mysteries*, 239; Bremmer, *Initiation into the Mysteries*, 11–16.
9. See Mylonas, *Eleusis and the Eleusinian Mysteries*, 261.

PHILO AND THE SEPTUAGINT

In view of the fact that Philo was an expositor of the Scriptures, it is interesting to see that not all of these terms are found in the Septuagint; the first (ἱεροφάντης) is used neither as a noun nor as a verb in the LXX. Μύστης is used only once (Wis 12:5), but μυστήριον is found thirty-one times; the terms μυσταγωγός/-γέω and ὄργια/ὀργιάζω are absent too, while τελέω is found twenty-four times, and τελετή six times. Hence, the terms found in the LXX are primarily μυστήριον and τελέω/τελετή. The first of these two is primarily used in the book of Daniel and in similar contexts; the other (τελετή) is used often as a term for heathen activities, like temple prostitution (1 Kgs 15:12) and unholy rites more broadly (Wis 14:15): sometimes it is translated 'initiations' (Wis 14:23; 3 Macc γ2:30). The verb τελέω is most often used to convey the relatively neutral meaning of 'to finish something', but also a few times as a term for yoking oneself with the heathens in their sins (Num 25:3,5; Ps 105:28; Hos 4:14).

The use of mystery terminology in Philo's works does not appear to have its primary origin in the Septuagint, as the latter lacks numerous central terms associated with Greek mystery cults that are employed by Philo. Consequently, the prominence of mystery terminology in Philo's Alexandrian social milieu emerges as the primary source domain. The question persists regarding the probability of Philo employing such terms merely as a matter of convenience, or whether his usage can be interpreted as stemming from a more intimate familiarity with them and specific purposes for them.

MYSTERY TERMS USED IN PHILO'S WORKS

This study examines the principal texts of Philo that contain—and thus demonstrate—his utilization of mystery terminology in his works.[10] Although a comprehensive analysis of how he employs these terms in his philosophical and theological arguments across various texts is beyond the scope of this investigation, an overview is provided. Emphasis will be placed on the diverse elements of the mystery cults that Philo incorporates rather than on his philosophical theology. This does not suggest that

---

10. Cf. ἱεροφάντης (24 times)/ἱεροφαντέω (16), μύστης (12)/μυστήριον (14)/ μυσταγωγός/-γέω (3/1), ὄργια/ὀργιάζω (7/4), and τελέω/τελετή (24/22), which are the major mystery terms in his works. For a comparable review, see Wolfson, *Philo*, 1:43–55; Cohen, "Mystery Terminology."

the latter is insignificant; however, the primary focus of this examination is on the mystery terminology he employs, specifically its relationship to the social context of mystery movements.[11]

The noun ἱεροφάντης is utilized as a descriptor or characterization of several individuals, predominantly Moses, who is considered the preeminent human ἱεροφάντης. However, God is regarded as the supreme hierophant, surpassing Moses. It was God who bestowed upon Moses the dual role of hierophant and prophet.

The time and place of the initiation of Moses as a hierophant was when he was on the mountain, conversing with God, as narrated in the book of Exodus. In *Mos.* 2:71 Philo retells this: "While he was still staying on the mount, he was being instructed in all the mysteries (ἐμυσταγωγεῖτο παιδευόμενος) of his priestly duties; and first in those which stood first in order, namely the building and furnishing of the sanctuary." In *Gig.* 54, Philo elucidates Moses's initiation further, employing several terms associated with the mysteries. Moses had established his tent outside the camp (Exod 33:7). According to the narrative in Exod 33, the tent—designated as the tent of meeting—was situated at a considerable distance from the encampment of the Israelites: "When Moses entered the tent, the pillar of cloud would descend and stand at the entrance of the tent, and the LORD would speak with Moses" as a friend, face to face (Exod 33:9 NRSV). In Philo's exposition (*Gig.* 54, cf. *Decal.* 18; *Spec.* 1:41–50), this is given in terms from the mysteries thus: "Then only does he begin to worship God and entering the darkness, the invisible region (εἰς τὸν γνόφον, τὸν ἀειδῆ χῶρον), abides there while he learns the secrets of the most holy mysteries (καταμένει τελούμενος τὰς ἱερωτάτας τελετάς). There, he becomes not only one of the initiated (μύστης) but also the hierophant and teacher of divine rites (ἱεροφάντης ὀργίων), which he will impart to those whose ears are purified." In this text, Moses's entry into the tent is described using terminology associated with mystery cults; notably, Moses enters the *darkness*, thereby acquiring knowledge of the esoteric teachings of the mysteries. Being a '*mystes*' he is becoming a hierophant, who is to minister to those "whose ears are purified."

This latter aspect is utilized multiple times: those who have been initiated are instructed not to disclose their experiences, but rather to retain and safeguard their experiences and knowledge in secrecy and silence (*Sacr.* 60–62; *Cher.* 42; 48), cf. *Fug.* 85: "Drive off, then, ye initiates

---

11. As for a more recent investigation of the use of these terms in Philo's discussion of the knowledge of God, see e.g., Ryu, *Knowledge of God*, 152–214.

and *hierophants* of holy mysteries (ὦ μύσται καὶ ἱεροφάνται θείων ὀργίων), drive off the motley crowd, flotsam and jetsam, souls hardly capable of cleansing and purifying, . . . longing . . . to tell out such things as should never find utterance." On the other hand, Philo admonishes his readers to grow in wisdom by seeking out the initiated: "But, if ye meet with anyone of the initiated (τινι τῶν τετελεσμένων), press him closely, cling to him, lest knowing of some still newer secret he hides it from you; stay till you have learnt its full lesson" (*Cher.* 48c).

Philo demonstrates awareness of the distinction between greater and lesser mysteries and employs this differentiation in his expositions. See *Sacr.* 62, cf. *Sacr.* 33. In *Leg.* 3:100, he says about Moses that "there is a mind more perfect and more thoroughly cleansed, which has undergone initiation into the great mysteries (τὰ μεγάλα μυστήρια μυηθείς), a mind which gains its knowledge of the First Cause not from created things . . . but lifting its eyes above and beyond creation obtains a clear vision of the uncreated One."

Then Philo, having admonished his readers to press forward in their search for knowledge, reveals that he struggled to gain more wisdom and considered himself to have become initiated: "I myself was initiated under Moses the God-beloved into his greater mysteries (μυηθεὶς τὰ μεγάλα μυστήρια), yet when I saw the prophet Jeremiah and knew him to be not only himself enlightened, but a worthy minister of the holy secrets (ὅτι οὐ μόνον μύστης ἐστὶν ἀλλὰ καὶ ἱεροφάντης ἱκανός), I was not slow to become his disciple" (*Cher.* 49). This is the only passage in which Philo describes himself in mystic terms, but it demonstrates very well how he could use as metaphors the terms from mystery cults. He became initiated by studying the books of Moses and Jeremiah.

In a couple of places it might at first seem unclear whether ἱεροφάντης refers to God or Moses, but most probably it denotes Moses (*Leg.* 3:151; *Somn.* 2:29).[12] Other texts clearly use this term to denote Moses (*Leg.* 3:173; *Sacr.* 94; *Post.* 16; 164(?)); 174; *Mos.* 2:153).

However, other individuals were also designated as hierophants. In Philo's exegesis of Num 11:16 in *Sobr.* 20, he elucidates that the seventy so-called elders described in Num 11 are not merely those whom the general populace regarded as older men (and also as hierophantes), but rather are those whom the wise man alone recognizes and deems worthy of the appellation of elder. Philo does not, however, provide any

---

12. *Fug.* 85 is also somewhat ambiguous as to whom it designates.

elucidation as to why they are also termed hierophantes. In *Spec.* 3:135 the high priest is designated as ἱεροφάντης. In *Mos.* 2:40 the translators of the Septuagint are referred to as both hierophantes and prophets, and in *Cher.* 49, the prophet Jeremiah is ascribed the designation ἱεροφάντης.

Consequently, several individuals from the Scriptures may be designated as hierophants; however, Moses is indeed preeminent among them. In the other approximately twenty occurrences, the term refers to Moses.[13] Moses was made a ἱεροφάντης on Mount Sinai, where God himself was the μυσταγωγός: "And while he was still up there (on the mountain), he was initiated, educated first of all in that concerning the priesthood" (*Mos.* 2:71).

Aspects of the Mystery Cults Not Used by Philo

Several critical aspects of mystery cults are notably absent from Philo's works. These omissions primarily pertain to certain institutional aspects of the mystery cults. This observation leads to the following hypotheses: Philo may have lacked comprehensive knowledge about where Greek mystery rites were conducted. Additionally, this absence might suggest that Philo did not consider that Jewish institutional settings might host performances of mystery-like rites. His terminology does not appear to be derived from firsthand knowledge of actual mystery practices.

To substantiate this suggestion, it is necessary to first examine the significant institutional terminology absent from Philo's vocabulary regarding the mysteries. If we take as our point of departure the major Greek mystery rites in Eleusis, for example, they were carried out in a complex called the τελεστήριον (*telesterion*), and the most holy location here was called the ἀνάκτορον (*anaktoron*). During the initiation rites, the people concerned were led through some physical and symbolic stages. Scholars emphasize that the most important rites here probably included three different elements: the δρώμενα (*dromena*: that which was enacted), the δεικνύμενα (*deiknymena*: the sacred objects that were shown), and the λεγόμενα (*legomena*: the words that were spoken). The act of seeing the sacred things was also called ἐποπτεια (*epopteia*), and those seeing it were called ἐπόπτης (*epoptes*). However, further description is complicated

---

13. See e.g., *Deus.* 156; *Migr.* 14; *Somn.* 2:3, 29, 109; *Mos.* 2:149, 153; *Decal.* 18, *Spec.* 1:41; 2:201.

because the central items, acts, and topics were among the secrets not to be revealed to those uninitiated.[14]

Of the seven institutional terms listed above, *none* are to be found in the works of Philo.[15] In addition, institutional leadership terms such as 'hierophantides' and 'hierokeryx' are not present in the works of Philo either. The noun δαδοῦχος (torch) and the verb δαδουχέω (bearing a torch), respectively, are only present in *Her.* 311 and in *Ebr.* 168. This lack of relevant institutional mystery terms indicates that Philo is not taking his point of departure from personal knowledge of relevant institutions and their inherent acts. Nevertheless, Philo is aware of the distinction between the greater and lesser mysteries (*Leg.* 3:100; *Cher.* 49; *Sacr.* 33, 62), and he writes about being a ἱεροφάντης (hierophantes) and being initiated as a μύστης (mystes). But it is somewhat astonishing that so many institutional mystery terms are lacking in his works.

PHILO AND THE MYSTERIES IN RECENT RESEARCH

The presence of terminology associated with mystery cults is evident in the works of Philo; however, the critical questions are: what do these terms represent? How should their presence and Philo's use of them be interpreted? These inquiries are not novel but warrant some reconsideration.

Jewish Mysteries in Alexandria?

Many reviewers have referred to an 1895 study by F. C. Conybeare on *De Vita Contemplativa*, in which he presented the bold statement that "from many hints up and down the works of Philo it is certain that among the Alexandrian Jews there existed a system of mysteries, perhaps in imitation of the Greek mysteries of Demeter which were celebrated year by year on the hill of Eleusis."[16] In most studies influenced by the history of religions school, this view was taken by several.[17]

---

14. Mylonas, *Eleusis and the Eleusinian Mysteries*, 261.

15. The more general words like δεικνύμενα and λεγόμενα are, of course, present in various forms, but not in a context of mystery acts.

16. The quotation is taken from Lease, "Jewish Mystery Cults Since Goodenough," 858.

17. On these, see especially Lease, "Jewish Mystery Cults Since Goodenough," 861–64.

One of those still referred to is *Joseph Pascher*.[18] He does not provide a detailed analysis of Philo's use of various mystery terms; instead, he constructs a comprehensive theology of Philo's mystery religion, which he purports to identify in Philo's works. Central to the author's perspective is the manner in which Philo delineates a royal path of the soul, a "Königsweg der Seele," as an *itinerarium mentis in Deum* (*Opif.* 69–71; *Mut.* 179–186; *Det.* 89). In his work Pascher applies both sophia-ideology and logos-theology, and Philo's allegories are pivotal: Here especially Philo's expositions of the high priest's garments (*Spec.* 1:84–97; *Mos.* 2:117–135; *QE* 2:107–163) become essential passages that Pascher reads in light of the Isis cult. He also finds that Philo's allegorical exegesis of the provision of manna demonstrates a "Mysterienmahl" known to the Jews (184–191), influenced by the gentile mystery meals. Pasher's summary, which also reveals how he works in this study as a whole, runs thus:[19]

> Philon kennt ein heiliges Mahl, in dem durch den Genuss von Licht-Logos-Pneuma-Manna der "Seiende" geschaut wird. In dieser Schau wird der Myste vergöttlicht. Die Lehre steht in engem Zusammenhang mit der Mysterientheologie, sie tritt teilweise sogar in der Terminologie der Mysterien auf und hat starke Parallelen in der Mysterienliteratur. Wir glauben uns daher zu der Annahme berechtigt, dass Philon oder seine jüdische Vorlage Idee und Praxis des Mysterienmahles aus einem wirklichen Mysterium kannte, weiterhin dann, dass in diesem Mahl die Liebesvereinigung als Genuss der Gottheit versinnbildet war. Darin sehen wir die geistige Brücke zwischen Synusie und Gottesschau.

Hence, Pascher sees Judaism as the target domain of Philo's use of such terms. But the one who, above all others, is associated with a comparable mystical interpretation of Philo is *Erwin R. Goodenough*.[20] Goodenough posited that the Judaism of the Diaspora differed significantly from that practiced in Palestine. However, as Jews throughout history have been influenced to varying degrees by their surrounding cultures, the Diaspora Jews during Philo's era were influenced by Greek mystery cults. Consequently, Goodenough asserted that Philo's works in particular must be interpreted within the context of these mysteries. He regarded Philo as the primary source for understanding the details of

---

18. Pascher, Η ΒΑΣΙΛΙΚΗ ΟΔΟΣ.
19. Pascher, Η ΒΑΣΙΛΙΚΗ ΟΔΟΣ, 191.
20. Goodenough, *By Light, Light*. See also Goodenough, *Introduction*, 134–61.

Judaism as a Jewish mystery cult, while acknowledging that Philo was not the sole representative of this perspective. According to Goodenough, "it is in terms of the Mystery that Philo alone becomes intelligible, for all his writing is oriented about it, and directed toward its explanation."[21]

Indeed, Goodenough's proposition suggests that as the Jewish people were unable to become initiates of Isis or other mystery cults, their own Judaism was transformed into a comparable esoteric tradition:

> Yet since a Jew could not now simply become an initiate of Isis and Orpheus and remain a Jew as well, the amazingly clever trick was devised, we do not know when or by whom, of representing Moses as Orpheus and Hermes-Tat, and explaining that the Jewish "Wisdom" figure, by translation "Sophia," was identical with that "Female Principle in nature" which Plutarch intensified as Isis! All that now needed to be done was to develop sufficient skill in allegory and the Torah could be represented as the ἱερὸς λόγος *par-excellence*, whereby Judaism was at once transformed into the greatest, the only true, Mystery. Moses became priest and hierophant as well as lawgiver. The door was wide open, and the Jews, without the slightest feeling of disloyalty, or the abandonment of cult practices, could and did take all of the esoteric ideology of the mystic philosophers about them, especially and inevitably the Pythagorean-Platonism of Alexandria. Indeed they early claimed, not that they had borrowed it from the Greeks, but that the Greeks originally had taken it from them.[22]

Goodenough, in this context, proposes that this form of Judaism functioned in a manner analogous to a mystery cult. His formulations, at the very least, lend themselves to such an interpretation. He said, however, that "how far such Jews organized themselves into cult groups, θίασοι, I have not been able to determine. The evidence seems to suggest that they may have had their mystic initiation, baptism, like the Christians later, and a 'sacred table' from which the uninitiated were rigorously kept away. The evidence for this is unsatisfactory because scanty and not in agreement."[23]

---

21. Goodenough, *By Light, Light*, 8.
22. Goodenough, *By Light, Light*, 7.
23. Goodenough, *By Light, Light*, 8.

Jewish Mysteries: A Literary Phenomenon?

Goodenough has been heavily criticized for his view of the reality and nature of a Jewish mystery cult,[24] and in a later volume, he had to admit, "There is no evidence whatsoever to support a view that mystic Jews had distinct rites of their own, distinct initiations, to which even Jews must be specially admitted."[25] The mystery evident in Philo's works is primarily one of learning; it is literal but also possesses literary qualities. Consequently, according to Goodenough, the process of being instructed in the teachings of Moses was akin to initiation for Philo, with Moses serving as the 'hierophant' or 'mystagogos.' Thus, it exhibits a predominantly scholarly or 'bookish' character.

It is not strange that Goodenough has been interpreted in this way. His formulations in *By Light, Light*, are open to such interpretations, and his appendices in the same volume, in which he searches for a kind of mystic liturgy, support such readings too.[26]

Harry A. Wolfson, in discussing Philo's attitudes towards central aspects of his environment as polytheism, mythology, and mysteries,[27] started with Philo's denunciations of the Greek mysteries (*Spec.* 3:119-123). But then again, Philo is found not to hesitate in making use of the vocabulary of these mysteries in his descriptions of the beliefs and institutions of Judaism: "He [Philo] had no objection to the use of all these terms because he knew fully well that, while in form they were borrowed from Greek popular religion, in substance they expressed certain characteristics of God which are to be found in Scripture."[28] Wolfson, furthermore, postulated two reasons why Philo liked to apply mystery terms in his expositions. First, they are called mysteries because the true knowledge of them lies hidden in the Scripture and has to be understood by way of allegorical interpretations. Second, "they are called mysteries as a challenge to the heathen mysteries."[29]

---

24. Nock, "Question of Jewish Mysteries," 463–65; Lease, "Jewish Mystery Cults Since Goodenough," 868–71.
25. Goodenough, *Introduction*, 154.
26. See Goodenough, *By Light, Light*, 306–58: Chapter XI: The Mystic Liturgy.
27. Wolfson, *Philo*, 1:27–55.
28. Wolfson, *Philo*, 1:38–39.
29. Wolfson, *Philo*, 1:49.

Another scholar who has dealt extensively with the mystery terminology in Philo is *Christoph Riedweg*.[30] In his work, Riedweg wants to focus on three aspects: First, "die Einwirkungen der Mysterien" on the works of Plato, Philo, and Clement; then, what conclusions (Rückschlüsse) can be drawn from the texts to the praxis of the cults, and "an Eigenleben gewinnenden Traditionslinien der Mysteriemetaphorik."[31] In the context of the present work, the first and third questions are considered the most important. When dealing with Philo's texts, Riedweg focuses primarily on a few texts he considers especially important.[32] In dealing with *Cher.* 40–50, Riedweg finds that Philo to some extent is influenced by Plato, especially his *Phaedrus*. But this is not sufficient to explain the use in this section. Hence, Riedweg suggests that—especially concerning *Cher.* 42— there probably is some sort of "Mysterienritual im Hintergrund."[33] When investigating Philo's terminology further, he finds that mystery terminology represents some of Philo's favorite metaphors for characterizing allegorical interpretations of Scripture. But "Mysterien-terminologie ist nun allerdings nur eine sprachliche Ausdrucksform Philons."[34] Furthermore, Riedweg suggests that Philo's own personal knowledge of mystery cults "geht kaum über rein äusserliche, allgemeinbekannte Elemente hinaus."[35] Hence, he states that Philo's mystery terminology "nur aus literarisch-rhetorischer Bildungstradition stammen, nicht direct einem Kult entnommen sein."[36] We will have to return to Riedweg's view in the sections below.

Finally, at the end of this review of recent research, I will briefly mention the view of *Naomi G. Cohen*. According to her, "Philo was following current usage, for 'mystery terminology' had entered common parlance to indicate not only the rites of mystery religions but also religious revelations in general, various aspects of philosophical rhetoric, and even the technical expertise of an occupation—in short, as a figure of speech."[37] Her descriptions may be valuable as long as it comes to the

---

30. Riedweg, *Mysterienterminologie*, especially 70–115.
31. Riedweg, *Mysterienterminologie*, xi.
32. Hence, he deals with *Cher.* 40–50 (pp. 71–92); *Somn.* 1:164–165 (pp. 96–98); *Gig.* 57 (pp. 98–99); *Spec.* 1:319–323 (pp. 99–104); *Gig.* 54 (pp. 104–105) and *Leg.* 3:10 (pp. 105–107).
33. Riedweg, *Mysterienterminologie*, 79, cf. 84.
34. Riedweg, *Mysterienterminologie*, 91.
35. Riedweg, *Mysterienterminologie*, 103.
36. Riedweg, *Mysterienterminologie*, 103.
37. Cohen, "Mystery Terminology," 175. See also Mazzanti, "'Mysteries' in Philo."

how of Philo's usage, but she does not tell us much about *why* Philo used this terminology.

Hence, given the perspectives presented here, I find that most of the scholars discussed above considered the Greek mystery cults to be the source domain for Philo's own use of mystery terms. Further, most of these same scholars appear to assume that his readers, whether Jews or Gentiles, were familiar with language from mystery religions, such that Philo employed it in order to reach his target domain. Only one scholar (Wolfson) mentioned that Philo employed these terms as a challenge to the heathen mysteries.

PHILO'S CRITICISM OF ALEXANDRIAN MYSTERIES

Philo was very familiar with the various cultural aspects of his Alexandria; this included having some knowledge of the Greek mystery cults of his time: On the one hand, the terminology found in his works reveals a knowledge of some concepts from mystery religions, but there are also sayings of his that reveal a closer familiarity with some aspects of the actual practice of the mysteries, possibly due to his observance of some of their members in the city of Alexandria.[38]

However, we must remember that Philo is no neutral or disengaged observer; his descriptions are sometimes rather derogatory and even somewhat competitive. Hence, we may also ask what perceptions he provides: that is, how does he—according to his symbolic universe—conceptualize the Greek mysteries? In *Spec.* 3:40 he seems to presuppose that his readers know that male prostitutes and castrates are involved in the mystery cults: "Certainly you may see these hybrids and women continually strutting about through the thick of the market, heading the processions at the feasts, appointed to serve as unholy ministers of holy things, leading the mysteries and initiations and celebrating the rites of Demeter (καὶ μυστηρίων καὶ τελετῶν κατάρχοντας καὶ Δήμετρος ὀργιάζοντας)." This is the only time he mentions Δήμετρος, who is so important in the Eleusinian mystery cult. Concerning the prominence of male prostitutes in

---

38. In addition to the studies mentioned above, see also Mazzanti, "'Mysteries' in Philo," 128.

the mysteries, however, Colson comments that he has found no other sources confirming this statement of Philo.[39]

Furthermore, in *Spec.* 1:323 Philo claims that persons are getting initiated into the mysteries for money: "we often find that no person of good character is admitted to the mysteries, while robbers and pirates and associations of abominable and licentious women, when they offer money to those who conduct the initiating rites, are sometimes accepted" (see *Fug.* 85). Such sayings reveal a negative attitude toward the mysteries comparable to some of his descriptions of the Greco-Roman clubs and associations in Alexandria.[40] We may also note that most of these critical sayings of Philo concerning activities related to the mysteries are in his non-allegorical works, belonging to the Exposition, and thus probably also belonging to his later works, written in or after his stay in Rome as part of the delegation sent from Alexandria in order to negotiate with the Emperor, Gaius Caligula.[41]

Spec. 1:319–323: Philo on Mystery Propaganda Contra Jewish Missionary Propaganda in the Agora of Alexandria

But we must take a closer look at the text of *Spec.* 1:319–323 in which Philo has some further descriptions concerning the activities of some mystery cults that are interesting in our context. The importance of this passage makes it relevant to provide a comprehensive quotation (*Spec.* 1:319–323):

> 319 Furthermore, he [Moses] banishes from the sacred legislation the lore of occult rites and mysteries and all such imposture and buffoonery (Πρὸς τούτοις ἔτι τὰ περὶ τελετὰς καὶ μυστήρια καὶ πᾶσαν τὴν τοιαύτην τερθρείαν καὶ βωμολοχίαν ἐκ τῆς ἱερᾶς ἀναιρεῖ νομοθεσίας,). He would not have those who were bred in such a commonwealth (πολιτεία) as ours take part in mummeries and clinging on to mystic fables (ὀργιάζεσθαι καὶ μυστικῶν πλασμάτων ἐκκρεμαμένους), despise truth and pursue things which have taken night and darkness for their province, discarding what is fit to bear the light of day.

---

39. See Colson et al. eds. and trans., *Philo*, vol. 7 (LCL), 634.

40. Seland, "Philo and the Clubs," 114–17.

41. Here I rely on the work of Niehoff and her dating of these works; see Niehoff, *Philo of Alexandria*.

Let none, therefore, of the followers and disciples of Moses either confer or receive initiation to such rites (μηδεὶς οὖν μήτε τελείτω μήτε τελείσθω τῶν Μωυσέως φοιτητῶν καὶ γνωρίμων). For both in teacher and taught such action is gross sacrilege. 320 For tell me, ye mystics (ὦ μύσται), if these things are good and profitable, why do you shut yourselves up in profound darkness (συγκλεισάμενοι ἑαυτοὺς ἐν σκότῳ βαθεῖ) and reserve their benefits for three or four alone, when by producing them in the midst of the market-place you might extend them to every man and thus enable all to share in security a better and happier life? 321 For virtue has no room in her home for a grudging spirit [*Phaedrus* 247]. Let those who work mischief feel shame and seek holes and corners of the earth and profound darkness (βαθὺ σκότος), there lie hid and keep the multitude of their iniquities veiled out of the sight of all. But let those whose actions serve the common weal use freedom of speech (παρρησία) and walk in the daylight through the midst of the marketplace (διὰ μέσης ... ἀγορᾶς), ready to converse with crowded gatherings, to let the clear sunlight shine upon their own life and through the two most royal senses, sight and hearing, to render good service to the assembled groups, who through the one behold spectacles as marvelous as they are delightful, and through the other feast on the sweet draught of words which are wont to gladden the minds of such as are not wholly averse to learning.
322 Cannot you see that nature also does not conceal any of her glorious and admirable works, but displays the stars and the whole heaven to delight by the sight and to foster the love of philosophy; so too the seas and fountains and rivers and the air so happily tempered by winds and breezes to make the yearly seasons, and the countless varieties of plants and animals and again of fruits—all for the use and enjoyment of men?
323 Were it not well, then, that we should follow her intentions and display in public all that is profitable and necessary for the benefit of those who are worthy to use it? ...

Some scholars[42] have suggested that this section is an exposition of the Septuagintal addition to Deut 23:17 (οὐκ ἔσται τελεσφόρος ἀπὸ θυγατέρων Ισραηλ, καὶ οὐκ ἔσται τελισκόμενος ἀπὸ υἱῶν Ισραηλ); this is possible but not probable, as the associations between Deut 23 and this text are not that obvious.

---

42. E.g., Colson et al., eds. and trans., *Philo*, vol. 7 (LCLf), 285; Pascher, Η ΒΑΣΙΛΙΚΗ ΟΔΟΣ, 7.

Then, what kind of activities is Philo focusing on here? Goodenough has suggested that the reference is to some Jews celebrating a rite in a Jewish mystery cult.[43] He further surmises that Philo criticizes them for "equating that truth [concerning God] with certain rites, and making the prerequisite for admission not the character or aspirations of the applicant, but ability to pay the initiation fee" (1:323). However, his suggestions that this passage as a whole concerns a Jewish mystery rite seems farfetched and is more likely based on Goodenough's reading of Philo's 'ideology' as a whole as a kind of Jewish mystery religion rather than on what Philo's text conveys.

Christoph Riedweg suggests that the fact that Philo deals so energetically here with these issues indicates that some Alexandrian Jews had been initiated into some mystery cults.[44] He also argues convincingly that Philo is not necessarily thinking about some of the greater official and public celebration ceremonies like that known from Eleusis but that he criticizes some minor and more private initiations in the city, carried out by itinerant mystery 'hierophants.'[45] Riedweg also claims that Philo's descriptions do not indicate that he had any personal knowledge of the mysteries he criticizes or that he had been initiated into a mystery cult. The aspects of mystery cults Philo criticizes are mainly such as most probably were evident and well known to many, namely, that those peddling such propaganda focused on the profit of being initiated, and that these initiations were carried out in darkness and in private.[46]

Philo seems instead to argue against any Jew who would want to be involved in some Greek mysteries. The following reading of the text supports such an understanding: First, the immediately proceeding passage about false prophets (1:315–318) seems to support such an interpretation. Second, a comparable negative attitude and stern warnings against participation in such mysteries are also voiced in *Spec.* 1:56.[47] In both cases, the problem is Jews getting involved in mystery activities leading to apostasy (compare 3 Macc 3:20).

---

43. Goodenough, *By Light, Light*, 123.

44. Riedweg, *Mysterienterminologie*, 99.

45. Riedweg points specifically to (Orphic-) Bacchic mystery cults and initiations. Riedweg, *Mysterienterminologie*, 100.

46. Riedweg, *Mysterienterminologie*, 102–3.

47. Note here the expression τελουμένος δὲ τὰς μυθικὰς τελετάς. See Seland, *Establishment Violence*, 134, note 88.

Third, darkness (see *Spec.* 1:320) is a feature associated with processes of initiation into the mysteries, especially at Eleusis. As the initiates were led into and through the *anaktoron*, they passed some areas of darkness and were then shown things not to be revealed or described to those uninitiated outsiders.[48] Philo criticizes this use of darkness above, as well as in 1:56c ("... they ... have chosen darkness in preference to the brightest light and blindfolded the mind which had the power of keen vision.") and praised those turning to Judaism, going out of darkness, and entering into the light (*Virt.* 179, 221; *Abr.* 70). Darkness is a description much used by Philo concerning the conditions of the pagans and of paganism as such and is thus a typical Philonic description of pagan cultic activities.[49]

At the same time, however, one should not overlook the possibility that Philo is here rather comparing the propaganda methods and secret initiations of the mystery-representatives with Jewish 'missionary' agents, thus emphasizing the usefulness of the message of the Jewish preachers for all and everyone and accentuating that it is preached in the open. Borgen[50] sees here an example of proselyte recruitment efforts being carried out in the agora, as Philo says:

> But let those whose actions serve the common weal use freedom of speech (παρρησία) and walk in the daylight through the midst of the marketplace, ready to converse with crowded gatherings (διὰ μέσης ἴτωσαν ἀγορᾶς ἐντευξόμενοι πολυανθρώποις ὁμίλοις).... Were it not well, then, that we should follow her intentions and display in public all that is profitable and necessary for the benefit of those who are worthy to use it? (*Spec.* 1:321, 323).

Whatever one might think of the extent of Jewish 'missionary activities' in the first century CE—an issue still debated—the 'we' in this text here most probably indicates Jewish propaganda agents and their openness in the agora concerning their doctrines and religion. Philo seems here to describe the activities of the mystery agents in contrast to the

---

48. Mylonas, *Eleusis and the Eleusinian Mysteries*, 261.

49. Here belongs also the descriptions saying that the converts are leaving the darkness "to behold a most radiant light" (*Virt.* 179). See Seland, *Establishment Violence*, 116-17; Seland, *Strangers in the Light*, 65-67; and Wilson, trans., *On Virtues*, 368-69.

50. See Borgen, *Philo of Alexandria, an Exegete*, 223; and Borgen, "Proselytes," 65-66. See also McKnight, *Light Among the Gentiles*, 55; and Bird, *Crossing over Sea and Land*, 103-9.

open and public preaching by Jews concerning the benefits of their Judaism (see 1:321).

Borgen has argued that "the sources demonstrate that some gentiles became proselytes because of attraction. In other cases, Jews actively presented their religion in gentile circles and even at times used military force to bring people into the Jewish religion."[51] Leaving the first and the third options out of view here, several observations support the view that Jews could actively present their religion in Gentile circles. Scholars have here pointed to the fact that Philo presents both Abraham (*Virt.* 211-219) and Moses (*Virt.* 177) as actively reaching out to the Gentiles, and other non-Jewish sources seem to state that in 139 BCE, the Jews were banished from Rome "because they attempted to transmit their sacred rites to the Romans."[52] According to Dickson, "The fact that Philo is so adamant Judaism must be proclaimed in the market-place ought to be taken as evidence of his own missionary activity or at least of a missionary ideal which found some historical expression in Alexandria and of which he thoroughly approved. Otherwise, the discussion would fail entirely to have any effect amongst his Jewish readers in Alexandria, for the dissonance between his words and reality would be plain to all."[53]

Thus, the passage of *Spec.*1 demonstrates Philo's disdain for—and opposition to—the Greek mystery cults. However, it is not possible to ascertain whether it indicates a comprehensive understanding of these cults based on personal experiences. Nonetheless, given the prevalence of mystery cults in nearly every town and certainly in a metropolis such as Alexandria, Philo would have had the opportunity to observe their various activities. In this passage, he characterizes their activities as indicative of the nature of their acquisitions. They engage in agitation in the streets, but upon gaining followers, they lead them into a darkness that is both spiritually and physically a withdrawal into obscurity, while the Jews discuss their wisdom openly in the agora, thereby illustrating that their wisdom is accessible and available to all.

---

51. Borgen, "Proselytes," 58. So also McKnight, *Light Among the Gentiles*, 55; and Dickson, *Mission-Commitment*, 38.

52. Borgen, "Proselytes," 66.

53. Dickson, *Mission-Commitment*, 38. It would also be in line with Philo's statement in *Mos.* 2:44 concerning the hope that one day each nation will abandon its peculiar ways and turn to (his) Judaism. See Dickson, *Mission-Commitment*, 18 and 75-77. See also Philo's positive characterizations of Joseph and his apologetic activities during his imprisonment in Egypt: *Ios.* 85-87.

Accordingly, as a summary so far, one might say that the passage indicates neither that Philo had been initiated into some mystery cults nor that he considered his Judaism as a kind of mystery, but that he had observed some activities of the non-Jewish 'mystagoges' in the streets, and contrasted them with the Jewish 'missionizing' agents both with regard to behavior and the results of the different 'initiations.' In addition, one should not say that Philo's descriptions here (and elsewhere in his works) are solely derived from literary traditions of education ("nur aus literarisch-rhetorischer Bildungstradition stammen"), as Riedweg surmises,[54] but that Philo could draw upon some local information and possible personal impressions from adherents of the cults and 'missionary' activities concerned.

PHILO'S USE OF "MYSTERIES" AS POSTCOLONIAL CULTURAL CRITICISM

One may contend that due to my limited examination of the role of mystery terminology in elucidating Philo's theological and philosophical perspectives, any comparative analysis and discussion like the one above of Philo's utilization of mystery terms is potentially problematic. Nevertheless, the primary challenge lies not with Philo but with the mysteries themselves, as there is a paucity of information regarding the teachings and revelations imparted to those initiated into the Greek mysteries, such as those at Eleusis. This study has focused on Philo's employment of certain key mystery terms to investigate their application in relation to the institutional aspects of Greek mysteries. However, the investigation of these mysteries is hindered by the silence imposed upon the initiates.

What, then, motivated Philo to employ mystery terminology in his expositions? It is evident that mystery terminology was prevalent in the temporal and environmental context of Philo's milieu. Comparisons of Philo with, e.g., Plato, are not to be neglected. There may have been many influences from Plato also in this regard. But still, why did Philo use mystery terms? The following views might be mentioned here.

The perspective of Erwin R. Goodenough is likely less tenable in contemporary scholarship than it was some decades ago. Current scholarly consensus suggests that Philo did not employ mystery terminology in his expositions due to Alexandrian Judaism, or even Diaspora Judaism

---

54. Riedweg, *Mysterienterminologie*, 103.

more broadly, adopting the form of a mystery cult. Goodenough's interpretations in this regard are now generally considered obsolete.

Henry Austin Wolfson has posited that Philo employed mystery terminology for two reasons. First, because the true knowledge of God and His Law is concealed within the Scriptures. "Second, they are called mysteries as a challenge to the heathen mysteries." This latter function exists because, according to Philo, communion with God, salvation, and a superior way of life are not attained through the esoteric rites of the mysteries but "by obedience to the teachings and practices of the Law of Moses" as the authentic mysteries.[55] Consequently, Philo presents a superior approach as a challenge to non-Jewish individuals. Moreover, regardless of the validity of Wolfson's perspective, it portrays Philo as a teacher and preacher. However, his role extended beyond these capacities.

A few decades later, Peder Borgen suggested that Philo was "a conqueror, on the verge of being conquered." Borgen explained this view by saying that Philo was not interested in a synthesis between Judaism and Hellenism, nor in transforming Judaism based on Hellenistic religion. Philo's intention was "to conquer the surrounding culture ideologically by claiming that whatever good there is has its source in Scripture and thus belonged to the Jewish nation and its heritage."[56] Borgen also considered Philo as thus representing those progressive Jews who infiltrated the gymnasium as reflected in the letter of Emperor Claudius to the Alexandrians.[57] Furthermore, he added the following observations in support of his view:[58] Philo thought that ideas found in Hellenistic philosophy of a Platonic, Pythagorean, or Stoic nature were already present in the writings of Moses; this is seen in several statements by Philo.[59] Borgen also finds his view supported by Philo's distinction between Jews as the chosen people and other men. Borgen's view has received a favorable reaction from some,[60] but is still open to some refinement.

Then, T. J. Lang, in an article on "Mystery Cults and Christian Associations in Early Alexandrian Theology," introduced and applied two other key terms in trying to catch the relations between Christian and

55. Both quotes are from Wolfson, *Philo* 1:49.
56. Borgen, "Philo of Alexandria," 151.
57. Concerning this letter, see Bell, ed., *Jews and Christians in Egypt*, 1–37.
58. Borgen, "Philo of Alexandria," 151–53.
59. Borgen mentions *Heres* 214; *Leg.* 1:108; *Spec.* 4:61; *Post.* 133; *QG* 4:152; *Congr.* 176.
60. See Runia, "Philo, Alexandrian and Jew," 16: "can hardly be bettered."

non-Christian associations as set forth by Clement of Alexandria in his works, especially in his *Protreptikos*.[61] Clement is found to depict Christian practices such as baptism, catechesis, and exegesis as forms of initiation into hidden mysteries. Lang characterizes Clement's procedures in *Protreptikos* thus: "As a sociological strategy, his is one of synchronized social *rupture* and cultural *recapture*." Furthermore, Lang explains the *rupture* as "a distancing of the Christian associations and non-Christian forms of communal life." He goes on: "The *recapture* is Clement's unyielding insistence on the intellectual and religious priority of the Christian way of life."[62] In this pursuit, Lang finds Philo to be a precursor to Clement.[63] To Philo, mystery associations "are depraved institutions forbidden by Torah. This is the social rupture in Philo's insistence on Jewish exclusivity." Moreover, Philo's depictions of Jewish institutions and practices by appropriating terminology and images from mystery associations are part of his recapturing.[64]

I find most of these various efforts of characterizing Philo's procedures of verbalizing how he tried to cope with his Greek social world in relation to his Judaism interesting and valuable. However, as most of the labels or characterizations applied by Wolfson, Borgen, and Lang (Judaism as a challenge, conquering on the verge of being conquered, rupturing-recapturing) are somewhat idiosyncratic, I would prefer to look for what the more structured studies of postcolonialism might provide as more solid ground for categorization and understanding. Accordingly, I suggest that mimicry and hybridity are the categories that capture most of the three above-mentioned scholars' efforts to describe what was going on in Philo's application of some mystery terms in his works.

In postcolonial studies, the use and understanding of these two terms are, inter alia, influenced by Homi K. Bhabha's view and use of them. According to Bhabha,[65] "colonial mimicry is the desire for a reformed, recognizable Other, as a subject of difference that is almost the same, but not quite. Which is to say, that the discourse of mimicry is constructed around an ambivalence." Mimicry emerges as the representation of a difference that is itself a process of disavowal. This process might evolve as a strategy on the side of the colonized to survive or

---

61. Lang, "Mystery Cults and Christian Associations."
62. Lang, "Mystery Cults and Christian Associations," 418.
63. Lang, "Mystery Cults and Christian Associations," 419–21.
64. Lang, "Mystery Cults and Christian Associations," 420.
65. Bhabha, *Location of Culture*, 122.

even to conquer the culture of the colonizer by enlarging on common aspects. But it is often emphasized that "by adopting the colonizer's cultural habits, assumptions, institutions and values, the result is never a simple reproduction of those traits. Rather the result is a 'blurred copy' of the colonizer that can be quite threatening."[66] Here the phenomenon of 'hybridity' enters. Hybridity denotes new transcultural forms that may develop in the meeting of the colonizer and colonized, especially as the latter mimics the former. It may take many forms, including linguistic, cultural, political, racial, and so on.[67]

Hence, my reasons for considering the practice of Philo in terms of these two postcolonial categories are that they concern Philo's copying of the many terms related to the Greco-Roman mystery cults, and that his use of these terms results in a labeling of some different social actions and institutions that should be characterized as hybridized versions of the originals. One might still endorse Wolfson's suggestion of characterizing Philo's use as a "challenge," Borgen's proposal of a "conqueror on the verge of being conquered," and Lang's suggestion of a "rupture" and a "recapture" to provide helpful suggestions. However, my preference for the terms "mimicry" and "hybridity" is due to my view of the social situation of Philo in Alexandria ("a city not their own"[68]), his view of the Jewish people, and his role as a politician negotiating with the emperor in Rome the Alexandrian situation of being colonized. But to provide a fuller discussion of these issues belongs in another setting.[69]

SUMMARY

Philo may be described as a teacher, theologian, and philosopher, but he was also a politician, deeply embedded in his social Diaspora world. Hence, many venues are available to investigate his life and work.

Peder Borgen coined a description of Philo in relation to his social world thus: "A conqueror, on the verge of being conquered." In this chapter, I describe Philo and his relationship with the world of mystery

---

66. Ashcroft et al., *Post-Colonial Studies*, 125.

67. Ashcroft et al., *Post-Colonial Studies*, 108.

68. This phrase is taken from Claudius's Letter to the Alexandrines, line 95. See Smallwood, *Jews Under Roman Rule*, 247-50.

69. Note here again my study of Philo and postcolonialism: Seland, "'Colony' and 'Metropolis,'" and the somewhat older study—Seland, "Philo and the Clubs"—both included in this volume, somewhat abbreviated.

terminology in Alexandria. Many studies take their point of departure from Philo's relation to Plato and his use of mystery terms. Admittedly, there are many similarities, and the influence of Plato cannot be denied. However, Philo lived in a city with several mystery cults and various clubs and associations. Hence, he could observe members of these institutions in his own city.

In his allegorical writings, he used several mystery terms in his interpretations and various descriptions of educational and scholarly activities. This terminology is much less frequent in his later and less allegorical works, especially in those considered to belong to his Exposition. His expository work *De Specialibus Legibus*, however, contains a harsh condemnation of the activities of some local mysteries (*Spec.* 1:319–323). Furthermore, we have seen above that there are several terms from the social and semantic fields of mystery cults that Philo does not use. The lack of some institutional terms in Philo's works is especially noteworthy.

However, several terms related to the process of initiation are used by Philo, cf. ἱεροφάντης/ἱεροφαντέω, μύστης/μυστήριον/μυσταγωγός/ (-γέω), ὄργια/ὀργιάζω, and τελέω/τελετή, which are the significant mystery terms in his works. This is comparable to the use of mystery terms in Plato, but also to their later use in works of some Christian writers, such as Clement of Alexandria.

As a politician Philo was wont to negotiate several Greek and Roman cultural issues and aspects. Furthermore, considering that Philo was a Jew living in the Diaspora and considering Jerusalem his mother city (*Flacc.* 46; *Legat.* 281), I suggest that the phenomena of mimicry and hybridity is illuminating when trying to understand some of Philo's reactions and attitudes toward some of the non-Jewish cultural expressions and institutions in Alexandria. Here also belong several of his statements applying the terminology of the mysteries.

7

Reimagining Philo on the Clubs and Associations in Alexandria
A Case of Cultural Criticism Seen from a Postcolonial Perspective

> "In the city there are clubs (θίασοι) with a large membership, whose fellowship is founded on no sound principle but on strong liquor and drunkenness and sottish carousing and their offspring, wantonness. 'Synods' (σύνοδοι) and 'divans' (κλῖναι) are the particular names given to them by the people of the country."
>
> (*FLACC.* 136)

INTRODUCTION

IN THE PRESENT CHAPTER, I continue my focus on cultural mimicry and the resulting hybridity. In writing about the Greco-Roman clubs and associations of Alexandria, Philo dealt with some very central aspects of the colonizing Roman Empire, as such clubs and associations had been around for a long time. My main points here are as follows: first, cultural criticism can take many forms; second, as the Romans had accepted the prevalent clubs and associations and thus accepted the phenomena as such, any criticism from the side of Philo, a Jew, was by definition a criticism of Greco-Roman culture.

However, according to my view, Philo did not tell his fellows to keep away from all such organizational structures, but he was critical of associational gatherings, as he also saw that they might represent dangerous milieus for those who wanted to maintain their Jewish monotheistic identity. He voiced his criticism by discussing the aspect of paying contributions as club members and by comparing the Greco-Roman clubs and associations with Jewish gatherings, thus lifting up the superiority of their own comparable institutions and gatherings. In these comparisons there are issues of both mimicry and hybridity.

The quotation above from one of the works of Philo of Alexandria (*Flaccum* 136) is one of several that mention the Greco-Roman clubs and associations in Alexandria. However, most of his comments have been noted only in passing by modern scholars.[1]

This is an astonishing circumstance, and that by reason of two facts: first, Greco-Roman clubs and associations were to be found in almost every town of the Roman Empire in the first century CE, Alexandria being no exception.[2] Second, there are several passages in Philo's works that deal with clubs and associations.

Thus, the purpose of this chapter is to deal with passages in the works of Philo related to the phenomenon of Greco-Roman clubs and associations, and to try to get a picture of how he conceived of these institutions and how he evaluated them *in comparison to* Jewish gatherings. I do this by continuing to use the postcolonial lenses of *mimicry and hybridity*. It is argued here that Philo had good knowledge of various clubs and associations in Alexandria. However, he used this knowledge in a specific manner. He does not strictly and totally forbid participation but

---

1. In 1996 I had an article published in which I discussed Philo's relations to the Greco-Roman clubs and associations: the present study is an abbreviated but also somewhat revised version of that study. See Seland, "Philo and the Clubs." The major changes in the present article compared to the 1996 version are that some minor sections have been left out (i.e., sections from pp. 111 and 113, most of p. 118, the last half of p. 120, the upper half of p. 121, and some of pp. 123–24. Then the two main sections, "Philo's Comparison" and "The Payment," are now given as the second and first parts respectively of this chapter. In addition, the introduction, and the summary have been rewritten).

2. See, for example, the older works of San Nicolò, *Ägyptisches Vereinswesen*), and Muszynski, "Les 'Associations Religieuses' en Égypte." See also Arnaoutoglou, "Collegia in the Province of Egypt"; and the lists of documentary evidence for associations in Egypt on pp. 213–216. Further: Brashear, *Vereine im griechisch-römischen Ägypten*.

is critical of the associations and skeptical of joining them. Although they may be frequented if the purpose is to acquire virtue, to Philo, nevertheless, they represented dangerous settings that might very easily lead to idolatry and apostasy.

Philo's arguments may therefore be said to have specific social functions: they are set forth to warn his fellow Jews, to keep them together, to discourage them from mingling with the 'many', and thereby to function as inducements to preserve their identity as Jews. All this is, in light of my postcolonial perspectives, to be considered vital in strengthening Jewish identity.

Philo's remarks on these societies in his own hometown of Alexandria can be studied and presented in several ways, but we shall here concentrate on two related sets of questions. First, what does Philo tell us about these clubs and associations compared to what we know from other sources? What does he tell us about their existence, structure, and activities? Second, how does he perceive various aspects of these clubs and associations? What are his evaluations of them? While this distinction may be difficult to substantiate consistently, it may function as a heuristic device in studying his works.

I present the relevant material found in Philo subsumed under four headings: (1) some aspects of recent research; (2) central aspects of the associations; (3) the payment of contributions; and (4) Philo's comparison of the Jewish gatherings and feasts with those of the associations. In order to set this study in the perspective of other research on the Graeco-Roman associations, however, I first outline some trends in earlier and more recent research.

SOME ASPECTS OF RECENT RESEARCH

Research on Greco-Roman clubs and associations flourished at the end of the nineteenth and in the first decades of the twentieth century. One of the main reasons for such great interest in the associations at that time was the many epigraphic findings that brought 'Light from the Ancient East' as Adolf Deissmann called one of his famous books (1908, ET 1927). Some of the important studies from this period are still impressive and indispensable reference works.[3] Most studies on the associations

---

3. See esp. Liebenam, *Zur Geschichte und Organisation*; Waltzing, *Etude historique sur les corporations*; Ziebarth, *Das griechische Vereinswesen*; Poland, *Geschichte des*

up to the end of the twentieth century relied on these older works and confirmed the basic picture we get in these studies.[4] The time for all-embracing works, however, like those of Waltzing and Poland, seems to have passed. More recent scholars have concentrated on various aspects or types of associations. Mention could here also be made of the older studies that tried to relate features of emerging Christian groups to those of the associations,[5] and some more recent, relating features of the associations to the Qumran community.[6]

When sociological and sociohistorical studies of the early churches gained popularity in the 1960s and '70s, comparisons with the associations were slowly renewed.[7] The importance of the clubs and associations for understanding comparable group gatherings in antiquity and the social life and structures of both Jewish Diaspora life and early Christian groups was revived.[8] However, it was not until the 1980s and the '90s that this interest led to greater research on both ancient clubs and associations and clubs, *and* their possible relevance for understanding the early churches. Pivotal in this research was a group established in Canada around Professor John S. Kloppenborg, working on both aspects mentioned above. An important result of their work was published in 1996, dealing with—and thus named—*Voluntary Associations in the Greco-Roman World*.[9] Further publications from several members of this group demonstrate the relevance of this research and its value for studies of both Jewish and

---

griechischen Vereinswesens; San Nicolò, *Ägyptisches Vereinswesen*, vol. 1; and Kornemann, "Collegium."

4. Here I am thinking of studies like Herrmann, "Genossenschaft"; Waszink, "Genossenschaft"; de Robertis, *Il Fenomeno Associativo Nel Mondo Romano*; Forbes, *Neoi*; and Burford, *Craftsmen*; Graeber, *Untersuchungen zum spätrömischen Korporationswesen*; Fisher, "Greek Associations"; and Fisher, "Roman Associations").

5. For example, Heinrici, "Die Christengemeinde"; Roberts, et al., "Guild of Zeus Hypsistos"; and Reicke, *Diakonie, Festfreude und Zelos*.

6. For example Bardtke, "Der Gegenwärtige Stand"; and Dombrowski, "HYHD in 1QS and to koinon."

7. See esp. Judge, *Social Pattern*; Judge, "Social Identity of the First Christians"; gives some of his reactions to the more sociologically oriented studies published in the period 1960–1980. See also Wilken, "Collegia"; Wilken, *Christians as the Romans Saw Them*, 15–25, 31–47; Malherbe, *Social Aspects of Early Christianity*, 60–91.

8. See Barton and Horsley, "Hellenistic Cult Group"; Klauck, *Herrenmahl und hellenistischer Kult*; Meeks, *First Urban Christians*. See also Seland, "Collegium kai Ekklesia."

9. Kloppenborg and Wilson, eds., *Voluntary Associations*. The volume contains fourteen studies by thirteen scholars.

Christian groups of the first century CE.¹⁰ By now we have an abundance of works dealing with the Greco-Roman clubs and associations and their relevance for life and social interactions of this period.¹¹ A comprehensive history-of-research presentation of this research in the last two centuries is still to be written; what we have is a few minor ones dealing with the most recent decades of research.¹² A main obstacle to more general access to this field has been the diversity of relevant source material, and especial the problem of accessing the epigraphic sources, located in so many and diverse places. This access is now about to be greatly improved by the publication of several sourcebooks that provide texts, translations, and commentaries on the relevant sources.¹³

At the beginning of the first century CE, Jews lived almost all over the Greco-Roman world, and they could not have overlooked the many clubs and associations that were also found in nearly every city of that world. It seems quite natural, therefore, to ask how these Jews related to such societies.

---

10. As an important study of the clubs and associations as such, I would point to Philip A. Harland's work: Harland, *Associations, Synagogues, and Congregations*. This has now been revised and published on the internet as Harland, *Associations, Synagogues, and Congregations*. This work also dealt with, as the title demonstrates, Jewish and Christian parallel phenomena. Another important publication of Harland's dealing with the same fields, is his collection of articles, published in 2009: Harland, *Dynamics of Identity in the World of the Early Christians*. Of works dealing even more directly with the New Testament, several works of Richard S. Ascough could be mentioned. See esp. Ascough, *Paul's Macedonian Associations*. See also his two more recent collections of articles: Ascough, *Christ Groups & Associations*; and Ascough, *Early Christ Groups and Greco-Roman Associations*.

11. See e.g., Egelhaaf-Gaiser and Schäfer, eds., *Religiöse Vereine in der römischen Antike*; and Gutsfeld and Koch, eds., *Vereine, Synagogen und Gemeinden*.

12. See Ascough, *What Are They Saying*, 71-94; Bendlin, "Gemeinschaft, Öffentlichkeit und Identität"; Schmeller, "Zum Exegetischen Interesse." As part of such a research history, one should also mention Perry, *Roman Collegia*.

13. Three volumes have their origins in a Greek seminar at the University of Toronto: Kloppenborg and Ascough, eds., *Greco-Roman Associations*, vol. 1, *Attica, Central Greece, Macedonia, Thrace*; vol. 2, *North Coast of the Black Sea, Asia Minor*; vol. 3, *Ptolemaic and Early Roman Egypt*. See also the following sourcebook, containing texts from Greco-Roman writers, descriptions of association buildings, and an annotated bibliography of secondary sources, including a number of translations of inscriptions and papyri: Ascough et al., eds., *Associations in the Greco-Roman World*. One should perhaps also mention the useful website made available by Philip A. Harland: Associations in the Greco-Roman World: A Companion to the Sourcebook (http://philipharland.com/greco-roman-associations).

Central Aspects of the Associations

Sociologically speaking, clubs and associations may be characterized as corporate groups, that is, as groups with fixed rules for admission and exclusion and with a fixed purpose for their existence.[14] A set of rules was sometimes inscribed on steles erected in their localities. Furthermore, with regard to financial matters, sometimes extending to leadership, associations were deeply involved in the patron-client structures typical of this world.[15] Rich men or women could serve as benefactors and patrons for several clubs. They again could draw upon the loyalty of the members if needed. The membership was diversified: on the one hand, club members could be drawn primarily from specific occupations—for example, weavers, bakers, and artists; on the other hand, they could consist of people from various age groups. An association could also consist of people from various segments of society, occupations, sexes, and various levels of influence and status. Women, freedmen, and slaves are found in several, though not all. Hence, membership could be characterized as based on fictive kinship: the members were fictive brothers and sisters.

The internal organization of the clubs and associations, especially in Greek cities, had the polis (i.e., the city) as its structural model; they had structured leadership and laws regulating activities, duties, and responsibilities. In this way, people who had little influence in their polis could find a setting where they were acknowledged. Club membership provided a feeling of belonging. Hence, whether the purposes of the clubs were convivial, political, or economic—most often these features were intertwined—the clubs also had socializing functions. They represented a part of the general *paideia*. This aspect is most evident in the clubs of young people that were associated with their educational and gymnasial settings,[16] but is probably to be considered inherent in others too.[17]

Scholars have also attempted to group and characterize the associations according to various types. This may be an artificial way of looking at the associations;[18] and no general consensus has evolved with regard to

14. See Boissevain, *Friends of Friends*.

15. See Eisenstadt and Roniger, *Patrons, Clients and Friends*; and Moxnes, "Patron-Client Relations and the New Community."

16. See Forbes, *Neoi*.

17. Schmitt-Pandel, "Collective Activities," esp. 206.

18. See Tod, *Ancient Inscriptions* (reprint 1974): "A satisfactory classification is well-night impossible." See, however, Kloppenborg, "Collegia and Thiasoi"; and Harland, *Associations, Synagogues, and Congregations*, 23-24.

the kinds or number of types.[19] Efforts have also been made to associate some of the most current terms with specific types of associations: most common is the opinion that θίασος signifies 'cultic association'; and ἑταιρία is viewed as a term typical of the convivial clubs and associations, especially the more politically active associations.[20] But as most of the clubs and associations known to us had both "cultic" and "convivial" aspects, such classification efforts are now less fruitful. At least it is not possible to see any consistent groupings in the ways Philo uses these terms. Furthermore, the danger of anachronistic characterizations is near at hand: for example, when dealing with the aspect of religion in ancient societies, one should consider the fact that religion was not something that can be isolated from general social life. "The Greek city knows no separation between sacred and profane. Religion is present in all the different levels of social life, and all collective practices have a religious dimension."[21] Participation in symposia and associations was a central part of collective life, but there were also other group formations.

Philip A. Harland has suggested another taxonomy for describing the various associations. He finds that there are several problems with purpose-centered typologies, and draws upon Kloppenborg, who has proposed that it is more helpful to categorize associations based on the profile of their membership; that is, on membership based on household connections, a shared occupation, and a common cult.[22] Furthermore, he expands on this, saying,[23]

---

19. The following classifications can be found in the older standard works: Handels- und Kaufmannsgilden, Verschiedene Vereine unter Industriellen Krämern und Handwerker, Vereine unter Gladiatoren und Schauspieler (Liebenam 1890); Kultvereine, Wissenschaftliche Vereine, Künstler vereine, Politische vereine, Berufsverbände, Vereine fur Leibesübung, Gesellige Vereine verschiedener Art (Ziebarth 1896); Kultvereine, Vereine unter Altersgenossen, Agonistische Vereine, Berufsvereine, Private und sonstige Vereine (San Nicolò 1913–15); le associzioni religiose, le associazioni conviviale, le associazioni politiche, le associazioni funerarie, le associazioni professionale (De Robertis 1955).

20. Poland, *Geschichte des griechischen Vereinswesens*, 16–28; San Nicolò, *Ägyptisches Vereinswesen*, 11–29; Ziebarth, *Das griechische Vereinswesen*, 92–95; see also Liebenam, *Zur Geschichte und Organisation*, 19–20, 165–66.

21. Schmitt-Pandel, "Collective Activities," 200. The model worked out by Bruce J. Malina may still be illuminating here in understanding the role of religion. See Malina, "Religion in the World of Paul."

22. Harland, *Associations, Synagogues, and Congregations*, 23.

23. Harland, *Associations, Synagogues, and Congregations*, 24.

Turning to social networks and structures in the societies of Roman Asia Minor, it is possible to distinguish five important sources of members for associations, and in some cases, certain groups drew members primarily from one particular type of social network. There were groups which drew membership primarily from 1) household or family connections, 2) ethnic or geographic connections, 3) neighborhood connections, 4) occupational connections, and 5) temple or ritual connections.

However, he emphasizes that such sets of social linkages were often interrelated with issues concerning the self-understandings or identities of particular associations.

CENTRAL ASPECTS OF THE ASSOCIATIONS AS DESCRIBED BY PHILO

The various terms used for clubs and associations in the Greek and Latin sources have been intensively studied by several scholars.[24] Philo uses three of the better-known terms from the Greek sources: σύνοδος, ἑταιρία and θίασος. And he adds a fourth, the somewhat rare term κλίνη. All of these terms can be found in several of Philo's texts, but in relatively few cases do the contexts unambiguously relate to the type of club or association.[25] Most regularly σύνοδος refers only to 'assembly,' 'gathering,' or 'union.'[26] The term ἑταιρία is frequently used in its more general sense of 'friendly connection,' 'friendship,' and 'comradeship.'[27] In *Flacc.* 136, θίασος is used in a way that suggests that Philo himself considered

---

24. See Liebenam, *Zur Geschichte und Organisation*, 63–158; Kornemann, "Collegium," cols. 380–81; Ziebarth, *Das griechische Vereinswesen*, 133–90, esp. 133–40; Poland, *Geschichte des griechischen Vereinswesens*, 8–172.

25. See esp. *Flacc.* 4; 136-137; *Contmpl.* 40–67; *Legat.* 312, 316; *Spec.* 2.193; 3.96.

26. See for example *Opif.* 161; *Cher.* 29, 50, 124; *Ebr.* 24; *Congr.* 12, 62; *Agr.* 145; *Abr.* 137; *Ios.* 43 (in the Loeb Classical Library edition, these are translated as "assembly"); *Spec.* 1:178; 3:170, 172, 187; 4:239; *Contempl.* 124; *Migr.* 26, 30, 63; *Fug.* 140; *Mut.* 38 (translated "gathering"); *Agr.* 49; *Deus.* 56; *Conf.* 40, 188; *Spec.* 2:40, 140; et al. (translated "union"). Consult Liddell et al., *Greek-English Lexicon*, 1720, which gives the following possibilities: 1. assembly, meeting; 2. national gathering; 3. company, guild; 4. in hostile terms, meeting of two armies; 5.=*synousia*, sexual intercourse; II. 1. of things, coming together, constriction; 2. astron., conjunction. Most of these are relevant for Philo's texts.

27. See *Agr.* 104; *Conf.* 97; *Migr.* 158; *Abr.* 126; *Decal.* 89; *Spec.* 2:95; *Contempl.* 18; In *Spec.* 3:96 and *Flacc.* 4, however, the contexts demonstrate that clubs/associations are denoted.

this word to be the most common, typical designation for 'association.' But even this term most frequently seems to demand the more general meaning of 'company,' 'gathering,' or 'group' without any connotations of 'association.'[28] In this way, all these terms turn out to be polysemous. 'Association' or 'club' is only one possible meaning, and in Philo it is not even one of the most frequent.

In *Flacc.* 136, however, Philo characterizes the terms σύνοδος and κλίνη as terms being "given to them by the people of the country." The word σύνοδος is well known from other sources. This might suggest that the other term, κλίνη, which is a rarely used for "club" or "association" in the other Greek sources,[29] in fact was also a much-used term in Egypt. Poland calls it "die Agyptische κλίνη," a "Spezialname," and "merkwürdigste Erscheinung."[30] However, this term is not often used by Philo. With the sole exception of *Flacc.* 136, he always uses it in a more general way, signifying 'that on which one lies,' 'couch.'[31] But Philo also uses the compound word κλινάρχης to name the function of Isidorus at the banquets (*Flacc.* 137). This might strengthen the interpretation that κλίνη really was a common term for association in Egypt.[32]

Several details about activities in various clubs and associations known to us from other sources can also be found in Philo's works.[33] In *Flaccum* 136, cited at the beginning of this study, Philo uses two well-known terms for associations (θίασος and σύνοδος). He also stated that they had many members. In the same passage, he also mentions one of their leaders (the leader?): Isidorus. Philo here shows that he was familiar with the fact that leaders or patrons could be at the head of more than one association. In *Flacc.* 136–138, further, we have one of the most vivid accounts from the first century CE of the kind of dependency members could be bound up with in the relation to their patron. According to *Flacc.* 137–138, "when he [Isidorus] wished to get some worthless project carried out, a single call brought them together in a body, and they

---

28. For example, *Post.* 101; *Plant.* 14, 58; *Ebr.* 70, 94; *Fug.* 32, 198, 205; *Somn.* 1:196; 2:10. 127. 139. 277; *Vita Mosis* 2:185, et al.

29. Poland, *Geschichte des griechischen Vereinswesens*, 358.

30. Poland, *Geschichte des griechischen Vereinswesens*, 152. He refers further to Ziebarth 1896, who refers to Philo's *Flacc.* 136. See Poland, *Geschichte des griechischen Vereinswesens*, 358.

31. See *Spec.* 2:20; *Somn.* 1:123, 125; 2:57.

32. See Westermann, "Entertainment," 24–25.

33. On the organization of the clubs in Greco-Roman Egypt, see Boak, "Organization of the Gilds."

said and did what they were bidden." Further on in the same treatise, Philo states that Isidorus once bade some of them to launch accusations and slanders against Flaccus. When some of them were arrested, it was revealed that they had been promised both money and wine as payment (*Flacc.* 140, 142).

Despite the evident coloring of the story by Philo, there is no compelling reason to doubt such a relationship between a patron and his association(s), for we have other evidence witnessing similar kinds of relationships. In the ruins of Pompeii there have been found placards telling whom various associations were supporting in the elections,[34] and it is well known that patrons not infrequently supported their associations with wine, food, or money.[35] That poor people could also be members of associations is substantiated by other sources.[36] The story of Philo is thus an admirable presentation of the patron-client relationship so well-known from the time of the Roman Empire, and of its practice of "do ut des."[37]

But Philo also knew that association members themselves had to pay dues, whether as entrance fees or as monthly contributions: ἐράνους or συμβολάς ... φέρειν are his expressions for these (*Ebr.* 14–15. 20–21. 35). In *Ebrietate* 20–26 he discusses the paying of contributions; and since this obviously is an important issue to him, we shall soon return to it. Philo was also familiar with the practice that payment of contributions might be necessary to make gatherings and feasts financially feasible (*Contempl.* 46).

Such feasts and gatherings were typical traits of the Greco-Roman clubs and associations, according to other sources.[38] In *Flacc.* 4 Philo mentions their sacrifices and conviviality. But it is in his descriptions of these aspects that he is most expressive and negative. He emphasizes eating and drinking (*Spec.* 2:193; *Legat.* 312), and he mentions intrigues and even poisoning as occurring in these associations (*Spec.* 3:96 see also *Contempl.* 40–41, perhaps also *Cher.* 91–92 and *Plant.* 100).[39] Philo's

---

34. Liebenam, *Zur Geschichte und Organisation*, 135.

35. See Roberts et al., "Guild of Zeus Hypsistos," where such a practice is codified in the laws of an association. See also Danker, *Benefactor*, 152–53.

36. Kornemann, "Collegium," 402, 410 and 414; Liebenam, *Zur Geschichte und Organisation*, 41, 260, and 264; and Wilken, *Christians as the Romans Saw Them*, 35–40.

37. Reicke, *Diakonie, Festfreude und Zelos*, 327; see Eisenstadt and Roniger, *Patrons, Clients, and Friends*, 43–63.

38. MacMullen, *Roman Social Relations*, 77; Poland, *Geschichte des griechischen Vereinswesens*, 502.

39. Note here the prohibition of sorcery given in the law of the association of

emphasis is especially notable when we study his comparisons of Jewish gatherings and feasts with those of the Greco-Roman associations.

The Payment of Contributions: *De Ebrietate* 20–26

In most of his references to clubs and associations, Philo concentrates on wine drinking and drunkenness. Hence, one might naturally ask whether there is further discussion of the clubs in his treatises on drunkenness and sobriety. This proves to be the case.

Philo uses the figure of Noah from Gen 9:20–29 in four treatises to present his discussions of wine and drunkenness.[40] In *De Plantatione* 140–141 he states other philosophers' views on drunknness, and in *De Ebrietate* he purports to "consider what the great law-giver in his never failing wisdom holds on this subject" (*Ebr.* 1). It is here that we find a discussion of the payment of dues.

In this work, however, Philo soon breaks away from the text of Gen 9:20–29 and concentrates on Deut 21:18–21: the case of the disobedient son. In *Ebr.* 14–95, he then discusses the four accusations launched against the son by his parents. These Philo finds to be disobedience, contentiousness, payment of contributions, and drunkenness (*Ebr.* 15).[41]

The Text

Ebr. 20–23 come with more extensive treatment of the payment of contributions. The passage deserves to be cited in full, since it is crucial to Philo and his argument:

> (20) As for contributions or club subscriptions, when the subject is to share in the best of possessions, prudence, such payments are praiseworthy and profitable (συμβολάς γε μὴν καὶ ἐράνους φέρειν ἐπὶ μὴν τῇ τοῦ ἀρίστου κτήματος μετουσίᾳ, φρονήσεως, ἐπαινετὸν καὶ συμφέρον). But when they are paid to obtain that supreme evil, folly (ἀφροσύνης) the practice is unprofitable and blameworthy.
>
> (21) We contribute to the former object by desire for virtue, by zeal for things noble, by continous study therein, by persistent

---

Philadelphia in Lydia (Barton and Horsley, "Hellenistic Cult Group," 8–10).

40. See *Agr.*; *Plant.*; *Ebr.*, and *Sobr.*

41. For a fuller exposition of this text, see Seland, "Philo and the Clubs," 117–25.

self-training, by unwearied and unflagging labor. We contribute to the opposite by slackness, indolence, luxury, effiminacy, and by complete irregularity of life (παντελὴς ἐκδιαίτησις).

(22) We can see indeed people preparing themselves to compete in the arena of wine bibbing and every day exercising themselves and contending in the contests of gluttony. The contributions they make are supposed to be for a profitable purpose, but they are actually mulcting themselves in everything, in money, body and soul. Their substance they diminish by the actual payments, their bodily powers they shatter and enfeeble by the delicate living, and by excessive indulgence in food they deluge their souls as with a winter torrent and submerge them perforce in the depths.

(23) In just the same way those who pay their contributions only to destroy training and education are mulcting their most vital element, the understanding, and cut away therefrom its safeguards, prudence and self-control, and indeed courage and justice to boot. It was for this reason, I think, that Moses himself used a compound word, "contribution cutting" (συμβολοκοπῶν), to bring out more clearly the nature of the thing he was describing, because when men bring their efforts like contributions or club-money, so to speak, (ὥσπερ τινὰς συμβολὰς καὶ ἐράνους εἰσφέροντες) to bear against virtue, they wound and divide and cut in pieces docile and knowledge-loving souls, till they bring them to utter destruction.

After having presented the four ways of relating to one's parents, Philo then returns to the payers of contributions in this way:

(95) It is with good reason, then, that the disobedient and contentious man who "brings contributions," that is contributes and adds sins to sins, new to old, voluntary to involuntary, and as though inflamed by wine drowns the whole of life in ceaseless and unending drunkenness, sodden with drinking deep of the unmixed cup of folly, is judged by the holy word to be worthy of stoning. Yes, for he has made away with the commands of right reason (τὰς ὀρθοῦ λόγου προστάξεις), his father and the observances enjoined by instruction (ταῖς παιδείας ... νομίμους), his mother, and though he had before him the example of true nobility in his brothers whom the parents honoured, he did not imitate their virtue, but contrariwise determined to be the aggressor in wickedness. And thus he made a god of the body, a god of the vanity most honoured among the Egyptians, whose symbol is the image of the golden bull.

A Brief Exposition of the Text

The integral place of cultic activities in the associations and comparable gatherings has been pointed out by several scholars.[42] In most such gatherings, it would have been very difficult, if not impossible, to participate without simultaneously being a participant in the libations and other cultic ceremonies.

Yet *Ebr.* 20–26 seems to indicate that Philo nevertheless accepts payment of contributions when one is driven by the right intention, that is, when the purpose is to gain *prudence*. What does Philo mean by this statement? What is the meaning of prudence for Philo? Where or how does one attain prudence? The answers to these questions inhere in his conception of prudence as a principal virtue and in his view of education as a means of acquiring it.

Both in the works of Plato and among the Stoics there are statements to the effect that prudence or wisdom is the leader among the virtues, and similar statements can also be found in Philo.[43] But more often in Philo the εὐσέβεια is the queen: "it approaches the role of philosophy and wisdom and thus φρόνησις."[44] This is probably a consequence of his work with the Scriptures and of his view of theology as an integrated and central part of his own philosophy, the ordinary philosophy being regarded as a handmaid of Scripture.[45] Thus, if Philo agrees to the payment of contributions when the object is to gain prudence, we may ask: How and whereby does one gain such prudence?

Philo's answer to the first part of this question must be conceived in accordance with his philosophical heritage: the ἀρητή, virtue, is firmly associated with the παιδεία; education. The goal of παιδεία is to make one gain virtues.[46] This firm connection of paideia and virtue is obviously the main reason for Philo's complaint in *Ebr.* 23 against those who pay contributions: "they are mulcting their most vital element, the understanding, and cut away therefrom its safeguards, prudence, self-control, and indeed courage and justice to boot." This linkage is also the key to an understanding of *Ebr.* 21 where he delineates how one may contribute to 'prudence.' The attitudes here enumerated are used several times in

---

42. Poland, *Geschichte des griechischen Vereinswesens*, 173; Bell, *Cults and Creeds*.
43. Wolfson, *Philo*, 1:215; Consult *Leg.* 1:70–71.
44. Mott, "Greek Ethics and Christian Conversion," 25–26.
45. Wolfson, *Philo*, 1:214–15.
46. Mott, "Greek Ethics," 25.

contexts of virtue and education.⁴⁷ Thus, the acquisition of prudence, of virtue, is also associated with παιδεία in Philo's writings.

The second part of our question, also the part most difficult to answer, remains to be considered: whence comes such education that promotes acquisition of the virtues?

That Philo here speaks about Jewish educational settings is rather implausible, and that for the following reasons: First, Jewish synagogues are repeatedly described by Philo as educational settings in which prudence is sought and taught. The synagogues are not only characterized as schools, but as schools of prudence (*Vita Mosis* 2:216; see *Spec.* 2:62; *Praem* 60; *Legatio* 312). Hence, a suggestion that *Ebr.* 20 relates to Jewish synagogal education would compose a kind of tautology: whereas the synagogues are schools of prudence, one then says that contributions are praiseworthy if their intention is to gain prudence. Second, evidence for other Jewish associations outside, or even in connection with, the synagogues is both scarce and ambiguous.⁴⁸ Accordingly, it might be more natural to relate the sayings of *Ebr.* 20–26 to Philo's attitude respecting non- Jewish clubs and associations.

According to the evidence presented above, Philo tends to be critical of the activities of gatherings of symposia and associations. On the other hand, several scholars have pointed out that Philo shows an excellent knowledge of Greco-Roman culture and many of its institutions. He appears to be well informed about encyclical education (*Congr.* 74–76), having participated in banquets, frequented the theater, heard concerts and watched boxing competitions, wrestling matches, and horse-racing (*Ebr.* 177; *Prov.* 58; *Prob.* 26, 141; cf. *Migr.* 116).⁴⁹ Thus he might have held the opinion that these 'settings' were not to be avoided by any means,

---

47. Ad *pothos aretes*, see *Spec.* 2:230; *Congr.* 112. 166; *Prob.* 22; ad *kalon zelos*, see *Contempl.* 68; *Somn.* 2:235; *Praem.* 22; ad *meletai synecheis*, *Gig.* 26; *Agr.* 160; ad *askesis epomonoi*, *Leg.* 1:89; *Sacr.* 63.

48. Mendelson, *Secular Education*, 33, says that "since there is no evidence that synagogue schools were open on weekdays, we may conclude that if the Jews encountered secular studies in an institutional setting, it would have been in the Greek gymnasium."

The evidence for Jewish associations is scarce. It is not obvious that the traditions in t.Sukkah 4.6 and b. Sukkah 51b; y.Sukkah 5,1.55a about the seats in the great synagogue of Alexandria being arranged according to the professions point to the existence of Jewish associations or guilds. See Ziebarth, *Das griechische Vereinswesen*, 101. Meeks (*First Urban Christians*, 39) and Applebaum, ("Social and Economic Status," 703) interpret them as witnessing Jewish associations. See further Seland, "Collegium kai Ekklesia," 54–55.

49. See Borgen, "Philo of Alexandria," 252–56; Mendelson, *Secular Education*, 31–33.

but that they could be used and frequented by Jews. We shall next present some material substantiating the interpretation that Philo did not strictly *forbid* participation, but that the clue to an accurate understanding of *Ebr.* 20 lies in his disclaimer about misusing such institutions.

The decisive support for such an interpretation lies in the text of *Ebr.* 20 itself. Here Philo says that contributions are praiseworthy if they are to gain prudence, and in 21 he states what purposes and activities make such participation blameworthy. In this section he points to "slackness, indolence, luxury, effeminacy and . . . complete irregularity of life" (cf. 22–23). Philo blames such gatherings as being those of pleasure lovers. This stance is further substantiated by *Ebr.* 95–96. Here Philo states that the disobedient son has in fact been disobedient to both his mother and his father: that is, to both the encyclia and right reason. Accordingly, it is not participation "per se" that is blameworthy, but the use of such gatherings for unworthy profit. Such participation is described as that of one who "drowns the whole of life in ceaseless and unending drunkenness," comparable to *Ebr.* 22 where such behavior is described as "excessive indulgence in food." Accordingly, the summation of such an attitude is formulated thus by Philo: "And thus he made a god of the body, a god of vanity most honoured among the Egyptians, whose symbol is the golden bull" (*Ebr.* 95).[50]

This last characterization does not differ very much from that of *Ebr.* 21b. When Philo in the last-mentioned passage writes of "complete irregularity of life" (παντελὴς ἐκδιαίτησις) he employs a description which in other contexts he invariably uses to denote idolatry or apostasy. In four of its occurrences it is used of unspecified apostasy,[51] and in *Vita Mosis* 2:167; 2:270 and *Spec.* 3:126 it is invoked in descriptions of idolatry of the golden calf in the desert. The term ἐκδιαίτησις is thus very strong, as is the description in *Ebr.* 25 where the contributor is characterized as one who purposes to do a wrongful act "in spite of the direct injunction of the Law, not to go with the many to do evil" (Exod 23:2).

The norm for considering the use of education is to be considered in light of the Law, having the study of the Law as its goal. Philo admits that the lower education should come first, but then philosophy is the higher

---

50. On the issue of making a god of the belly, see Sandnes, *Belly and Body*; on the "Banquets—opportunities for the belly," see Sandnes, *Belly and Body*, 79–96; on 'The Belly in Philo's writings', see Sandnes, *Belly and Body*, 108–132.

51. See *Praem.* 98; *Vita Mosis* 1:31, 278; *Somn.* 2:123, consult 4 Macc 4:19; 18;5; and Josephus, *War* 7:264.

(*Congr.* 74–80).⁵² This aspect of education, as posited by Philo, which also constitutes the practical component (cf. *Ebr.* 82–83), encompasses the progression from lower to higher education and is to be implemented in the context of daily life, including the appropriate utilization of clubs and associations (*Ebr.* 20–21).

The purpose of *Ebr.* 20–26 is thus not totally to forbid participation and payments of contributions to non-Jewish institutions, but to be deliberate in the use of such institutions and to strive for the acquisition of virtues rather than for their ruin. And to strive for the virtues, is to live with the Torah as one's guide. The virtues are promoted by the Torah (*Spec.* 1:299; 2:224; 4:134; *Praem.* 162), and they cannot in fact be gained save through the service of God (*Sacr.* 37).

This attitude may be further illuminated by pointing to a passage in which Philo discloses his own participation in banquets: *Leg.* 3.155–156. The context here is how to overrule passion by reason, and the argument from his own experiences runs thus:

> When we are present at entertainments (συνουσίαις), and are about to take and enjoy the viands provided, if we take our places at table with reason (σὺν λόγῳ) like some weapon to parry blows, we shall neither gourge ourselves with food beyond measure like cormorants, nor overdosed with unlimited strong drink shall we succumb to intoxication with its resultant foolish talk: for reason will curb and bridle the impetuous rush of the passion.
>
> I, to mention myself in proof of what I say, know by frequent experience (πολλάκις παθῶν οἶδα) how true it is. Many a time have I been present at a gathering with little that was sociable about it or at costly suppers. When I did not arrive with reason for my companion, I found myself the slave of the enjoyments provided, at the mercy of harsh masters, entertainments for eye and ear and all that brings pleasure by way of taste or smell. But whenever I arrive with convincing reason at my side, I find myself a master not a slave, and, putting forth all my strength, win the noble victory of endurance and self-mastery, in a vigorous and pertinacious encounter with everything that incites the unruly desires.

This may seem as only an example of how to manage at a party without getting too drunk and satiated. But when read in the light of *Ebr.* 95 and Philo's view of the pleasure-lover as comparable to an idolator, the passage brings us closer to his intention as set forth in *Ebr.* 20–26. Those

---

52. Mendelson, *Secular Education*, 35–38; Borgen, *Bread from Heaven*, 108–15.

who intend to participate only to drink and to live according to their pleasures are in fact indulging in the worship of the created instead of the creator and therefore are to be blamed and avoided (see *Spec.* 1:176). But with reason as one's companion, one will succeed and make progress in one's education. Hence, as described in our sociological characterizations of the clubs and associations, they also had socializing aspects, even when read in light of Philo's view of education.

PHILO'S COMPARISON OF JEWISH GATHERINGS AND FEASTS WITH THOSE OF THE GRAECO-ROMAN CLUBS AND ASSOCIATIONS: ISSUES OF MIMICRY AND HYBRIDITY

To the Roman colonizers who watched Jews coming together in their synagogues, these gatherings might resemble those of the associations. In fact, we have evidence to substantiate such a supposition. In *Ant.* 14 Josephus refers to letters and edicts that either compare the Jewish synagogal gatherings to the clubs (θίασοι) or designate them as σύνοδοι (*Ant.* 14:215–216, 235–236, 259–260).[53]

A similar use of these terms can also be found in *Legat.* 312 and 316. Here Philo argues against Gaius that his predecessors had not forbidden gatherings of Jews. In 312–313, which he says renders "the substance if not the actual words" of a letter from the emperor, Philo writes:

> He ordered that the Jews alone should be permitted by them to assemble in synagogues. These gatherings, he said, were not based on drunkenness and carousing to promote conspiracy and so to do grave injury to the cause of peace, but were schools of temperance and justice where men while practicing virtue subscribed the annual first-fruits to pay for the sacrifices which they offer and commissioned sacred envoys to Jerusalem according to their ancestral practice.

In *Legat.* 316 then he cites from a letter of Gaius Norbanus Flaccus to the Ephesians declaring what the emperor had written to him. From this Philo concludes: "He [i.e., the emperor] did not think that the form generally adopted about meetings (τῷ κοινῷ τύπῳ τῶν συνόδων) should be applied to do away with the assemblages of the Jews (τὰς τῶν Ἰουδαίων)." These passages are informative. They disclose Philo's

---

53. See further on this issue, Smallwood, *Jews Under Roman Rule*, 133–37.

knowledge of the tendency toward political unrest in some of the associations (see *Flacc.* 4 and *Spec.* 4:46–47), and they disclose the fact that the Roman authorities were critical of such 'collegia,' sometimes prohibiting their existence. This restrictive attitude of the Roman authorities is also witnessed in Pliny's letters.[54]

Philo further plays on the aspect of "drunkenness and carousing" of the associations in his defense of the Jewish synagogal gatherings. In this comparison the synagogues are described as "schools of temperance and justice," that is, places where the virtues are nourished and practiced.[55]

We here get a glimpse of the Jews' insecure position in the Diaspora. While some emperors might have been of a favorable mind toward the Jews, others were certainly not; and the standings of the Jews varied from place to place, from city to city.[56] To place the Jewish synagogues in the same category as the colonizers' associations was not without danger, and Philo is concerned with showing the differences between synagogues and associations, in order to secure the peace of the synagogues. What is of special importance to our present topic is his pinpointing the issue of political unrest and drunkenness as a feature of the other associations.

In *Vita Contemplativa* Philo describes a Jewish group of which we might know almost nothing if we lacked his account. This group, the Therapeutae, lived near Alexandria, and Philo seems to have had a good knowledge of them.

In *Contempl.* 40–47, he contrasts their gatherings (τὰς κοινὰς συνόδους) and meals (συμποσίοις) with the Greek symposia (των ἄλλων συμπόσια). In this comparative account the other symposia are described almost as orgies in wine-drinking, drunkenness, and strife. The gatherings of the Therapeutae, however, are sober, in fact of quite another kind and quality. They are not disturbed by drunkenness and intrigues; no slaves are serving at the tables (71–72), and no drinking of wine occurs (73–74), but the participants listen in silence to the expositions of holy Scriptures, sing hymns, and offer prayers (see 80, 83–84, 89–90).

It must be admitted that Philo here most probably gives a somewhat exaggerated description of both the excesses of the Greek symposia and

---

54. See Liebenam, *Zur Geschichte und Organisation*, 29; Ziebarth, *Das griechische Vereinswesen*, 95; Reicke, *Diakonie, Festfreude und Zelos*, 325; and Wilken, *Christians as the Romans Saw Them*, 12–15.

55. Note his descriptions of the synagogues in *Vita Mosis* 2:216; *Spec.* 2:62 and *Praem.* 60.

56. Rajak, "Jewish Rights."

the sobriety of the Therapeutae. There is also criticism of the symposia in Greek present in non-Jewish literature; to some degree Philo is applying a literary topos.[57] But he is most expressive and articulate in *Contempl.* Hence, his tendency is obvious: his attitude toward the Greek symposia is one of contempt and rejection. But there are surely elements of mimicry and hybridity present here in these comparisons.

This description of the symposia would not have been so valuable to the present study had it not been for the fact that the symposia activities were similar to those of the associations—even though they were not necessarily identical—and for the fact that the term συμπόσιον plays a considerable role in other passages dealing more explicitly with the activities of wine-drinking and drunkenness so closely associated with the gatherings of the clubs and the associations.

The word συμπόσιον is not a common word signifying 'association' in our sources stemming from this period, but some compound forms, especially συμποσίαρχος and συμποσιασταί are found not infrequently.[58] The term συμπόσιον itself has a long history as a term signifying 'drinking party.'[59] Usually it refers to the second half of a gathering. First came the meal; then, when this was finished and the women and the children had left, the symposium began. Such a symposium contained some cultic elements too, especially in connection with the three first drinking cups, which were for the gods and the heroes. Then hymns were sung. These cultic aspects have led Peter von der Mühl to go so far as to say that "Jener kultische Character besagt ferner, dass die Symphosiasten keine 'Gesellschaft' in unserem Sinne, sondern eine Gemeinde sind, ein Thiasos, der so wenig wie jeder andere sakraler Bindung entbehren kann."[60] In this way, these symposia closely resemble the gatherings of the clubs and associations, indeed represent one aspect of their gatherings. Philo probably does not use the word συμπόσιον to mean 'association,' but he makes use of it to emphasize one aspect of them: the wine-drinking. This enables us to draw into our consideration the text of *Contempl.* 40–47 (cf. above), as important for his understanding of this aspect, as well as the texts presented in the preceding section.

---

57. Collins, *Between Athens and Jerusalem*, 143.

58. See the index in Poland, *Geschichte des griechischen Vereinswesens*. On wine-drinking, see esp. Poland, *Geschichte des griechischen Vereinswesens*, 262–64. Consult further Henrichs, "Changing Dionysiac Identities," esp. 140–42.

59. Mühl, "Das griechische Symposion."

60. Mühl, "Das griechische Symposion," 489.

The excesses of food consumption and wine-drinking in non-Jewish gatherings is also dealt with in Philo's presentations of various Jewish feasts as he contrasts them with Graeco-Roman feasts and associations.[61] In *Spec.* 2:145-146 he is considering Passover, and in 2:148 he describes the actual gatherings in Jewish homes. Here he makes it explicit that they "are not as in other festive gatherings (τὰ ἄλλα συμπόσια) to indulge the belly with wine and viands, but to fulfill with prayers and hymns the custom handed down by their fathers" (2:148). The word used by Philo for 'feast' is ἑορτή, and in *Spec.* 2:193 the great Day of Atonement is described as a feast:

> Perhaps some of the perversely minded who are not ashamed to censure things excellent will say, What sort of a feast is this in which there are no gatherings to eat and drink, no company of entertainers or entertained, no copious supply of strong drink nor tables sumptuously furnished, nor a generous display of all the accompaniments of a public banquet.

Philo then adduces three arguments in favor of the ascetic features of this feast: first, the self-restraint (ἐγκράτεια) which it entails (2:195); second, the centrality of devotion to prayer and supplication (2:196); third, the season in which the celebration occurs, namely, when all the fruits of the earth have been gathered in (2:197).

The first argument is the most interesting for us here. Philo points to the self-restraint this feast entails, namely "in controlling the tongue and the belly and the organs below the belly" (2:195). This is something the Jews are exhorted to do every day, but especially on the occasion of the fast. But his emphasis on this aspect is more important, since it represents one of the more outstanding duties ignored in the other symposia. To Philo, those who liked to participate in the symposia were persons who could not control their tongues, their belly, or their sexual behavior (*Spec.* 1:192; *Contempl.* 52, 55; *Somn.* 2:167-168). Such lack of self-restraint could very easily lead into apostasy from the Law. In *Virt.* 182 he is in fact pointing to the observation that among persons who become apostates are those "ministering to the delights of the belly and the organs below it." Participation in the symposia, whether in an association or not, could, according to Philo, easily end up in apostasy.

Thus, his comparisons of Jewish gatherings with the symposia and his praise of the former could certainly function as a warning to his fellow

---

61. On Philo's comparisons, see also Sandnes, *Belly and Body*, esp. 123-32.

Jews. The 'other gatherings' represented dangerous 'milieus' and as such they could easily lead into situations of apostasy.

SUMMARY AND CONCLUSIONS

The purpose of this study has been to investigate Philo's descriptions and his attitudes respecting some part of the social life of Alexandria. The phenomenon of various clubs and associations has been neglected in previous research on Philo.

Philo describes various aspects of the activities of Greco-Roman associations: he uses several terms known to us from other sources and describes practices of belonging to an association such as paying dues, offering sacrifices, attending symposia, cultivating political unrest, and experiencing consequent anxiety of Roman officials, and being aware of the authorities' limited tolerance of associations.

In his comparisons of Jewish feasts and gatherings with those of the Greeks and Romans, Philo emphasizes wine-drinking and drunkenness in the latter. In *Ebr.* 20–26 he discusses the payment of dues, a discussion that shows that he does not totally forbid participation. Hence, he is in a way an 'infiltrator' in these Greco-Roman settings. Nevertheless, he is cautious about joining such associations; in fact, he seems to believe that participation could easily lead to idolatry and apostasy by fostering love of pleasure. Hence, we do not have a case of blunt mimicry here, but a *cultural criticism* that argues in preference to Jewish counterparts instead of the Greco-Roman symposia and associations. Philo's descriptions thus have sociopolitical aims: It's better to stick to the Jewish settings than to be involved in the associations so influenced by the colonizers' excessiveness. But that there also is some mimicry here resulting in hybridity is hardly to be denied.

Philo's restrictive attitude can thus be summed up by quoting his own remarks characterizing non-Jewish symposia, in contrast to the Jewish Sabbath gatherings (*Spec.* 1:176):

> All these things should be held in little account by those who are minded to live with God for their standard and for the service of Him that truly IS—men who, trained to disregard the pleasures of the flesh and practiced in the study of nature's verities, pursue the joys and sweet comforts of the intellect.

8

Reimagining Philo's Views of Magic

A Study of Cultural Criticism as Antimagical Apologetic

> "Moses demands that one who is registered in the commonwealth of the laws should be perfect not in the lore, in which the many are schooled, of divination and voices and plausible conjectures, but in his duties towards God in which there is nothing doubtful or ambiguous but undoubted, naked truth."
>
> SPEC. 1:63

INTRODUCTION

IN THE INTRODUCTION TO his book on *Jews in the Mediterranean Diaspora*, J. M. G. Barclay begins with a quotation from Num 23:9: "Behold, a people who will dwell alone, and will not be reckoned among the nations." He then asserts: "Balaam's oracle, cited above, encapsulates the sense of distinction which lies at the heart of the Jewish tradition."[1] Barclay proceeds to briefly outline the interpretations of this saying provided by Philo

---

1. Barclay, *Jews in the Mediteerranean Diaspora*, 1.

and Josephus respectively. At the conclusion of his concise introduction, Barclay states: "Balaam's oracle, with its divergent interpretations in Philo and Josephus, thus poses some key questions about the social and cultural strategies of Jews in the Mediterranean Diaspora."[2]

Barclay's observation is to the point. Philo's presentation and explication of Balaam and his work constitutes a component of Philo's cultural strategies, primarily manifested in the form of criticism directed towards magical practices, whether Jewish or Greco-Roman. In the present context, I have called Philo's strategy of cultural criticism as "antimagical apologetics."[3] Antimagical apologetics is a kind of "apologetic counter-interpretation"; Philo is presenting a kind of antimagical apologetics on behalf of biblical characters in order to oppose the magicians' interpretations of his heroes (Moses and others), that is, those who accuse other nonmagicians of magi. In the pages to follow I will first deal with magic more generally in the works and world of Philo, then focus on his use of Balaam in his works as part of Philo's social and cultural strategies.

The figure of Balaam (Hebrew: Bileam) presents an enigmatic character within the traditions of the Hebrew Scriptures/Old Testament. Consequently, it is unsurprising that some ambiguity persists in later Jewish works and traditions, including those of Philo of Alexandria, and extends further into other Jewish and certain early Christian literature of the Common Era (CE). Philo addresses and utilizes the Balaam figure in multiple contexts within both his allegorical commentaries and his Expositio. Within the allegorical commentaries, references to Balaam are found in *Cher.* 32–33: *Det.* 71; *Deus* 181; *Conf.* 159; *Migr.* 113–115, and in *Mut.* 202. In the context of the Expositio, Philo provides an extensive retelling of the Balaam narrative from Num 22–24 in his *De vita Mosis* (sections 1:263–299), with additional aspects of Balaam's message addressed in *Praem.* 95–97. As a procedure of criticism, it is given in a Jewish context, but it has some wider ramifications as it also becomes a criticism of magical practices in general, Greco-Roman practices included.[4]

---

2. Barclay, *Jews in the Mediteerranean Diaspora*, 3.
3. Adopted from Keener, *Acts*, 2:1508.
4. Seland, "Expository Use."

PHILO ON MAGIC IN THE GRECO-ROMAN WORLD

In Philo's era, magic was a pervasive phenomenon in the Greco-Roman world.[5] Pliny the Elder (23–79 CE), for instance, provides extensive information regarding magical procedures, rituals, and artifacts in his *Historia Naturalis* 28–30. An examination of Philo's works reveals his familiarity with the various magical practices prevalent in the social milieu of Alexandria. This is most evident in the following passage from *Spec.* 3:100–102:

> 100 Now the true magic (ἀληθῆ μαγικήν), the scientific vision by which the facts of nature are presented in a clearer light, is felt to be a fit object for reverence and ambition and is carefully studied not only by ordinary persons but by kings and the greatest kings, and particularly those of the Persians, so much so that it is said that no one in that country is promoted to the throne unless he has first been admitted into the caste of the Magi (τοῦ μάγων). 101 But there is a counterfeit of this, most properly called a perversion of art, pursued by charlatan mendicants (μηναγύρται) and parasites and the basest of the women and slave population, who make it their profession to deal in purifications and disenchantments and promise with some sort of charms and incantations to turn men's love into deadly enmity and their hatred into profound affection. The simplest and most innocent natures are deceived by the bait till at least the worst misfortunes come upon them and thereby the wide membership which unites great companies of friends and kinsmen falls gradually into decay and is rapidly and silently destroyed. All these things our lawgiver had in view, I believe, when he prohibited any postponement in bringing poisoners (φαρμακευτῶν) to justice and ordained that the punishment should be exacted at once.

In this section, Philo reveals several aspects of his knowledge and views of the magicians of his time and their activities. He knew about the ancient association of the Magi with Persians. This was common knowledge, at least among the literati of his time, and Philo has a similar description in *Prob.* 74. He also reveals that he can distinguish between science and magic or, to use his way of stating it: there was a positive scientific version of magic and a negative and perverse version. Furthermore,

---

5. For a brief, but informative review of recent literature on magic at the beginning of the first century CE, see Keener, *Acts*, 2:1500–1507. For a collection of relevant sources in translation, see Ogden, *Magic*. On Jewish magic, see Bohak, *Ancient Jewish Magic*.

his descriptions seem to be so detailed that they are probably not only derived from his knowledge of the prohibitions of Moses but also from personal observations. Another important aspect of his statement is the association of magic with the poor and the uneducated. While this might be a derogatory statement of Philo as a member of the (Jewish) elite in Alexandria, we find similar convictions in other sources.[6] In addition, as David E. Aune pinpoints, "The Greek of the magical papyri is the unpretentious common language of the people, not the cultivated, literary and atticistic language of the educated."[7] Lastly, this passage demonstrates that Philo obviously knew various sorts of aggressive and malevolent magic: "charms and incantations to turn men's love into deadly enmity and their hatred into profound love affection," consult here also *Spec.* 1:62. Hence, this is an important passage in Philo's works.

However, scholarly studies concerning the phenomenon of magic and magical practices as reflected in Philo's works are very rare.[8] Furthermore, among the many studies published on magic in ancient Egypt,[9] very little can be found on Philo's views and attitudes. The present chapter attempts to remedy some of this lack of research by focusing on magic and magical divination in the works of Philo. Here, I explore what he might tell us about magical practices by investigating how he dealt with texts of the Bible related to magic, how he himself conceptualized it, and eventually how he thus advised his readers to cope with magic. In the first section below, I briefly review some issues discussed in recent studies of ancient magic. In the following sections, I investigate how Philo dealt with various aspects of his expository use of magic in his works.[10]

---

6. Aune, "Magic in Early Christianity," 1521, points to Origen's *Contra Celsum* 6.41; 7.4, and Philostratus *Vit. soph.* 523, 590. Aune's study is reprinted in his collection of articles, published in 2008, as Aune, "Magic in Early Christianity," in *Apocalypticism, Prophecy, and Magic*.

7. Aune, "Magic in Early Christianity," 1521.

8. In fact, I have found a few studies of magic in the works of Philo, all by Robert M. Berchman. See Berchman, "Arcana Mundi: Magic and Divination in the *De Somniis*" (1998); this is identical to his earlier SBL paper: Berchman, "Arcana Mundi: Magic and Divination in the *De Somniis*" (1987). Furthermore, see Berchman, "Arcana Mundi: Prophecy and Divination in the *Vita Mosis*" (1988). See also Berchman, "Arcana Mundi Between Balaam and Hecate." Bohak, *Ancient Jewish Magic*, deals with Philo on pp. 78–80, i.e., only two and a half pages.

9. On magic in ancient Egypt, see e.g., Ritner, "Egyptian Magical Practice"; Luck, trans., *Arcana Mundi*; Assmann, "Magic and Theology"; Frankfurter, "Ritual Expertise."

10. In the present article I draw on three former studies of mine; Seland, *Establishment Violence*, 143–51; and especially Seland, "Philo, Magic and Balaam"; and Seland,

ANCIENT MAGIC: SOME ISSUES

Social anthropologists emphasize the embedded nature of religion in cultures of the Greco-Roman world;[11] the Greeks did not even have a term for 'religion.' Robert K. Ritner has indeed argued that "Egyptian magic was traditionally neither unorthodox, illegal, nor 'socially deviant,' but had a commonplace within Egyptian religion."[12] On the other hand, however, one can find that magic is not only present in descriptions by outsiders, but that there existed in antiquity individuals who considered themselves magicians: "The category of magic is not merely the expression of an ideological prejudice against 'the other'; it was also a profession and a practice understood by its practitioners as being something different from the official cult of the gods."[13] Hence Jonathan Z. Smith has stated that "the social approach, ironically, cannot seem to handle those cultural instances where 'magicians' function as a craft, as a profession, either as an hereditary office or as a guild with procedures for both training and incorporation."[14] Thus, when dealing with magic in the Greco-Roman world, some scholars have emphasized that the distinction between religion and magic was already observed by those writing in the Greco-Roman epochs as far back as in the works of Plato.[15]

There is thus no consensus on these issues in recent research: "Magic's relation both to religion and science has never been clearly delineated."[16] However, the common opinion emerging during the last decades seems to favor the view that magic and religion might be distinguished, but not viewed as or studied as quite separate entities.[17] Alan F. Segal speaks for many when he says that "all definitions of magic are

---

"Expository Use."

11. Malina, "Religion in the World of Paul."

12. See Ritner, "Egyptian Magical Practice," 3,353–58, here quoted from p. 3,353. See further Ritner, "Religious, Social, and Legal Parameters."

13. Thomassen, "Is Magic a Subclass of Ritual?," 57.

14. See Smith, "Trading Places," 20. He uses this observation, however, to claim that there is "little merit in continuing the use of the substantive term 'magic' in second-order, theoretical, academic discourse" (16). It is not quite clear to me, alas, how he then would describe what is generally now labeled magic.

15. See e.g., Graf, "Excluding the Charming."

16. Segal, "Hellenistic Magic," 349.

17. Klauck tries to see magic and religion as two contrary poles on a continuum or as the two endpoints of a line. See Klauck, *Die religiöse Umwelt des Urchristentums*, 1:174–75.

relative to the culture and subculture under discussion. Furthermore, it is my contention that we have been misled by our own cultural assumptions into making too strict a distinction between magic and religion in the Hellenistic world."[18] Jan N. Bremmer pointed out that the birth of the magic-religion opposition is quite recent and can be dated fairly exactly to the end of the nineteenth century.[19] However, we can hardly do without some kind of distinction, but our definitions should not be too rigid at the outset. Applied to a study like this of 'magic' in the works of Philo, it should be appropriate to investigate how he conceptualizes these issues and let the various points of view voiced in recent research be tested on his material. In this way, we may arrive at an understanding of what 'magic' represents in his symbolic universe.

I have included the issue of 'divination' in the present study, but with a clear emphasis on what is to be called *'magical* divination.' Aune defines divination as "the art or science of interpreting symbolic messages from the gods."[20] But if magic is hard to define, so is necessarily magical divination. Following Aune again, we might define *oracular* divination as "messages from the gods in human language, received as statements from a god, usually in response to inquiries."[21] *Magical* divination, however, is characterized by the search for divine guidance through various means: Among the most common here are lamp divination (lychnomanteia); bowl divination (lekanomanteia); saucer divination (phialomanteia); divination by dreams (oneiromanteia); the casting of lots (kleromancy); watching the flight and behavior of birds (ornitomancy); the condition and behavior of sacrificial animals, or their vital organs before or after sacrifice (hepatoscopy, hieromancy); or various omens or sounds.[22] Several of these types are mentioned by Philo.

---

18. See Segal, "Hellenistic Magic," 351; see p. 359 where he says that "when magic was viewed as benign it might easily be coterminous with religion, whereas in the crucial contexts where magic was viewed as antagonistic and illegal it was carefully differentiated." See also now Bremmer, "Birth of the Term 'Magic.'"

19. See Bremmer, "Birth of the Term 'Magic,'" 11–12. See p. 12 where he says: "The opposition, then, is a typical product of the Victorian middle-classes with their strong need for positive self-definition against the colonial subjects abroad and the peasants at home. It has no place in a discussion of magic in antiquity." While he may be right in his first assertion, I am not so sure about his last statement. 'Magic' may still have some heuristic value for our studies today.

20. Aune, *Prophecy in Early Christianity*, 23.

21. Aune, *Prophecy in Early Christianity*, 23.

22. Aune, *Prophecy in Early Christianity*, 23–24 and 44–47.

PHILO AND THE MAGIC OF HIS HOLY SCRIPTURES

Philo was an expositor of the Law of Moses—the Torah—in its Greek version. He may have known some Hebrew, but scholars seem to agree that he did not read the Scriptures in Hebrew, but in Greek. Most of his works are commentaries on topics and/or writings from the Pentateuch.[23]

Septuagintal and Philonic Vocabulary Around Magic

References to magical practices are found scattered in most of the Hebrew Scriptures, and in a wide range of text types.[24] The most specialized and technical vocabulary, however, appears in the legal material of the Pentateuch. As this is the section of the Bible primarily dealt with by Philo, these references are also the most interesting for the present study (see Exod 7:11; 22:17; Lev 19:26, 31; 20:6. 27; Deut 18:9–14).[25] Most informative about the variety of terms in the Pentateuch having to do with magic is Deut 18:10–11:

> 10 οὐχ εὑρεθήσεται ἐν σοὶ περικαθαίρων τὸν υἱὸν αὐτοῦ ἢ τὴν θυγατέρα αὐτοῦ ἐν πυρί, μαντευόμενος μαντείαν, κληδονιζόμενος καὶ οἰωνιζόμενος, φαρμακός, 11 ἐπαείδων ἐπαοιδήν, ἐγγαστρίμυθος καὶ τερατοσκόπος, ἐπερωτῶν τοὺς νεκρούς.
> 10 No one shall be found among you who makes a son or daughter pass through fire, or who practices divination, or is a soothsayer, or an augur, or a sorcerer, 11 or one who casts spells, or who consults ghosts or spirits, or who seeks oracles from the dead. (NRSV)

---

23. See further on these issues Borgen, *Philo of Alexandria, An Exegete*; Borgen, "Philo of Alexandria as Exegete"; Adams, *Greek Genres*, 277–290.

24. For an overview of the various texts, one might check the various articles in *The Anchor Bible Dictionary* on "Amulet," "Augury," "Charmer," "Conjuring," "Divination," "Medium," "Necromancy," "Soothsayer," "Sorcery," "Witchcraft," and "Wizard"—and especially Kuermmerlin-McLean, "Magic: Old Testament." See further Klutz, ed., *Magic in the Biblical World*; Ricks, "Magician as Outsider"; Schäfer, "Magic and Religion in Ancient Judaism"; and Yamauchi, "Magic in the Biblical World."

25. There are also many other references to magic and magicians in the Hebrew Scriptures both in the historical books and in the books of the prophets. We also find a variety of attitudes to magicians and magical practices exhibited in these works. See for instance esp. 2 Kgs 9:22–23; 2 Chr 33:6; 1 Sam 28; Isa 8:19; 57:3; Ezek 22:28; and Mal 3:5. In some texts there obviously are magical aspects inherent in the ancient Israelite practices described; e.g., clothing (2 Kgs 2:13–14); mandrakes (Gen 30:14–18); instruments (2 Kgs 5:11); hair (Judg 16:17); spells (Josh 10:12); belomancy (1 Sam 20:20–22) and hydromancy (Exod 15:25).

With the addition of one term (in Lev 19:26: ὀρνιθοσκοπέω), we have here presented all the various terms for 'magic' used in the Pentateuch.

The primary Greek terms belonging to the semantic field of magic are the words grouped around μάγος, φαρμακεύς, and γόης. Μάγος and its related terms (μαγεία, μαγικός) are probably the most common terms denoting magicians or magical practices. The φαρμακεύς or φάρμακος group (see φαρμακεία, φάρμακον, φαρμακεύω) denote figures more like our 'witch', 'sorcerer', 'poisoner' and their actions, while the γόης group represents terms with a more derogatory value, denoting also sorcerer, but especially with a flavor of 'swindler', 'cheater', and all that they represent. According to Gerhard Delling "the only distinction between μάγος and γόης is that the latter is mostly used for the lower practitioner."[26]

We find that the μαγ- terms do not occur in the Septuagintian version of the Pentateuch at all, but 8 times in the book of Daniel (1:20; 2:2, 10, 27; 4:4; 5:7, 11, 15); Philo uses these terms 8 times.[27] The φαρμακεύς group is found 14 times in the LXX, including in Exod 7:11, 22; 9:11; and Deut 18:10; in Philo these terms are much more common, appearing a total of 41 times. Not all of these arise in contexts of magic, however. Γόης or terms belonging to this stem are not present in the LXX at all. Philo, however, uses γόης 6 times and γοητεία 13 times.

When it comes to terms denoting *magical divination*, there is an even richer terminology available, denoting most of the various kinds of divination mentioned above. The word ἐπαοιδός ('enchanter') is one of the terms that are much more frequent in the LXX than in Philo: In Philo ἐπαοιδός is found only once in a section dealing with the sophists (*Migr.* 83). In the LXX ἐπαοιδός is found 21 times. Here it is especially used as the primary term describing the magicians of Pharaoh in Egypt, competing with Moses. Among the other terms denoting various forms of magical divination, we find that ἐγγαστρίμυθος (belly-speaker, to speak as a medium) is found 14 times in the LXX.[28] Here it is especially prominent in the descriptions of Saul consulting the 'witch' in Endor. It is only found once in Philo; that is in *Somn.* 1:220 where it is one of several terms describing the sorcerers competing with Moses before Pharaoh. Terms

26. See γόης, *TDNT* 1:737.

27. See μάγος; *Mos.* 1:92. 276; *Spec.* 3:93, 100; *Mut.* 106 and 110; μαγικός, *Mos.* 1:277; *Spec.* 3:100. See the most recent Philo index: Borgen et al., eds., *Philo Index*.

28. Lev 19:31; 20:6. 27; Deut 18:11; see also 1 Sam 28:3, 7, 8, 9; 1 Chr 10:13; 2 Chr 33:6; 35:19; Isa 8:19; 19:3; 44:25. See further on this term; Torallas Tovar and Maravela-Solbakk, "Between Necromancers and Ventriloquists."

belonging to the κληδονίζω group, meaning 'to give a sign or omen' as a medium or to be a 'diviner' are found only a few times in both the LXX and Philo.[29] Μαντεύομαι, denoting 'to prophesy,' 'to divine,' 'to give an oracle,' or 'to consult an oracle'; and μάντις, denoting 'soothsayer,' 'diviner,' or 'prophet,' are found 30 times in LXX;[30] only two of these are in the Pentateuch (Num. 22:7; 23:23), both belonging to the Balaam narrative. In Philo these terms are even more frequent (35 times),[31] also here as a favorite term describing Balaam. Οἰωνοσκόπος, usually lexicalized as 'soothsayer,' and 'one who takes omens from the flight and screams of birds' (ornitomancy), is not present in the LXX; Philo uses it in *Mut.* 202 (Balaam); *Spec.* 1:60; 4:48, cf. the οἰωνοσκοπία in *Mos.* 1:264 (Balaam). The term οἰωνίζω, and its derived terms, having the same meaning of taking omens from birds, are present in the LXX in Gen 30:27; 44:5, 15; Lev 19:26; and Deut 18:10 (see also 1 Kgs 20:33; 2 Kgs 17:17; 21:6; and 33:6). In Philo we find not οἰωνίζω but οἰωνόμαντις in *Conf.* 159 and *Somn* 1:220, and οἰωνός 6 times, especially in *Mos.* 1:263-287, as a term describing Balaam. The word ὀρνιθοσκόπος, a synonym to οἰωνοσκόπος, present in Lev 19:26, is not present in the works of Philo.

There is thus a variety of terms denoting 'magic' and 'magical divination' in both the LXX and in the texts of Philo; almost all the terms found in the LXX are also found in Philo, and just a few terms are present in the LXX only and not in Philo, or vice versa. All this demonstrates that Philo is strongly influenced by the vocabulary of the LXX. On the other hand, there is also enough variety in Philo to trigger a further investigation of how he understands and uses descriptions of magic and magicians, and possibly, how he advises readers to cope with it.

THE EXPOSITORY USE OF THE BALAAM FIGURE IN PHILO'S *DE VITA MOSIS*[32]

Our focus on 'expository use' indicates that we are not interested in all Philo has to say about Balaam, but more in how he uses him—that is, for

---

29. In the Pentateuch (LXX), κληδονίζω is found in Deut 18:10 and 14 (see also 2 Kgs 21:6; 2 Chr 33:6; and Isa 2:6). In Philo we find the terms from this group in *Mos.* 1:287; *Spec.* 1:60, 63; and *Flacc.* 177.

30. μαντεία 3x; μαντεύομαι 12x; μαντικός 11x; μάντις 5x.

31. μαντεία 7x; μαντεύομαι 6x; μαντικός 11x; μάντις 11x.

32. The following is adopted from my article, published in 2016: Seland, "Expository Use."

what purposes Philo puts Balaam to use. The question of *how* Philo uses Balaam will thus determine the questions of what Philo says about him. Hence, we may ask: What does Philo tell us about the words and deeds of Balaam? How does he use the figure of Balaam? In what contexts does he use him? Are there any patterns of expository contexts and purposes to be found?

In recent years, some major studies and anthologies of studies on Balaam have been published,[33] but not many have focused on the role of Balaam in the works of Philo,[34] and even fewer have treated Philo's expository use of the Balaam figure. Several studies have also dealt with the Balaam text from Deir 'Alla, and its possible relevance for understanding the Balaam of the biblical tradition and related traditions.[35] However, our primary focus in what follows is on Philo's expository use of this enigmatic figure in *De vita Mosis*.

A Short Review of Balaam in Pre-Philo Traditions

In the Hebrew Bible, the main story of Balaam is given in the three chapters of Numbers 22–24. In addition, Balaam is mentioned in Num 31:8, 16; Deut 23:5–6; Josh 13:22; 24:9–10; Neh 13:2; and Micah 6:5. As the primary focus of our study is not the Balaam traditions of the Hebrew Scriptures as such, and as Philo probably did not know Hebrew, but used Greek translation(s), our primary focus is on the Greek texts.

A few comments on the Hebrew version might nevertheless be pertinent: It is clear from a reading of Num 22–24 (and the other text segments dealing with Balaam) that there are several traditions about Balaam represented here. Some will argue that the whole of Num 22–24 is a later insertion into the book of Numbers;[36] other focus on the vari-

---

33. See Moore, *Balaam Traditions*; Greene, *Balaam and His Interpreters*; and partly Lichtenberger and Mittmann-Richert, eds., *Biblical Figures*.

34. Several of these are dealing with Balaam as a magician: Greene, "Balaam: Prophet, Diviner and Priest"; Greene, "Balaam as Figure"; Greene, "Balaam Figure and Type." See also Berchman, "Arcana Mundi: Prophecy and Divination in the *Vita Mosis*"; and Seland, "Philo, Magic and Balaam."

35. See e.g., Moore, *Balaam Traditions*, 66–96; Hoftizer and van der Kooij, eds., *Balaam Text from Deir 'Alla*; Puech, "Bala'am and Deir 'Alla."

36. Consult Rösel, "Wie einer vom Propheten zum Verführer wurde," 508: "Der Bericht in den Kapiteln 22–24 des Numeribuches ist mit dem Kontext nicht weiter verknüpft; wenn man ihn entfernen würde, wäre sein Fehlen wohl nicht zu bemerken." See also the references in his footnote 10.

ous probable traditions present within these three chapters.[37] Applying the old literary views and history-of-tradition criticism associated with the source designations JEDP, or a modified version of this, some have suggested rather elaborate source-critical descriptions of the various traditions inherent in these chapters.[38] However, as Philo used neither these nor any comparable source theories, and given that he did not use Hebrew text versions, these theories are of little interest here. The traditions represented by the Balaam texts outside Num 22–24, however, are still interesting as evidence of various views (traditions) concerning Balaam in vogue in ancient Israel.

Another aspect of Num 22–24 relevant for our study is the fact that Balaam as a whole is presented as a rather positive figure in this text segment.[39] He does not dispute the LORD's order, and he is consistent in his replies to Balak that he can only bring forth what the LORD gives him to say. Even though the story of Balaam and the donkey might represent a somewhat different picture of Balaam, it is not Balaam who changes his mind, but the LORD is depicted as getting angry because Balaam was going to Balak (22:22), even though the LORD had accepted his going a few verses earlier (22:20). No wonder scholars see this as an indication of the presence of different sources.

Thirdly then, and in light of the discussion to follow in this chapter, it is important to note that Balaam most probably is not described as a magician in Num 22–24 of the Hebrew Bible, but more as a prophet of YHWH. He converses with God, and gets his messages from God (e.g., 22:9–12, 20). He is not *called* a prophet in the text of Num 22–24, but he "sees": his eyes are opened by the LORD, and he hears the word of God (see 22:31, and esp. 24:3–4; 15–16). There are, however, two issues in the text that might be open for an interpretation pointing towards

---

37. See e.g., Zsengellér, "Changes in the Balaam-Interpretation," 487–88: Zsengellér finds at least three Balaam pictures in Num 22–24: "1. a non-israelite curse reciter who deals with magic as well; 2. an obedient prophet of God, who knows and follows his words, and who was called to curse but went to bless; 3. a ridiculous prophet who far from being in contact with God does not see the angel sent by God though seen by his ass" (page 487).

38. One of the most comprehensive source-critical description is probably the one by Greene: see Greene, "Balaam: Prophet, Diviner, and Priest"; see Greene, *Balaam and His Interpreters*, 6–68. See also Rösel, "Wie einer vom Propheten zum Verführer Wurde"; and Hackett, "Balaam (PERSON) [Heb Bil'am]," esp. pp. 569–71.

39. Not all have seen this, especially not if they read Num 22–24 in light of Deut 23:5–6. However, read on its own, Num 22–24 is basically positive. See Frankel, "Deuteronomic Portrayal of Balaam," 30–31.

an understanding of Balaam as a magician: In Num 22:7 it is said that the elders came to Balaam "with the fees for divination in their hands" (NRSV). This translation of the Hebrew קסם is possible and traditional,[40] but several scholars have lifted up another translation as more probable, namely, not "fees for divination" but "instruments of divination"[41] that Balaam was to use. Then there is the somewhat unexpected statement of Num 24:1, where a reader would have expected Balaam to go to meet God in order to seek his advice as in the two former cases; instead it says, "Now Balaam saw that it pleased the LORD to bless Israel, so he did not go, as at other times, to look for omens, but set his face towards the wilderness." But the narrator adds: "Then the spirit of God came upon him, and he uttered his oracle" (24:2). The expression "to look for omens," open to a magical interpretation, is balanced by the more prophetic-related "the spirit of God came upon him." However, the connotations of 'magic' inherent here are further developed in later traditions.

As stated above, Balaam is mentioned in seven other text segments (Num 31:8, 16; Deut 23:5–6; Josh 13:22; 24:9; Neh 13:2; and Micah 6:5), and some of these provide a somewhat different picture of Balaam. The most negative of these, and containing some new issues of Balaam's activities, is Num 31:8, 16. In 31:8 it is said that the Israelites killed Balaam; this is very similar to Josh 13:22, which states that Balaam was killed and adds the explanation that this happened because "Balaam practiced divination." In Num 31:16, however, it is said, "These women here [i.e., the Midianites, see 31:9], *on Balaam's advice*, made the Israelites act treacherously against the LORD in the affair of Peor, so that the plague came among the congregation of the LORD." This is the most negative statement of them all about Balaam in the Hebrew Bible and tells us something that is not inherent in Num 22–24, nor in Num 25, as these chapters tell us nothing about any such advice from Balaam. In Deut 23:3–5 (NRSV), furthermore, (quoted in Neh 13:1–2), it is said that "No Ammonite or Moabite shall be admitted to the assembly of the LORD. Even to the tenth generation, none of their descendants shall be admitted to the assembly of the LORD, 4 because they did not meet you with food and water on your journey out of Egypt, and *because they hired against you Balaam son of Beor, from Pethor of Mesopotamia, to curse you*. 5 (Yet the LORD your God refused to heed Balaam; the LORD your God turned the curse into

---

40. Vermes, "Story of Balaam," 130.

41. See e.g., Barré, "Portrait of Balaam," 256; Moberly, "On Learning to Be a True Prophet," 3–4.

a blessing for you, because the LORD your God loved you)." This latter statement is comparable to Josh 24:10 where God says that "I would not listen to Balaam, therefore he blessed you." All of these statements are negative in what they tell about Balaam; only one text has a more positive view of him (Mic 6:5: "remember what King Balak of Moab devised, what Balaam son of Beor answered him.") It is outside the range of this chapter to discuss these passages further;[42] they are referred to here because they represent the material Philo had at his disposal, though in the form of the Greek translation(s). Hence, we now turn to the Septuagint.

Balaam in the Septuagint

Philo used the biblical traditions in their Greek form. We know that he knew about the translation of the Torah from Hebrew into Greek as he provides his version of the translation story (*Mos.* 2:25–44). Hence it is the Greek version of the Torah that is to be the focus here, that is, what we call the Septuagint (LXX).

In the main, there are several differences but just a few major deviations in the LXX from the Hebrew 'Vorlage' in the Balaam texts. According to Zsengellér, "the number of differences between the text of Num 22–24 in the Masoretic Text (MT) and the LXX amounts to 177."[43] Wevers finds that the most striking differences between the two accounts lies in "the use of the divine name, more particularly of κύριος versus (ὁ) θεός in the LXX over against אלהים (or אל) vs יהוה in the Hebrew. In the book as a whole יהוה usually becomes κύριος in the LXX (360 times), whereas אלהים is rendered by (ὁ) θεός 24 times out of 29." What Wevers finds particularly significant here is that אלהים never becomes κύριος in the LXX.[44] Concerning Num 22–24 he suggests that his findings indicate that to the translator(s), it is not יהוה who meets Balaam, but ὁ θεός. Hence, the translator did not consider Balaam a real prophet of יהוה.[45]

Considering Num 22–24 as a whole, however, the greatest differences between the LXX and the Hebrew text are probably to be found

---

42. Further discussion can be found in Greene, "Balaam: Prophet, Diviner, and Priest," 92–95; Greene, "Balaam as Figure and Type," 84–91; Rösel, "Wie einer Vom Propheten Zum Verführer Wurde," 515–18. See also Frankel, "Deuteronomic Portrayal of Balaam."

43. Zsengellér, "Changes in the Balaam-Interpretation," 488.

44. See further Wevers, "Balaam Narrative," 135.

45. Wevers, "Balaam Narrative," 144.

in parts of Balaam's messages, particularly in the more eschatological sections. In Num 23:10d, there is a change in expression as the Hebrew text, from "Let me die the death of the upright, and let my end be like his!" into the Greek: ἀποθάνοι ἡ ψυχή μου ἐν ψυχαῖς δικαίων, καὶ γένοιτο τὸ σπέρμα μου ὡς τὸ σπέρμα τούτων—that is: "Let my soul die with the souls of the righteous, and let my descendants be as their descendants." Zsengellér reads this as indicating that "Seeing Israel's future, he would like to assure something similar for his own progeny."[46] However, one should perhaps not pay too much attention to this difference.

In 24:7 and 24:17 the translator has made some more obvious changes, which emphasize the Messianic color of these sayings.[47] According to Wevers, "By this reinterpretation, the Septuagint rendered more concrete and in a sense brought near, the rather distant and cautious Messianic perspective of the Hebrew text, and made Balaam a prophet of a coming Messiah."[48] In the coming centuries, the Balaam pericope would play a central role in the messianic expectations of several Jewish and Christian texts.

In the other texts mentioning Balaam (Num 31:8, 16; Deut 23:5–6; Josh 13:22; 24:9, and Mic 6:5), there are only some minor differences, but no major deviations in the LXX from the Hebrew text. Hence, we now turn to Philo of Alexandria, and his use of the Balaam figure.

THE BALAAM FIGURE IN THE WORKS OF PHILO

In the following sections, we will primarily deal with Philo's use of the Balaam figure in his *De vita Mosis* 1 (*Mos.* 1). This work is not properly a part of the Expositio, but on the other hand, it may have been intended as a kind of introduction to it.[49] Peder Borgen seems to consider it more as

---

46. Zsengellér, "Changes in the Balaam-Interpretation," 489.

47. In 24:7 we get a change from (MT): Water shall flow from his buckets, and his seed shall have abundant water, his king shall be higher than Agag, and his kingdom shall be exalted, to (LXX): A person will come forth from his offspring and he shall rule over many nations, and his reign shall be exalted beyond Gog, and his reign shall be increased. In 24:17 the Messianic overtones are strengthened too: (MT): I see him, but not now; I behold him, but not near—a star shall come out of Jacob, and a scepter shall rise out of Israel; (LXX): I will point to him, and not now; I deem him happy, but he is not at hand. A star shall dawn out of Iacob, and a person shall rise up out of Israel.

48. Wevers, "Balaam Narrative," 490.

49. Royse, "Works of Philo," 47, drawing on Goodenough, "Philo's Exposition."

a companion work.⁵⁰ The other texts dealing with Balaam (*Cher.* 32–33: *Det.* 71; *Deus* 181; *Conf.* 159; *Migr.* 113–115 and in *Mut.* 202) will be dealt with as far as they are considered relevant for understanding *De vita Mosis*.

The *Vita Mosis* and the Balaam Figure

De vita Mosis is a two-volume work of a strong biographical nature. In the first volume, Philo gives a mainly biographical and chronological account of Moses, focusing on Moses as a king. In the second volume, topological viewpoints are more dominant, as Moses is described as a lawgiver, high priest, and prophet. Philo's work is based on the life of Moses as found in Exodus, Numbers, and Leviticus. Philo himself, in his introduction, calls his work a βίος (*Mos.* 1:1: "I purpose to write the life of Moses"; see 2:292). This same passage indicates other aspects of *De vita Mosis*, as Philo says, "Such, as recorded in the Holy Scriptures, was the life and such the end of Moses, king, lawgiver, high priest, prophet." Because of this and other observations in the text, *De vita Mosis* might be characterized as deserving the label 'rewritten Bible' or 'rewritten scripture.'

The Genre of *De vita Mosis*

These labels have been hotly debated. The first use of them and the ensuing debate are often considered as originating with Geza Vermes in his book *Scripture and Tradition in Judaism* (1961, 1973).⁵¹ In addition to such works as for example Ps.-Philo and Jubilees, the focus of the genre debate around Mos. has often been on the writings from the Dead Sea Scrolls. Peder Borgen was probably one of the earliest to offer a classification of 'rewritten Scripture' for some of Philo's works, especially those of the Expositio.⁵² Few followed in his tracks immediately after him, but in more recent time Philo has once again come back in focus.⁵³

---

50. Borgen, "Philo—An Interpreter of the Laws of Moses," 76.

51. See Vermes, *Scripture and Tradition*, 95, where he points to how "the Palestinian Targum and Jewish Antiquities, Ps.-Philo and Jubilees, each in their own way show how the Bible was rewritten."

52. See especially Borgen, *Philo of Alexandria, An Exegete*, 46–79; Borgen, "Philo of Alexandria: Reviewing," 37–53.

53. Consult e.g., Fraade, "Between Rewritten Bible"; Damgaard, "Philo's Life of Moses as 'Rewritten Bible.'"

The debate is too extensive and the studies too many for us to dig into these issues here and now; in addition to the debate to some extent still marred by disagreements over definitions and the most pertinent label(s) to use ('rewritten Bible,' 'rewritten Scripture/scripture,' 'parabiblical' or 'parascriptural' materials and so forth), questions arise whether these writings belong to a separate genre or typify an interpretative strategy, or whether the labels 'rewritten Scripture' and the like should be considered emic or etic classifications,[54] so more study should certainly be done on the works of Philo.

However, if one understands a label such as 'rewritten Scriture' as signifying that an author, on the basis of some biblical text(s)—whether smaller or larger units—reworks these not only by retelling them, but by rewriting them (rephrasing, paraphrasing, omitting, or adding material) and thus ending up with some 'new' (re)written texts, then the label should be considered functional. In addition, I consider this focus to be most relevant concerning Philo's rewriting of the story of Balaam from Num 22–24 in his *De vita Mosis* 1:263–299. Such a view finds some strong corroboration from Philo himself, as in a famous saying, at the beginning of the work, he says this about his writing process (1:4):

> I will . . . tell the story of Moses as I have learned it, both from the sacred books, the wonderful monuments of his wisdom which he has left behind him, and from some of the elders of the nation; for I always interwove what I was told with what I read, and thus believed myself to have a closer knowledge than others of his life's story.

An interesting issue in this saying is his mentioning of interweaving "what I was told with what I read"; that is, he uses traditions carried over from "the elders of the nation" and merges it with what he himself had read. Hence, in Philo we find both oral and written traditions transmitted, stories and laws as well as expositions taught by others and fruits of Philo's own reading. Reading his works today demonstrates that he must have had access to a large library, possibly both private and public. Gregory E. Sterling has set forth an interesting hypothesis about Philo's scholarly activities: "that Philo had a private school in his home or personally owned

---

54. Consider the deliberations represented by, inter alia, these works: Klostergaard Petersen, "Rewritten Bible"; Zahn, "Talking About Rewritten Texts"; Zahn, "Genre and Rewritten Scripture"; Koskenniemi and Lindqvist, eds., *Rewritten Biblical Figures*; Laato, ed., *Rewritten Bible Reconsidered*; and esp. the quite recent work: Zsengellér, ed., *Rewritten Bible after Fifty Years*.

structure for advanced students which were similar to schools of higher education run by individuals throughout the Greco-Roman world."[55] Evidence for this is, certainly, circumstantial, as Sterling himself admits. But Sterling provides nevertheless several arguments of plausibility for this view. First, he points to the plausibility that Philo worked within an exegetical tradition, as his references to other exegetes, whether literalists or allegorists, seem to indicate. Second, Philo probably employed some types of sources (cf. *Mos.* 1:4); third, he was probably aware of other extant Diaspora-Jewish works (Aristobolus, Pseudo-Aristeas, Ezekiel the Tragedian); hence, he was working within a tradition that also continued after him. Philo certainly worked within a variety of traditions, including various ways of (re)using and applying the Scriptures.

Having said that, this does not mean that *De vita Mosis* as such is to be characterized as 'rewritten scripture.' *De vita Mosis* surely is a *biography* on Moses, as Philo himself states ("I purpose to write the life of Moses..."1:1).[56] But this work contains several sections that draw rather closely on biblical passages by ways of retelling and rephrasing, and thus can best be characterized as "rewritten scripture."[57] Hence, we proceed to have a closer look at Philo's Balaam narrative in *Mos.* 1:263–292.

Expository Uses of Balaam in *De vita Mosis*

Why did Philo spend so much space and so many comments on Balaam? For what expository reasons did he deal with his activities? Below I shall discuss three expository contexts that may have triggered Philo's expositions of the Balaam narrative. But first are some general observations regarding Philo's text.

---

55. Sterling, "School of the Sacred Laws," 150.

56. James R. Royse calls it "an encomiastic biography of the Jewish legislator." Royse, "Works of Philo," 34, but also as "an apologetic and historical work." See pp. 34, 47, 50–51. See also Borgen, "Philo of Alexandria," 235: "Thus the book was written to tell the Gentile readers about the supreme lawgiver whose laws they are to accept and honor. It was also to strengthen the Jews for their universal role." "Philo has added features which resemble a Greek *bios*, a biographical novel." See further on these issues Damgaard, *Recasting Moses*, 1–21; 49–87.

57. See for instance the following examples in the immediate context of his Balaam narrative: *Vita Mos* 1:250–254 draw on Num 21:1–2; *Vita Mos* 1:255–256 on Num 21:16–18; *Vita Mos* 1:258–262 on Num 21:20–25; *Vita Mos* 1:263–293 draw on Num 22–24 (Balaam narrative); *Vita Mos* 1:294–299 elaborates on Num 31:16; *Vita Mos* 1:300–304 on Num 25; and so forth.

It might be argued that one obvious reason for Philo to deal with Balaam, is the place he occupies in the biblical traditions (Num 22–24; 31:8, 16; Deut 23:5–6; Josh 13:22; 24:9, and Mic 6:5). However, why did Philo include him in *Vita Mosis*? It has been pointed out that Moses is not mentioned in *Mos* 1:263–299, although this section is one of the longest and most detailed in *De vita Mosis*;[58] but neither is Moses mentioned in Num 22–24. Another somewhat remarkable feature in Philo's text is that Balaam is not mentioned by name in *Mos.* 1:263–299, not even once.[59] Is that a kind of derogatory omission by Philo? The ways Philo presents and describes Balaam's sayings (that is, his blessings) are also somewhat enigmatic. Several scholars have argued that Balaam is described as a kind of counterfigure to Moses, but there are no explicit comparisons of Balaam with Moses or vice versa. However, Philo is probably not retelling the story of Balaam for no purpose; Philo's expositions and elaborations in the text indicate that he wants to use the figure of Balaam for some very specific expository purposes.

The Balaam Story as Criticism of Magicians

To Philo, the main story in the LXX dealing with magical divination seems to be the narrative about Balaam (Num 22–24). In the Hebrew Bible and in the LXX, Balaam is not explicitly described as a magician, and the picture we get of Balaam in Num 22–24 in the Hebrew Scriptures is mainly positive.

The presentation of Balaam in the works of Philo is complex. However, the complexity of Philo's view of Balaam comes into clearer light when we consider more closely the framework of Philo's expositions of Balaam's oracles in *Vita Mosis*, and when further works of Philo are drawn upon. Here Balaam is described much more as a magician, that is, as a magical diviner.[60]

First; in the framework sections of Philo's work, it is not only said concerning Balak that as "he shrank from a war of destruction waged freely and openly with arms, he had recourse to augury and soothsaying" (*Mos.*

---

58. Zsengellér, "Changes in the Balaam-Interpretation," 492.

59. Philo mentions Balaam by name, however, in several other texts; see *Cher.* 32–33; *Det.* 71; *Deus* 181; *Conf.* 64–66. 159; *Migr.* 113–115 and *Mut.* 202. Just as in *Mos.* 1:263–299, Balaam is mentioned but unnamed in *Conf.* 72 too.

60. Rösel, "Wie einer vom Propheten zum Verführer Wurde." I also draw here on Seland, "Philo, Magic and Balaam," 241–45.

1:263), but Balaam is presented as just such a diviner. He was one "who had learned the secrets of that art in every form" (τὰ μαντικῆς), "but was particularly admired for his high proficiency in augury" (οἰωνοσκοπίαν; *Mos.* 1:264). In the introductory text segments, Balaam's proficiency is further elaborated on: "the report of him was continually spreading and reaching to every part" (265). Throughout the narrative too, Balaam is repeatedly called a μάντις (*Mos.* 1:282, 283, 285), but also a μάγος (*Mos.* 1:276). In *Mos.* 1:277 he is said to be sent away by Balak "to seek good omens through birds and voices (ἐξέπεμπε τὸν μάντιν ἐπ' οἰωνοὺς καὶ φήμας αἰσίους). When he becomes possessed by "the truly prophetic spirit" (1:277) and utters the oracles from God to Balak, his own art of wizardry (ἔντεχνον μαντικὴν) being banished from his soul: "For the craft of the sorcerer (μαγικὴν σοφιστείαν) and the inspiration of the Holiest might not live together" (*Mos.* 1:277). Hence Balaam is here obviously considered a magician who for the moment is possessed by the truly prophetic spirit and forced to give prophetic utterances (*Migr.* 114). In *Mos.* 1:286 Philo says that Balaam "in his heart longed to curse, even if he were prevented from doing this with his voice." Then, after the third oracle, Balaam almost immediately proceeded to utter his own advice to Balak, namely, how to seduce the Israelites (*Mos.* 1:294-299); "Hereby he convicted himself of the utmost impiety" (*Mos.* 1:294). Philo here more than hints at the magical and malevolent aspects of Balaam's divinatory work (cf. *Mos.* 1:263).

Second; these elaborations on the magic nature of Balaam's profession are even more present in several of the other texts where Philo mentions Balaam (cf. *Cher.* 32-33; *Deus* 181; *Conf.* 159; *Migr.* 113-115, and *Mut.* 202-203). In *Deus* 181 he is described as one who followed "omens and false soothsayings" (οἰωνοῖς καὶ ψευδέσι μαντείαις; cf. Ezek 22:28), and he did evil things (ἀδικεῖν). Therefore he is an example of a creature of earth, not of heavenly growth. In *Conf.* 159, Balaam is described as a "dealer in auguries and prodigies and in the vanity of unfounded conjectures" (οἰωνόμαντιν καὶ τερατοσκόπον περὶ τὰς ἀβεβαίους εἰκασίας ματαιάζοντα), and it is emphasized that there is a natural hostility between conjecture and truth, between vanity and knowledge, and between the divination (μαντεία) which has no true inspiration, and sober wisdom. Philo here does not do away with divination as such, as that would disparage the Israelite prophets, but he disapproves of the means and nature of Balaam's divinations. In *Migr.* 113 Balaam is said to have been "adjudged impious and accursed even by the wise lawgiver" (i.e., Moses), because he became the 'mantis' of evil things. This evidently draws upon the fact that Balaam is identified as one who in fact did not want to bless but to curse Israel, and who at last gave Balak evil advice (*Migr.* 114; *Mut.* 200). In *Mut.* 202–203 Balaam is called an οἰωνοσκόπος, and because of his divination he "defaced the stamp of heaven-sent prophecy" (διότι σοφιστεία μαντικῇ τὴν θεοφόρητον προφητείαν παρεχάραξε).

This brief review demonstrates that Philo's picture of Balaam is highly complex. On the one hand, Philo has to cope with the biblical and related traditions about the great prophecies of Balaam. On the other hand, he cannot escape other traditions emphasizing the magical aspects of Balaam's activities. Philo solves this dilemma by retelling the prophetic oracles while portraying Balaam as so possessed by the prophetic spirit of God that he can do nothing but obey this inspiration (*Migr.* 114). Nevertheless, when released from this prophetic possession, Balaam is and remains for Philo a magical diviner. It is telling that some of the descriptive terms he uses as characterizations of Balaam are used almost exclusively in these texts, and in other texts indisputably dealing with magicians. Furthermore, several of the terms applied to Balaam belong to the pentateuchal law of Deut 18:10–11 that describes magical actions forbidden in Israel. Hence Balaam is to be considered not merely a diviner, but a magical diviner of the kind prohibited in Israel (Num 23:23; see *Mos.* 1:284). Given Philo's high view of prophecy, it comes as no surprise to discover the great focus in his texts on the issue of magical divination. The social life of Alexandria probably surfaces when Philo cautions and says: "Moses demands that one who is registered in the commonwealth of the laws (κατὰ τοὺς νόμους πολιτεία) should be perfect not in the lore, in which many are schooled, of divination and voices and plausible conjectures, but in his duties towards God" (*Spec.* 1:63; cf. 1:319). He seems to have been well acquainted with various forms of magical divination: he mentions divination by interpreting dreams (oneiromanteia), bird-watching (ornitomancy), examining sacrificial animals, and deciphering various other omens.[61] Hence I suggest that Philo's struggles with the Balaam figure, resulting in his emphasis on Balaam's magic (only vaguely presented in the Pentateuch) should be understood as part of Philo's struggle against the magical divination of his own times—that is, as part of his cultural criticism of Greco-Roman Alexandria.

61. Consult *Spec* 1:62: "such as birds and wings and their flight hither and thither through the air, and groveling reptiles which crawl out of their holes to seek their food; and again entrails and blood and corpses which deprived of life at once collapse and decompose."

The Balaam Story as a Criticism of the Sophists

In dealing with Balaam, Philo sometimes applies to him terms related to the sophistic movement before and probably of his own time.[62] In *Mos.* 1:277 he says about the seer that he became possessed, and the truly prophetic spirit fell upon him and thus banished from his soul the art of wizardry: "For the craft of the sorcerer (μαγικὴν σοφιτείαν) and the inspiration of the Holiest might not live together." The Loeb Classical Library translation of Philo hides the allusion to the sophists somewhat. Furthermore, looking outside Philo's retelling of Num 22–24, we find sophistic terminology used in two more passages dealing with Balaam. In *Mut.* 202–203 Philo states that "that dealer in augury Balaam" (τὸν οἰωνοσκόπον Βαλαάμ) "perished because with his soothsayer's mock wisdom he defaced the stamp of heaven-sent prophecy" (διότι σοφιστείᾳ μαντικῇ τὴν θεοφόρητον προφητείαν παρεχάραξε). Furthermore, in *Det.* 71, having dealt with Cain and Abel, Philo compares Cain to Balaam: "He was a sophist (ὁ σοφιστὴς Βαλαάμ), an empty conglomeration of incompatible and discordant notions." Important here is that Philo immediately continues by dealing with the sophists in terms of their activities (71–76). According to Bruce W. Winter, "There are . . . forty-two references to 'sophist' (σοφιστής) in Philo, apart from fifty-two references to cognates, and numerous comments on the sophistic movement. His evidence constitutes the single most important witness for the first half of the first century on the Greek side, and nothing comparable exists elsewhere for this period in the empire."[63]

Winter argues strongly that Philo was a critic of the sophistic movement of his times, and that he conducted his discussions "within a framework of OT characters and texts."[64] One of Philo's arguments against the sophists was that they were using their rhetorical skills to seduce their hearers with sophistic 'magic.' Hence many of Philo's invectives against the magicians of ancient Egypt were in reality arguments against the sophists of his own time. Accusations of magic were thus central to his arguments against the sophists. In this Philo could lean on Platonic

---

62. Three studies are especially relevant here: Winter, *Philo and Paul Among the Sophists*; van Kooten, "Balaam as the Sophist par Excellence"; and Koskenniemi, "Philo and the Sophists."

63. Winter, *Philo and Paul Among the Sophists*, 7. Concerning the statistics, see also Koskenniemi, "Philo and the Sophists," 261.

64. Winter, *Philo and Paul Among the Sophists*, 80; see esp. 80–94.

criticism.⁶⁵ In his summary of Philo's concern, Winter stresses that it is threefold: the sophists' use of *paideia* hindered the development of virtue both in teachers and in pupils; the sophists' rhetorical skills were not used to present the truth but to seduce the hearers with sophistic 'magic', and the sophists' involvement in *paideia* was often more motivated by money than by the welfare of the students.⁶⁶

Winter's study is important as he has here provided further and better evidence than was available before for the plausibility of a Sophistic movement at the time of Philo, and he has made it plausible too that Philo was an opponent of the sophistry of his time. Winter also emphasizes that Philo uses OT characters as examples and types for the sophist of his own time—that is, for the sophists his readers might know. For example, Philo described, Moses's opponents in Egypt, as well as Balaam, as sophists; they were also labeled magicians. The common aspect of their procedures, however, was their efforts to deceive their hearers, to lure their hearers into falsehoods and illusions. To Philo, both the sophists and the magicians were real social phenomena, and both groups were deceivers to be avoided and opposed.⁶⁷ Here his exposition of the Balaam of the Scriptures had some of its 'Sitz im Leben.'

George H. van Kooten takes his point of departure from Winter's study and elaborates on some of his views.⁶⁸ According to van Kooten, "By anachronistically attributing the term 'sophist' to past opponents of Israel, Philo rewrites the history of Israel in philosophical terms."⁶⁹ But not only that, but such a rewriting is due to his concerns about the contemporary movement known as the Second Sophistic. Hence, as Philo treats several OT figures as sophists, they "function . . . as a chiffre of the (perceived) attack of sophistry on Philo's Platonic philosophy, thus giving a concrete and realistic urgency to Philo's scholarly work."⁷⁰ Van Kooten then shows how Philo draws on the Scriptures in his arguments against the sophists; he describes several events in the Scriptures in light

---

65. See Winter, *Philo and Paul Among the Sophists*. Winter, on his side, is here heavily dependent upon the work of J. de Romilly, *Magic and Rhetoric in Ancient Greece*.

66. Winter, *Philo and Paul Among the Sophists*, 80–81.

67. Winter, *Philo and Paul Among the Sophists*, 89: "Magic, sophistry and illusion were treated by Philo as virtual synonyms."

68. Van Kooten, "Balaam as the Sophist par Exellence."

69. Van Kooten, "Balaam as the Sophist par Exellence," 131.

70. Van Kooten, "Balaam as the Sophist par Exellence," 133.

of contemporary sophistic procedures,[71] and suggests the sophistic threat reached its climax in the figure of Balaam. Van Kooten highlights the importance of the Balaam figure by suggesting that "this focus on Balaam the Sophist becomes more understandable if one realizes that Philo's invective against Balaam is part of his comprehensive program of refuting the sophists."[72]

That Philo saw the sophists as a feature of his own day is hardly to be doubted, according to van Kooten. Several expressions in Philo's works support such a view; Philo experiences them as a problem of his own day (see esp. *Her.* 304–306; *Contempl.* 31; *Agr.* 136, 143; *Congr.* 64; *Det.* 38–39): the road which leads to God, according to Philo, is "philosophy, not the philosophy which is pursued by the sophistic group of present-day people (ὁ νῦν ἀνθρώπων σοφιστικὸς ὅμιλος)," but what is called in the Law the utterance and word of God (*Post.* 101–102). The ὁ νῦν marks the problem as contemporary, as also his descriptions of their activities as something to be found everywhere indicate (*Agr.* 136). Hence both Winter and van Kooten underscore the expository context of Philo's exposition of the Balaam figure to be closely related to his arguments against the sophists, and hence his antisophistic reading of so many narratives in the Scriptures.

The consensus represented by these works of Winter and van Kooten has been challenged on two fronts: The Finnish scholar Erkki Koskenniemi has questioned two of the premises used by Winter and van Kooten by arguing that it is not at all certain that there was any movement in Philo's time called the Second Sophistic movement, and that Philo's use of the term 'sophist' or its derived terms, does not denote such real sophists.[73]

Koskenniemi argues that there are several methodological problems inherent in Winter's and van Kooten's methods. Firstly, he claims, the word σοφιστής has a long history, and these two scholars are not sufficiently thorough when dealing with the term philologically; secondly, the concept 'Second Sophistic' is not at all clear; and thirdly, 'sophistic' is a difficult term to use, not least because it often is merged with rhetoric,

---

71. Van Kooten suggests that sophistic arguments are to be found in Philo's expositions of the creation, of the serpent and Eve, of the story about Cain and Abel, of the story of Abraham versus the Chaldeans, of Hagar and Ishmael versus Sarah and Isaac, and of the account of Israel in Egypt—of Joseph versus the sophists in Egypt, of Moses versus the sophists, and of Israel in the wilderness, including Balaam. See van Kooten, "Balaam as the Sophist par Exellence," 145–53.

72. Van Kooten, "Balaam as the Sophist Par Exellence," 141.

73. Koskenniemi, "Philo and the Sophists."

though not all rhetoricians were 'sophists.' Hence it is not apparent what Philo is referring to when using terms like 'sophists.'[74]

Koskenniemi is probably right that the term σοφιστής κτλ can be used positively, and as such even in the Septuagint, without pointing to a certain movement. Philo uses the term mostly, if not always, negatively. But Koskenniemi argues that it can be used and is often used by Philo to mean a 'quibbler' or an 'opponent,' a figure without genuine contact with real sophists. Hence, it seems that Philo had no fixed sense for the term 'sophist': "However, he could also use it very seriously, rebuking people who knew much but rejected good ethics. These people were often able to excel with their rhetorical skills. In these instances, Philo continues an old debate more than referring to a certain movement that proudly called themselves 'sophists.'"[75]

When such strong disagreements are represented in scholarly studies focusing on the one and same historical phenomenon as that demonstrated above, it is most often an indication of the need for more research. This seems to be the case with the quest of the plausibility of a Sophistic movement at the time of Philo of Alexandria, and with Philo's possible relation to it. On the one hand it is hard to find 'hard' evidence for the presence of Sophists in Alexandria;[76] on the other hand, the use of σοφιστής κτλ in the works of Philo needs an explanation. He obviously not only projected them back into the biblical world and literature but also considered them a part of his own day and of his own world (see the νῦν in *Post.* 101). Furthermore, considering the many Philonic references to σοφιστής κτλ, and the various contexts they are used in, including the references to Balaam, we would still suggest that Philo's discussions of the Sophists remain one of the expository contexts of Philo's elaborations of the Balaam narrative.

The Role of Balaam Contra the Role of Moses as a Prophet

Some scholars argue that Philo's picture of Balaam is drawn in opposition to that of Moses; that is, by describing Balaam and his activities in

---

74. Note here the similar reservations aired in Sterling, "'Jewish Philosophy,'" 147, when he says that "it is not clear that Philo actually refers to a distinct tradition, but uses sophist as a category for any who place rhetoric over reason. Even if Winter is right, it only indicates that Philo opposed the group."

75. Koskenniemi, "Philo and the Sophists," 261–66, quote taken from p. 266.

76. See, e.g., Karadimas, "Alexandria and the Second Sophistic."

negative terms, Moses and his work was to be enhanced. Hence one more expository context and purpose of Philo's text is to show that Moses was the one who was great in prophecy, not Balaam.[77]

Balaam is never directly called a 'prophet' in *De vita Mosis*, but his activities are described in related or comparable terms. The primary word describing Balaam is μαντίς or cognate terms (1:264, 277, 282, 285).[78] Though he is not called a 'prophet', his activities are nevertheless described in terms associated with prophetic work: He "wanted to pose as a distinguished prophet" (1:266). Having arrived in the presence of Balak, and as Balaam is about for the first time "to inquire God what I should say," Philo states that Balaam "straightway became possessed, and there fell upon him the truly prophetic spirit (ἔνθους αὐτίκα γίνε αι, προφητικοῦ πνεύματος ἐπιφοιτήσαντος) which banished utterly from his soul his art of wizardry" (1:277). After he had spoken, the possession left him (ὁ δὲ τῆς κατοκωχῆς ἀνεθεὶς 1:281). Then, when Balak sent Balaam away "to seek good omens through birds or voices, . . . he was suddenly possessed, and, understanding nothing, his reason as it were roaming, uttered these prophetic words which were put into his mouth" (ἐξελάλει προφητεύων τάδε; 1:283).

In the Hebrew 'Vorlage' (Num 22–24) as well as in the Septuagintal translation, Balaam is described in positive ways and terms; this is, however, changed in Philo's version. Not only does he elaborate on Balaam's advice to Balak on how to seduce the Israelites (Num 31:16; cf. *Mos.* 1:294–299), but several other descriptions of him are not very flattering. When the emissaries of Balak arrive where Balaam is, asking him for help, Philo states that Balaam "actuated not by any honourable or sincere feelings, but rather by a wish to pose as a distinguished prophet whose custom was to do nothing without the sanction of an oracle, declined" to aid them (1:266). Then when the second group arrived from Balak, Balaam seems to have been flattered, and "enticed by those offers present and prospective, and in deference to the dignity of the ambassadors, he gave way, again dishonestly alleging a divine command" (1:268). The episode on the road with the donkey is also described in a way discrediting the integrity of Balaam: as Balaam did not see the angel, "the unreasoning animal showed a superior power of sight to him who claimed to see not

---

77. Note here esp. Feldman, *Philo's Portrayal of Moses*, 188-96; and the works of Remus and Zsengellér presented below.

78. Balaam is repeatedly called a μάντις (*Mos.* 1.282, 283, 285), but also a μάγος (*Mos.* 1.276). See above.

only the world but the world's Maker" (1:272). As Balaam is possessed, and presenting his prophetic sayings, Philo emphasizes several times that during these possessions, Balaam prophesies "as one repeating the words which another had put into his mouth" (1:277, cf. also 1:281, 283, 286). In the third case, Philo even—as a comment from aside—says that Balaam pressed forward more eagerly than his conductor Balak, "partly because he was dominated by the worst of vices, conceit, partly because in his heart he longed to curse, even if he was prevented from doing so with his voice" (1:286). Balaam's evil comes to a peak in Philo's descriptions elaborating on Num 31:16, when Balaam tells Balak how to seduce the Israelites: "Hereby he convicted himself of the utmost impiety" (ἀσέβημα κατηγορῶν αὑτοῦ μέγιστον). Hence, at the end, it seems that Philo considers Balaam one who indeed wanted to curse and destroy the Israelites.

As mentioned above, some scholars suggest that Philo's version of Balaam in *De vita Mosis* 1:263–299 is to be read as an effort to present Balaam in a derogatory way, and especially as a lesser prophet than Moses. His biography of Moses, according to Harold Remus, and in particular the section about Balaam, "serves to rescue Moses from possible misunderstandings of Moses as a mere thaumaturge or as a magician, a reputation attested in a variety of sources."[79] Remus is able to point to several sources documenting an ambivalent attitude from pagans toward both Judaism and Moses. In not a few places, Moses is described as a thaumaturge and magician.[80] That Philo, a resident of a cosmopolitan city, would have been acquainted with such traditions about Moses, is suggested by various passages in his writings.[81] Hence, still according to Remus, "Philo's detailed portrait of Balaam as a counterfeit prophet offers a foil to Moses, the true prophet, and thus would serve to distance Moses from Balaam-like figures in Philo's own time and place to whom his readers, Jewish or pagan, might be attracted."[82] Philo's exposition of Balaam is thus not only to save the Moses of the past from charges of magic, but also to help his readers to identify present-day Balaams still practicing their 'art' in the streets and marketplaces of Alexandria.

---

79. Remus, "Moses and the Thaumaturges"; here quoted from the summary given on page 665.

80. Remus, "Moses and the Thaumaturges," 666–68. See also Gager, *Moses in Greco-Roman Paganism*, 134–61.

81. Remus, "Moses and the Thaumaturges," 668.

82. Remus, "Moses and the Thaumaturges," 666.

Louis H. Feldman, in his massive book *Philo's Portrayal of Moses*, also argues that the fact that Balaam had a great reputation as a prophet meant that Philo had to show that Moses was superior in prophecy.[83] That Balaam was important to Philo can be deduced from the great amount of space he is given in Philo's narrative (*Mos.* 1:263–299, in addition to several other brief references, cf. above). Furthermore, Philo considers Moses the greatest of the prophets, and as both Moses and Balaam were known among the pagans, Philo had to confirm Moses's greatness.

Philo does not mention the figure of Balaam by name in *De vita Mosis*, but in several texts he stresses that Balaam's name means empty.[84] In his introduction to the Balaam story, Philo describes an unnamed great prophet (*Mos.* 1:264–265):

> Now, there was at that time a man living in Mesopotamia far-famed as a soothsayer, who had learned the secrets of that art in its every form, but was particularly admired for his high proficiency in augury, so great and incredible were the things which he had revealed to many persons and on many occasions. To some he had foretold rainstorms in summer, to others drought and great heat in mid-winter, to some barrenness to follow fertility, or again plenty to follow dearth, to some rivers full or empty, ways of dealing with pestilences, and other things without number. In every one of these, his reputation for prediction made his name well known and was advancing him to great fame, since the report of him was continually spreading and reaching to every part.

Feldman suggests that Philo knew some oral traditions according to which Balaam was held to be a great prophet. Furthermore, the fact that Balaam is mentioned in an inscription discovered in 1967 indicates that Balaam was well known also among non-Israelites.[85] Hence Philo had to distinguish between Moses and Balaam. One way he was able to do this was by calling Moses a προφήτης, while Balaam is called a μάντις.

---

83. Feldman, *Philo's Portrayal of Moses*, 188–96. Here Feldman is also able to draw on some of his earlier articles, see esp. Feldman, "Philo's Version of Balaam."

84. See Colson et al., eds. and trans., *Philo* (LCL) 10:291: Balaam, foolish or vain (μάταιος) people (*Cher.* 32, *Conf.* 159; *Migr.* 113), a sophist, an empty (μάταιος) conglomeration of incompatible and discordant notions (*Det.* 71), a dealer in auguries and prodigies and in the vanity of unfounded conjecture (*Deus* 181; *Conf.* 159; *Mut.* 202), dwells in Mid-River Land, for his understanding is submerged (*Conf.* 66); he is no heavenly growth, but a creature of earth (181).

85. See Hoftizer and van der Kooij, eds., *Balaam Text from Deir 'Alla Re-Evaluated*; Puech, "Bala'am and Deir 'Alla."

Balaam could speak only what God put in his mouth, while Moses was the mediator between Israel and God, serving both as God's spokesperson to the Israelites and Israel's spokesman to God.[86] In sum then, according to Feldman, Philo devotes much space to the Balaam narrative in *De vita Mosis* because he felt that he had to demonstrate that Moses was superior in prophecy even to Balaam. However, Feldman notes the fact that Balaam had little to do with Moses, and Balaam is not mentioned by name in *Mos.* 2:263–299.

József Zsengellér for his part acknowledges that Moses is not mentioned in the Balaam narrative, but he nevertheless argues that "the description of Balaam's character becomes the counterpart of Moses' characterization that appears in other passages in Philo's work."[87] However, Moses is not so much here the hero to be defended. But why Balaam? It is in answering this question that Zsengellér tries to contribute new insight into the Balaam enigma. Philo could escape neither the Balaam narrative in Num 22–24, nor the other traditions of the Bible, nor other texts and traditions fashionable in his day. In his descriptions, as Philo merges positive and negative biblical traditions, the prophetic oratory emerges clearly, conformed to Philo's purposes. According to Zsengellér, Balaam's prophecies play an important role. They are to be read as a mixture of biblical thought and Philo's own message. Here Jewish ethics is given an account; Jewish monotheism is introduced to readers (1:284); in the future a Jewish 'man' is to appear, becoming the ruler of many nations; and by expanding on the evil counsel of Balaam Philo gives a warning to Greek-speaking Jews of his own time. Zsengellér summarizes this as follows:

> In contrast to the previous writings the reason for including Philo's Balaam-story in *De vita Mosis* is not its messianic prophecy but the figure of Balaam itself. For Philo the figure of the pagan fortune-teller appears to be useful in three different ways. First, as a kind of anti-Moses he presents an excellent contrast to the main hero of the exodus-narrative. Second, declaring his faith as a non-Israelite he is just the right person to interpret for the Gentiles the notion of Israel as the chosen people. Finally, Balaam the ungodly man is a deterring example and the symbol of uselessness for people arising against God and Israel.[88]

---

86. Feldman, *Philo's Portrayal of Moses*, 191.
87. Zsengellér, "Changes in the Balaam-Interpretation," 492.
88. Zsengellér, "Changes in the Balaam-Interpretation," 496.

C. T. R. Hayward, on the other hand, has argued that Philo portrays Balaam's oracles as prophecy of the highest order, and Balaam as a remarkable prophet indeed.[89] Hayward argues his view by pointing to the fact that Philo reduces Balaam's oracles from four to three, which to Philo is a figure of completeness.[90] Furthermore, he finds that Philo emphasizes the issue of sight in his descriptions of Balaam. Balaam is described as "the one who saw in sleep a clear presentation of God with the unsleeping eyes of the soul" (*Mos.* 1:289): "Something extraordinary has happened. By so speaking of Balaam, Philo has invested him with the character of Israel, whose name at first was Jacob."[91] Balaam is thus made into a mouthpiece of Jacob-Israel. In doing this, Philo drew upon Jewish traditions later to be codified in the Targums.[92] Furthermore, according to Hayward, that Balaam was to be considered a prophet is also emphasized by describing his divinations as *prophecies*: the first oracle is described as uttered by one possessed by the prophetic spirit (προφετικοῦ πνεύματος ἐπιφοιτήσαντος; *Mos.* 1:277); in the second he was 'prophesying' (προφητεύων; *Mos.* 1:283), and in the third he spoke inspired by God (ἔνθους γενόμενος; *Mos.* 1:288). The LXX does not use such terms when describing Balaam, but both Philo and the Targums do.

The Balaam narrative of *De vita Mosis* 1:263–299 is highly complex, comprising Philo's fashionable traditions and interpretations, intertwined in the Septuagintal text: "for I always interwove what I was told with what I read" (*Mos.* 1:4). Hence it is no wonder that the interpretations of the Balaam narrative and its importance are highly complicated too.

What is Philo's purpose in using this enigmatic story from Num 22–24? The scholars mentioned in this last section all focus—in one way or another—on the relationships of Balaam to Moses in Philo. We turn to them because, after all, the Balaam discussion at issue is given in a biography of Moses. Is a picture of Moses as the greatest prophet the one that is to be defended? Is Philo's picture of Balaam drawn in opposition to that of Moses; that is, by describing Balaam and his activities in negative terms are Moses and his work to be enhanced? In the following we shall present two issues that make this view problematic, and both are issues that are not satisfactorily dealt with in the studies presented above.

---

89. Hayward, "Balaam's Prophecies as interpreted," 19–36.
90. Hayward, "Balaam's Prophecies as interpreted," 20.
91. Hayward, "Balaam's Prophecies as interpreted," 22.
92. See on this also Vermes, "Story of Balaam."

First: Balaam Contra Moses. Major obstacles to the view that Balaam as a prophet is set in opposition to Moses as a prophet include that on the one hand Balaam is not mentioned by name in *Mos.* 1:263-299; and that on the other hand Moses is not within the horizon of that section either. *Mos.* 1 does not deal with Moses as a prophet but presents Moses as a king (cf. 1:334). First at the end of *Mos.* 2 Philo is dealing with Moses's prophetic office (2:187-287). Hence it would not be easy for readers to discover what relationship they were to see between Balaam and Moses as they are working their way through *Mos.* 1. It is telling that when scholars try to posit Balaam as a counterprophet to Moses, they have to use texts from several of Philo's other writings to establish their case. It cannot be established from *De vita Mosis* alone. One must admit, however, that if Philo's presentation of Balaam as a prophet differed widely—in a negative way—from his presentation of the other prophets inhabiting the Scriptures, including Moses, then this view of Balaam contra Moses had some plausibility. But is that the case?

Second: Balaam's prophetic inspiration compared with those of other prophets. Balaam's prophetic inspiration is several times described as being characterized by Balaam not quite knowing what he is saying—that is, his mouth utters what he is prompted to say. The first statement is given by the angel who stops the donkey. Philo describes it thus (*Mos.* 1:274, cf. 1:281):

> I shall prompt the needful words without your mind's consent, and direct your organs of speech as justice and convenience require. I shall guide the reins of speech, and, though you understand it not, employ your tongue for each prophetic utterance.

And then, as Balaam is to prophesy for the first time (*Mos.* 1:277):

> He advanced outside, and straightway became possessed, and there fell upon him the truly prophetic spirit (ἔνθους αὐτίκα γίνεται, προφητικοῦ πνεύματος ἐπιφοιτήσαντος) which banished utterly from his soul his art of wizardry. For the craft of the sorcerer and the inspiration of the Holiest (ἱερωτάτῃ κατοκωχῇ) might not live together.

Then, as Balaam is to prophesy the second time (1:283) Philo writes thus:

> In this solitude, he was suddenly possessed, and, understanding nothing, (ὁ δὲ μονωθεὶς ἐξαίφνης θεοφορεῖται καὶ μηδὲν συνιείς) his reason as it were roaming, uttered these prophetic words which were put into his mouth . . . .

As these are descriptions of Balaam's prophetic inspiration, it is important to compare them with those describing the other prophets of Israel, and Moses. How does Philo describe these? Two passages are especially relevant here: *Spec.* 1:65 and 4:49. In the first passage, Philo presents his exposition of Deut 18:15 and 18, about the great Prophet that is to appear, including a characterization of his prophetic inspiration as well as of prophets in general. The other is from Philo's description of prophetic inspiration in contrast to magical divination, which is a counterfeit of divine prophetic inspiration:

> A prophet possessed by God will suddenly appear and give prophetic oracles. Nothing what he says will be his own, for he that is truly under the control of divine inspiration has no power of apprehension when he speaks but serves as the channel for the insistent words of another's prompting. For prophets are the interpreters of God (ἑρμηνεῖς γάρ εἰσιν οἱ προφῆται θεοῦ), who makes full use of their organs of speech to set forth what he wills. (*Spec.* 1:65)

Feldman[93] notes that Philo does not say that the prophet will be like Moses, and the statement that he will suddenly appear is not in the Deuteronomic passage (18:15, 18). The important part in our context here, however, is his description of prophetic inspiration compared to that of Balaam above. The next passage (*Spec.* 4:49) runs thus:

> For no pronouncement of a prophet is ever his own; he is an interpreter prompted by Another in all his utterances (ἀλλ' ἔστιν ἑρμημεὺς ὑποβάλλοντος ἑτέρου πάνθ' ὅσα προφέρεται), when knowing not what he does he is filled with inspiration, as the reason withdraws and surrenders the citadel of the soul to a new visitor and tenant, the Divine Spirit which plays upon the vocal organism and dictates words which clearly express its prophetic message.

The similarities between these descriptions and those concerning Balaam are overwhelming, and the conclusion seems unavoidable: Balaam's prophetic inspirations are described in exactly the same ways as those of the Israelite prophets. Hence Balaam's prophetic inspirations and his role as a prophet are not different from those of the other prophets in Hebrew Scripture. Balaam is taken over by the spirit of God, he utters what the spirit/God prompts him to say, his own will being set aside;

---

93. Feldman, *Philo's Portrayal of Moses*, 308.

both Balaam and the Israelite prophets are spokespersons and interpreters (ἑρμηνεῖς) of God.[94]

If we then consider Philo's exposition of Moses as a prophet in *Mos.* 2:187–287, we will get the same picture. Philo here distinguishes between three different ways God speaks to Moses: one is represented by the divine utterances spoken by God in his own person (*Mos.* 2:188); another is represented by or comes through questions and answers (*Mos.* 2:188, 191–245), and the third is characterized by Moses speaking in his own person, "when possessed by God and carried away out of himself" (τὰ δ᾽ ἐκ προσώπου Μωυσέως ἐπιθειάσαντος καὶ ἐξ αὐτοῦ κατασχεθέντος; *Mos.* 2:188c, cf. 246–287; *Her.* 263). The latter is described in similar, partly identical terms, to those used in *Mos.* 1:263–299 to describe the prophecies of Balaam. Moses has been given of "God's power of foreknowledge and by this he will reveal future events" (2:190; compare the blessings of Balaam). Furthermore, Moses is "under divine inspiration" (2:246, 258, 263, 270).

This is not to argue that Philo did not consider Moses to be a special prophet; he did stand in a special and rather unique relationship to God,[95] but his prophetic inspiration was comparable to that of Balaam and vice versa. However, David Winston and John R. Levison have argued that while the prophets, Abraham, and Balaam experience "possession trances in which they become passive, ... Moses' ecstasy is a milder form which leads him to receive impressions of the future without a complete displacement of his rational faculties."[96] Nevertheless, this thesis is hard to substantiate from Philo's descriptions of Moses. Levison here draws on Philo's four examples of Moses's ecstatic inspiration as narrated in *Mos.* 2:246–287. In these four narratives, Levison finds a pattern that includes Moses's emotional response to a situation; his experience of possession; and his subsequent oracular utterance.[97] Hence Levison argues that Moses here does not experience an intrusion or a displacement of reason in the way that we find in Philo's descriptions of other prophets (*Spec.* 1:65; 4.49) and Balaam (*Mos.* 1:277, 283). Levison, however, is here drawing a very fine distinction between these

---

94. For an older exposition of Philo's views on prophecy in his Greek and Jewish context, see Wolfson, *Philo*, 2:24–36.

95. Especially emphasized in Feldman, *Philo's Portrayal of Moses*, 297.

96. Winston, "Two Types of Mosaic Prophecy"; Levison, "Two Types of Ecstatic Prophecy," here quoted from the latter, p. 83.

97. Levison, "Two Types of Ecstatic Prophecy," 84.

descriptions, which, I think is not convincing in light of Philo's expressions in *Mos* 2:188, where Philo describes the third kind of prophecy Moses experiences—utterances "spoken by Moses in his own person, when possessed and carried away out of himself" (τὰ δ' ἐκ προσώπου Μωυσέως ἐπιθεισάντος καὶ ἐξ αὐτοῦ κατεσχεθέντος, see also *Mos.* 2:246: Τὰ κατ' ἐνθουσιασμὸν τοῦ προφήτου κατωχῆς). However, the cases Philo uses to illustrate this kind of inspiration are clearly different from those in which Balaam was involved. Hence though Moses stood in a unique relationship with God, this uniqueness is never presented in opposition to the particularity of God's relationship with Balaam or with the other prophets, nor is Balaam's inspiration set in opposition to that of the Israelite prophets, Moses included.

It is thus hard to establish that a part of Philo's expository context was to establish the superiority of Moses vis-a-vis Balaam or his prophecies. Balaam's prophecies were genuine and God-inspired, but as it turned out, Balaam himself was a charlatan and a specialist in augury. He was, however used by God, by getting a temporary share in the same kind of prophetic inspiration as the Israelite prophets.

CONCLUSIONS

In the introductory sections of this chapter, it was noted that the distinction between 'magic' and 'religion' is not always easily maintained when examining texts from the time of, for example, Philo of Alexandria. On one hand, we observed that some professions and practitioners at that time considered themselves distinct from the official cults of the gods. Furthermore, it could be argued that magical procedures were considered legitimate in certain religious contexts. Hence, a rigid distinction between magic and religion might be problematic in some cases. However, in other cases, it could at least be heuristically valuable if applied with caution.

In analyzing the works of Philo, it is evident that he considered magic incompatible with 'true religion,' specifically with his Judaism. Magic facilitated impiety (ἀσεβεία; *Spec.* 1:61). Whether he regarded it as an inherent component of other 'religions' in his Alexandrian social context is probable, albeit difficult to ascertain due to the absence of direct statements on this matter. According to Philo, magical divination constitutes a transgression of both the first and ninth commandments of the Decalogue (*Spec.* 1:59–63; 4:48), and as such represents "corruption of art, a counterfeit of the divine and prophetic possession" (*Spec.* 4:48). Consequently, with respect to his own form of religion, magic is prohibited in the Torah, which serves as the constitution of his Judaism. For individuals aspiring to be Torah-observing Jews, magic should not be considered a viable option. Accordingly, his expositions can be interpreted as demonstrating that magic was a characteristic not only of the opponents of Moses in Egypt and of the non-Jewish Balaam, but also of the non-Jewish milieu surrounding the Jews in Alexandria.

Philo's *De vita Mosis* is a biographical work in which, primarily based on Exodus, Leviticus, and Numbers, he portrays Moses as a king, lawgiver, high priest, and prophet. The first volume is biographical and chronologically structured, while the second is more topical. Certain sections in this two-volume work are revised "editions" of biblical texts, representing what may be termed 'rewritten scripture.' The narrative concerning Balaam of Num 22–24, retold in *Mos.* 1:263–299, exemplifies such a rewritten account.

In Philo's rewriting of the Balaam narrative, we meet a person quite different from the one in Num 22–24; while the main story line of the biblical narrative is retained, the identity of Balaam is changed as he turns out to be more of a magician and more eager to curse the Israelites.

Philo's writings did not emerge in isolation; they were situated within a specific social and literary context. This study has examined the expository context of his interpretation of the Balaam figure, seeking to elucidate the rationale behind his particular portrayal of Balaam.

Scholars have proposed three expository contexts and purposes: Balaam as a practitioner of divination (a magical diviner), Balaam as a 'sophist,' or Balaam as a prophet to be interpreted as a counterfeit prophet in contrast to Moses, the authentic great prophet.

However, Philo's description of Balaam's prophetic inspirations is phrased in much the same ways as he describes the inspirations of the Israelite prophets, Moses included. Hence, it is not plausible that Balaam is to be read as a magical background figure in order to enhance the status of Moses.

Although the prophecies of Balaam are presented as divinely inspired, the portrayal of Balaam beyond his prophetic activities is predominantly negative.

Characterizing Balaam as a magical diviner and a 'sophist,' Philo utilizes his expositions of Balaam as a cautionary message to his contemporary readers, urging them to maintain their Jewish identity within the pluralistic and colonial environment of Alexandria.

Epilogue

IN THE *PROLOGUE* TO the present volume, I stated that "this volume represents an experimental approach in multiple respects."[1] Furthermore, I admitted that the application of postcolonial categories, models, and perspectives to the study of Philo of Alexandria may elicit skepticism from certain readers who might say: "Is Philo not considered one of the most assimilated Jews of the Diaspora? Is he not to be regarded as the first-century Jew most influenced by Greco-Roman philosophies, an eclectic thinker significantly shaped by philosophical currents such as Platonism, Stoicism, and Epicurean philosophy, to name the most prominent?"

However, considering Philo primarily as a philosopher is one-sided. In a recent collection of studies on *The Reception of Philo of Alexandria*, he is characterized as "a Jewish statesman, philosopher, and religious thinker."[2] In another context, I have characterized him as "a Jewish scholar, philosopher, politician, and author."[3] Anyway, he is indeed a philosopher, and significantly so. However, this aspect of his personality and work has not been emphasized in the preceding pages. I have chosen to focus on his political life and work, primarily because politics constituted a central component of the later years of his life (while simultaneously acknowledging that one should likely never disregard Philo as a philosopher). Nevertheless, despite the potential of being considered one-sided, I have chosen to concentrate on Philo the politician.

1. P. vii.
2. Friesen et al., eds., *Reception of Philo of Alexandria*, description given on the back cover.
3. Seland, *Why Study Philo?*, 158.

Three scholars and their work have been in my mind and have partly functioned as conversation partners during my writing on Philo as a politician. First, the person most of my co-scholars will associate with a focus on Philo as a politician is probably Erwin R. Goodenough (1893–1965). To him, Philo became an ardent opponent of the Romans; "he loved the Romans no more than the skipper of a tiny boat loves the hurricane" is one of his poignant characterizations.[4] Although Goodenough's work may be considered outdated, it nevertheless contains numerous observations that warrant further consideration. Consequently, Goodenough's work has received somewhat disproportionate attention in the preceding chapters.

The second scholar who has influenced my inquiries concerning Philo as a political figure is my former mentor, the Norwegian scholar Peder J. Borgen (1928–2023). Several decades ago, he posited that Philo was "a conqueror, on the verge of being conquered." Borgen elucidated this perspective by asserting that Philo was not interested in a synthesis of Judaism and Hellenism, nor in transforming Judaism based on Hellenistic religion. Philo's intention was "to conquer the surrounding culture ideologically by claiming that whatever good there is has its source in Scripture and thus belonged to the Jewish nation and its heritage."[5] Borgen also considered Philo to be representative of the progressive Jews who infiltrated the gymnasium, as reflected in the letter of Emperor Claudius to the Alexandrians in the 40s CE. Furthermore, he provided the following observations in support of his view: Philo believed that ideas found in Hellenistic philosophy of Platonic, Pythagorean, and Stoic nature were already present in the writings of Moses; this is evident in several statements by Philo. Borgen also finds his perspective supported by Philo's distinction between Jews as the people chosen by God and other peoples. Borgen's interpretation has received favorable responses from some scholars but remains subject to further refinement.

The third scholar has not been examined to the same extent above as the two aforementioned persons. Nevertheless, she is a highly esteemed scholar known for her numerous significant publications: Maren R. Niehoff. Her research primarily focuses on Philo's philosophy; however, it would have been beneficial to see a more extensive exploration of her perspective on Philo as a political figure, particularly in her biographical work on Philo. While her work is impressive, her assertion that Philo

---

4. Goodenough, *Politics*, 7.
5. Borgen, "Philo of Alexandria," 151.

became more Romanized during his years in Rome is not entirely convincing to me. Rather, it appears that Philo's experiences with Roman authorities during his time in Rome had a profound impact, leading to diminished admiration for Rome thereafter.

The first part of the present volume dealt with the methodology and perspectives to be applied, as well as with a presentation and discussion of central issues and events involving the Jews and Roman authorities. I will not repeat my procedures and results from these chapters here, but they present and thus represent my views of the social world of Philo and his life, attitudes, and actions in that world. The most novel aspect of my methodology is my emphasis on the Roman Empire as a colonizing power, and my efforts to adopt and apply perspectives represented by the postcolonial concepts of *mimicry* and *hybridity*. However, these chapters also represent, of course, my view of Roman politics at the time, how Philo was involved in it, how it shaped his life, and what roles we may say mimicry and hybridity played in Philo's expositions, and thus in our understanding of his view of the Romans.

In the second chapter, I first examined the key aspects of the Roman Empire in Alexandria. Subsequently, I briefly discussed certain issues pertaining to Philo's social position in Alexandria, addressing topics such as his familial background and status, education, and function(s) in his society.

Then, in the third chapter, my focus was on the genres, dates, and intended readers of Philo's writings, and relevant reading strategies. This was followed (in Chapter 4) by a treatment of Philo as a politician, especially focusing on his views of and attitudes toward the Roman Empire, and possible developments in that view; this chapter took a closer look at texts dealing with Jews and Roman authorities.

Part 2, then, is constructed to represent four test cases regarding the view on Philo and politics set forth in chapters 1–4. Three of these studies were previously published but have been adapted here to fit into the main focus of this volume. The first one deals primarily with Philo's use of the terms 'metropolis,' 'apoikia' and 'diaspora,' asking how a Jew like Philo evaluated the diaspora situation. Was it considered a favorable living condition? Was it perceived as a temporary circumstance with the expectation of returning to Eretz Israel? Was it regarded as a calamity? Was it even interpreted as a form of punishment? If we here read Philo as writing back from the Empire, we see a Philo who mimics the Roman Empire in his descriptions of the Jewish settlements by calling them ἀποικίαι and describing Jerusalem as their μητρόπολις. Mimicry does not focus on complete identity but on similarities. Therefore, assertions that Philo's use of terms such as ἀποίκια and μητρόπολις is anachronistic or disconnected from the historical context of his era are inaccurate. He used both ἀποίκια and μητρόπολις because he wrote in Greek, the lingua franca of the period, and because he employed an intentionally mimetic approach. Moreover, because mimicry does not imply complete equivalence, the outcome frequently manifests as hybridity. When interpreted in the context of Roman colonization activities during Philo's time, Philo's portrayal of Jewish settlements as colonizing endeavors may indeed have appeared as a hybrid description to a Roman reader.

The next three studies dealt with some 'social institutions' of Philo's world: his view of the mysteries, by some also called mystery cults; then, Philo's view of and attitudes toward the clubs and associations of Alexandria; and finally, Philo's views of magic as part of his cultural criticism. In the first of these three, the one concerning the mysteries, it is concluded that as a politician, Philo negotiated across several Greek and Roman cultural issues and aspects. Furthermore, considering that Philo was a Jew living in the Diaspora, having Jerusalem as his mother city (*Flacc.* 46; *Legat.* 281), I suggested that the phenomenon of mimicry and hybridity is illuminating when trying to understand Philo's reactions to and attitudes toward some of the non-Jewish cultural expressions and institutions in Alexandria. Here also belong several of his statements that apply the terminology of the mysteries and those that characterize his views of and attitudes toward the Greco-Roman clubs and associations in Alexandria.

The phenomenon of magic in Alexandria represents a distinct subject; consequently, the final study in this collection, which examines "Philo's views of magic as cultural criticism," diverges somewhat from the preceding analyses, but is still a study of cultural criticism. Upon examination of Philo's works, it becomes evident that he regarded magic as incompatible with true religion, specifically with his Judaism. Magic was considered to facilitate impiety (ἀσεβεία; *Spec.* 1:61). According to Philo, magical divination constitutes a violation of both the first and the ninth commandments of the Decalogue (*Spec.* 1:59–63) and was consequently regarded as a "corruption of art, a counterfeit of the divine and prophetic possession" (*Spec.* 4:48). Mimicry and hybridity are close at hand here. Furthermore, concerning his own religious tradition, magic is prohibited in the Torah, which serves as the foundational text of Judaism. Engaging in magical practices is not considered permissible for individuals striving to adhere to the Torah observance. Consequently, Philo's expositions can be interpreted as demonstrating that magic was a characteristic of not only Moses's adversaries in Egypt and of the non-Jewish figure Balaam, but also of the non-Jewish communities surrounding the Jews in Alexandria. Whether magical practices were also prevalent in Alexandria's Jewish sectors during his time remains a separate inquiry. Nevertheless, considering other sources documenting magical activities within Jewish circles, it may be posited that this phenomenon was more familiar to his readership than he ever acknowledged.

Philo of Alexandria was a Jewish scholar, philosopher, politician, and author. However, I am not ready to, or even able to, determine in what field he was greatest. What I do think, however, is that none of these functions or abilities of his should be played out against the others. That is, I think, one of the reasons why he still fascinates his readers.

Bibliography

Adams, Sean A. *Greek Genres and Jewish Authors: Negotiating Literary Culture in the Greco-Roman Era*. Waco, TX: Baylor University Press, 2020.
Alon, Gedalyahu. "On Philo's Halakha." In *The Jews, Judaism and the Classical World*, 89–132. Translated by Israel Abraham. Jerusalem: Magnes, 1977.
Amir, Yehoshua. *Die hellenistische Gestalt des Judentums bei Philon von Alexandria*. Forschungen zum jüdish-christlichen Dialog 5. Neukirchen-Vluyn: Neukirchener, 1983.
Ando, Clifford. "The Administration of the Provinces." In *A Companion to the Roman Empire*, edited by David S. Potter, 177–92. Blackwell Companions to the Ancient World. Ancient History. Malden, MA: Blackwell, 2006.
Applebaum, Shimon. "The Social and Economic Status of the Jews in the Diaspora." In *The Jewish People in the First Century: Historical Geography, Political History, Social, Cultural and Religious Life and Institutions*, edited by S. Safrai and M. Stern, 1:701–27. 2 vols. Compendia Rerum Iudaicarum ad Novum Testamentum, sec. 1, vol. 2. 1974. Reprint, Philadelphia: Fortress, 1988.
Arnaoutoglou, Ilias N. "Collegia in the Province of Egypt in the First Century AD." *Ancient Society* 35 (2005) 197–216.
Ascough, Richard S., ed. *Christ Groups & Associations: Foundational Essays*. Waco, TX: Baylor University Press, 2022.
———. *Early Christ Groups and Greco-Roman Associations: Organizational Models and Social Practices*. Eugene, OR.: Cascade Books, 2022.
———. *Paul's Macedonian Associations: The Social Context of Philippians and 1 Thessalonians*. Wissenschaftliche Untersuchungen zum Neuen Testament 2/161. Tübingen: Mohr Siebeck, 2003.
———. *What Are They Saying About the Formation of Pauline Churches?* New York: Paulist, 1998.
Ascough, Richard S., et al., eds. *Associations in the Greco-Roman World: A Sourcebook*. Waco, TX: Baylor University Press, 2012.
Ashcroft, Bill, et al., *The Empire Writes Back: Theory and Practice in Post-Colonial Literatures*. London: Routledge, 2002.
———. *Post-Colonial Studies: The Key Concepts*. 2nd ed. Routledge Key Guides. London: Routledge, 2007.

Assmann, Jan. "Magic and Theology in Ancient Egypt." In *Envisioning Magic: A Princeton Seminar and Symposium*, edited by Peter Schäfer and Hans G. Kippenberg, 1–18. Studies in the History of Religions 75. Leiden: Brill, 1997.

Atkinson, John. "Ethnic Cleansing in Roman Alexandria in 38 CE." *Acta Classica* 49 (2006) 31–54.

Aune, David E. "Magic in Early Christianity." In *Apocalypticism, Prophecy, and Magic in Early Christianity: Collected Essays*, 368–420. Grand Rapids: Baker Academic, 2008.

———. "Magic in Early Christianity." In *Aufstieg und Niedergang der Römischen Welt II. 23,3 Religion*, edited by Hildegard Temporini and Wolfgang Haase, 1507–57. Berlin: de Gruyter, 1980.

———. *Prophecy in Early Christianity and the Ancient Mediterranean World*. Grand Rapids: Eerdmans, 1983.

Barclay, John M. G. "The Empire Writes Back: Josephan Rhetoric in Flavian Rome." In *Flavius Josephus and Flavian Rome*, edited by Jonathan Edmondson et al., 315–32. Oxford: Oxford University Press, 2005.

———. "The Empire Writes Back: Josephan Rhetoric in Flavian Rome." In *Pauline Churches and Diaspora Jews*, 301–16. Wissenschaftliche Untersuchungen zum Neuen Testament 275. Tübingen: Mohr Siebeck, 2011.

———. *Jews in the Mediterranean Diaspora: From Alexander to Trajan (323 BCE—117 CE)*. Edinburgh: T. & T. Clark, 1996.

———. "Why the Roman Empire Was Insignificant to Paul." In *Pauline Churches and Diaspora Jews*, 363–87. Wissenschaftliche Untersuchungen zum Neuen Testament 275. Tübingen: Mohr Siebeck, 2011.

Bardtke, Hans. "Der Gegenwärtige Stand der Erforschung der in Palästina neu gefundenen hebräischen Handschriften 44: Die Rechtsstellung der Qumran-Gemeinde." *Theologische Literaturzeitung* 86 (1961) 94–103.

Barnett, P. W. "The Jewish Sign Prophets—A.D. 40–70: Their Intentions and Origin." *New Testament Studies* (1980/81) 679–97.

Barraclough, Ray. "Philo's Politics: Roman Rule and Hellenistic Judaism." In *Aufstieg und Niedergang der römischen Welt II 21,1: Geschichte und Kultur Roms im Spiegel der neueren Forschung. 2, Principat. Religion: (Hellenistisches Judentum in römischer Zeit: Philon und Josephus)*, edited by Hildegard Temporini and Wolfgang Haase, 417–553. Berlin: de Gruyter, 1984.

Barré, Michael L. "The Portrait of Balaam in Numbers 22–24." *Interpretation* 51 (1997) 254–66.

Barton, Stephen, and G. H. R. Horsley. "A Hellenistic Cult Group and the New Testament Churches." *Jahrbuch für Antike und Christentum* 24 (1981) 7–41.

Bekken, Per Jarle. *The Lawsuit Motif in John's Gospel from New Perspectives: Jesus Christ, Crucified Criminal and Emperor of the World*. Supplements to Novum Testamentum 158. Leiden: Brill, 2014.

———. "Philo's Relevance for the Study of the New Testament." In *Reading Philo. A Handbook to Philo of Alexandria*, edited by Torrey Seland, 226–67. Grand Rapids: Eerdmans, 2014.

Belkin, Samuel. *Philo and the Oral Law: The Philonic Interpretation of Biblical Law in Relation to the Palestinian Halakah*. Harvard Semitic Studies 11. **1940**. Reprint, New York: Johnson Reprint Group, 1968.

Bell, H. Idris. *Cults and Creeds in Greco-Roman Egypt*. Liverpool Monographs in Archaeology and Oriental Studies. Liverpool: Liverpool University Press, 1953.

———, ed. *Jews and Christians in Egypt: The Jewish Troubles in Alexandria and the Athanasian Controversy*. Westport, CT: Greenwwod, 1924. Reprint, 1976.

Bendlin, Andreas. "Gemeinschaft, Öffentlichkeit und Identität: Forschungsgeschichtliche Anmerkungen zu den Mustern sozialer Ordnung in Rom." In *Religiöse Vereine in der römischen Antike*, edited by Ulrike Egelhaaf-Gaiser and Alfred Schäfer, 9–40. Studien und Texte zu Antike und Christentum 13. Tübingen: Mohr Siebeck, 2002.

Berchman, Robert M. "Arcana Mundi: Between Balaam and Hecate; Prophecy, Divination, and Magic in Later Platonism." In *Society of Biblical Literature 1989 Seminar Papers*, edited by David J. Lull, 107–85. Society of Biblical Literature Seminar Papers Series 28. Atlanta: Scholars, 1989.

———. "Arcana Mundi: Magic and Divination in the *De Somniis* of Philo of Alexandria." In *Society of Biblical Literature 1987 Seminar Papers*, edited by Kent H. Richards, 403–28. SBL Seminar Papers Series 26. Atlanta: Scholars, 1987.

———. "Arcana Mundi: Magic and Divination in the *De Somniis* of Philo of Alexandria." In *Mediators of the Divine. Horizons of Prophecy, Divination, Dreams and Theurgy in Mediterranean Antiquity*, edited by Robert M. Berchman, 115–54. South Florida Studies in the History of Judaism 163. Atlanta: Scholars, 1998.

———. "Arcana Mundi: Prophecy and Divination in the *Vita Mosis* of Philo of Alexandria." In *SBL Seminar Papers Annual Meeting 1988*, edited by David J. Lull, 385–423. SBL Seminar Paper Series 27. Atlanta: Scholars, 1988.

Berthelot, Katell. *Jews and Their Roman Rivals: Pagan Rome's Challenge to Israel*. Princeton: Princeton University Press, 2021.

———. "Philo's Perception of the Roman Empire." *Journal for the Study of Judaism* 42 (2011) 166–87.

Betz, Hans Dieter. *Der Apostel Paulus und die sokratische Tradition*. Beiträge zur historischen Theologie 45. Tübingen: Mohr Siebeck, 1972.

Bhabha, Homi K. *The Location of Culture*. London: Routledge, 1994. Reprint 2004.

Bilde, Per. *Collected Studies on Philo and Josephus*. Edited by Eve-Marie Becker et al. Studia Aarhusiana Neotestamentica. Göttingen: Vandenhoeck & Ruprecht, 2016.

———. "Filon som polemiker og politisk apologet. En undersøgelse af de to historiske skrifter Mod Flaccus (In Flaccum) og Om delegationen til Gaius (De legatione ad Gaium)." In *Perspektiver på jødisk apologetik*, edited by Anders Klostergaard Petersen and Kåre Sigvald Fuglseth, 155–80. Antikken og Kristendommen 4. Copenhagen: Forlaget ANIS, 2007.

———. "Der Konflikt zwischen Gaius Caligula und den Juden über die Aufstellung einer Kaiserstatue im Tempel von Jerusalem." In *Collected Studies on Philo and Josephus*, edited by Eve-Marie Becker et al., 225–62. Studie Aarhusiana Neotestamentica 7. Göttingen: Vandenhoeck & Ruprecht, 2016.

———. "Philo as a Polemist and a Political Apologist: An Investigation of His Two Historical Treatises *Against Flaccus* and *The Embassy to Gaius*." In *Alexandria: A Cultural and Religious Melting Pot*, edited by George Hinge and Jens A. Krasilnikoff, 97–114. Aarhus Studies in Mediterranean Antiquity 9. Aarhus: Aarhus University Press, 2009.

———. "Philo as a Polemist and a Political Apologist: An Investigation of His Two Historical Treatises *Against Flaccus* and *The Embassy to Gaius*." In *Collected*

Studies on Philo and Josephus, edited by Eve-Marie Becker et al., 207–24. Studia Aarhusiana Neotestamentica. Göttingen: Vandenhoeck & Ruprecht, 2016.

Bird, Michael F. *Crossing over Sea and Land: Jewish Missionary Activity in the Second Temple Period*. Peabody, MA: Hendrickson, 2010.

Birnbaum, Ellen. "Allegorical Interpretation and Jewish Identity Among Alexandrian Jewish Writers." In *Neotestamentica et Philonica: Studies in Honor of Peder Borgen*, edited by David E. Aune et al., 307–29. Supplements to Novum Testamentum 106. Leiden: Brill, 2003.

———. "A Leader with Vision in the Ancient Jewish Diaspora." In *Jewish Religious Leadership: Image and Reality*, edited by Jack Wertheimer, 1:57–90. 2 vols. New York: Jewish Theological Seminary, 2004.

———. "Philo on the Greeks: A Jewish Perspective on Culture and Society in First-Century Alexandria." In *In the Spirit of Faith: Studies in Philo and Early Christianity in Honor of David Hay*, edited by David T. Runia and Gregory E. Sterling, 37–58. Brown Judaic Studies 332. Studia Philonica Annual: Studies in Hellenistic Judaism 13. Providence: Brown Judaic Studies, 2001.

———. *The Place of Judaism in Philo's Thought: Israel, Jews, and Proselytes*. Brown Judaic Studies 290. Studia Philonica Monographs 2. Atlanta: Scholars, 1996.

Birnbaum, Ellen, and John Dillon, trans. *On the Life of Abraham*, by Philo of Alexandria: *Introduction, Translation, and Commentary*. Philo of Alexandria Commentary Series 6. Leiden: Brill, 2020.

Bitter, Rudolf A. *Vreemdelingschap bij Philo van Alexandrie: Een Onderzoek naar de betekenis van PAROIKOS*. Paroikos. N.p., 1982.

Bloch, René. "Alexandria in Pharaonic Egypt: Projections in *De vita Mosis*." In *The Studia Philonica Annual*. Studies in Hellenistic Judaism, edited by David T. Runia and Gregory E. Sterling, 69–84. Atlanta: Scholars, 2012.

Boak, A. E. R. "The Organization of the Gilds in Greco-Roman Egypt." *Transactions of the American Philological Association* 68 (1937) 212–20.

Bohak, Gideon. *Ancient Jewish Magic: A History*. Cambridge: Cambridge University Press, 2008.

Boissevain, Jeremy. *Friends of Friends: Networks, Manipulators and Coalitions*. Pavilion Series. Social Anthropology. Oxford: Blackwell, 1974. Reprint, 1978.

Borgen, Peder. "Application of and Commitment to the Laws of Moses. Observations on Philo's Treatise *On the Embassy to Gaius*." In *In the Spirit of Faith: Studies in Philo and Early Christianity in Honor of David Hay*, edited by David T. Runia and Gregory E. Sterling, 86–101. *Studia Philonica Annual*. Studies in Hellenistic Judaism 13. Providence: Brown University, 2001.

———. "Autobiographical Ascent Reports: Philo and John the Seer." In *Early Christianity and Hellenistic Judaism*, 309–20. Edinburgh: T. & T. Clark, 1996.

———. "Autobiographical Ascent Reports: Philo and John the Seer." In *Illuminations by Philo of Alexandria*, by Peder Borgen, 249–60. Edited by Torrey Seland. Studies in Philo of Alexandria 12. Leiden: Brill, 2021.

———. *Bread from Heaven: An Exegetical Study of the Concept of Manna in the Gospel of John and the Writings of Philo*. Supplements to Novum Testamentum 10. Leiden: Brill, 1965. Reprint, 1981.

———. *Early Christianity and Hellenistic Judaism*. Edinburgh: T. & T. Clark, 1996.

———. *The Gospel of John: More Light from Philo, Paul and Archaeology; The Scriptures, Tradition, Exposition, Settings, Meaning*. Supplements to Novum Testamentum 154. Leiden: Brill, 2014.

———. "Heavenly Ascent in Philo: An Examination of Selected Passages." In *The Pseudepigrapha and Early Biblical Interpretation*, edited by James H. Charlesworth and Craig A. Evans, 246–68. Journal for the Study of the Pseudepigrapha 14. Sheffield: Sheffield Academic, 1993.

———. "Heavenly Ascent in Philo: An Examination of Selected Passages." In *Illuminations by Philo of Alexandria*, by Peder Borgen, 211–34. Edited by Torrey Seland. Studies in Philo of Alexandria 12. Leiden: Brill, 2021.

———. *Illuminations by Philo of Alexandria: Selected Studies on Interpretation in Philo, Paul and the Revelation of John*. Edited by Torrey Seland. Studies in Philo of Alexandria 12. Leiden: Brill, 2021.

———. "Judaism: Judaism in Egypt." In *The Anchor Bible Dictionary*, edited by David Noel Freedman et al., 3:1061–72. 6 vols. New York: Doubleday, 1992.

———. "Philo—An Interpreter of the Laws of Moses." In *Reading Philo: A Handbook of Philo of Alexandria*, edited by Torrey Seland, 75–101. Grand Rapids: Eerdmans, 2014.

———. "Philo of Alexandria: A Critical and Synthetical Survey of Research since World War II." In *Aufstieg und Niedergang der römischen Welt II 21,1: Geschichte und Kultur Roms im Spiegel der neueren Forschung. 2, Principat. Religion: (Hellenistisches Judentum in römischer Zeit: Philon und Josephus)*, edited by Wolfgang Haase, 98–154. Berlin: de Gruyter, 1984.

———. *Philo of Alexandria, An Exegete for His Time*. Supplements to Novum Testamentum 86. Leiden: Brill, 1997.

———. "Philo of Alexandria as Exegete." In *A History of Biblical Interpretation. Vol. 1, The Ancient Period*, edited by Alan J. Hauser and Duane F. Watson, 1:114–43. 2 vols. Grand Rapids: Eerdmans, 2003.

———. "Philo of Alexandria." In *Jewish Writings of the Second Temple Period: Apocrypha, Pseudepigrapha, Qumran Sectarian Writings, Philo, Josephus*, edited by Michael E. Stone, 233–82. Compendia rerum Iudaicarum ad Novum Testamentum 2/2. Assen: Van Gorcum, 1984.

———. "'There Shall Come Forth a Man': Reflections on Messianic Ideas in Philo." In *The Messiah: Developments in Earliest Judaism and Christianity*, edited by James H. Charlesworth et al., 341–61. Minneapolis: Fortress, 1992.

———. "'There Shall Come Forth a Man': Reflections on Messianic Ideas in Philo." In *Illuminations by Philo of Alexandria: Selected Studies on Interpretation in Philo, Paul and the Revelation of John*, by Peder Borgen, 105–27. Edited by Torrey Seland. Studies in Philo of Alexandria 12. Leiden: Brill, 2021.

———. "Two Philonic Prayers and Their Contexts: An Analysis of *Who Is the Heir of Divine Things* (*Her.*) 24–29 and *Against Flaccus* (*Flac.*) 170–175." *New Testament Studies* 45 (1999) 291–309.

———. "Proselytes, Conquest, and Mission." In *Recruitment, Conquest, and Conflict: Strategies in Judaism, Early Christianity, and the Greco-Roman World*, edited by Peder Borgen et al., 57–77. Emory Studies in Early Christianity 6. Atlanta: Scholars, 1998.

———. "'Yes,' 'No,' 'How Far?': The Participation of Jews and Christians in Pagan Cults." In *Early Christianity and Hellenistic Judaism*, 15–43. Edinburgh: T. & T. Clark, 1996.

Borgen, Peder, et al., eds. *The Philo Index: A Complete Greek Word Index to the Writings of Philo of Alexandria*. Grand Rapids: Eerdmans, 2000.

Bowden, Hugh. *Mystery Cults in the Ancient World*. London: Thames & Hudson, 2010.

Bradley, Guy, and John-Paul Wilson, eds. *Greek and Roman Colonization: Origins, Ideologies and Interactions*. Swansea: Classical Press of Wales, 2006.

Brah, Avtar. *Cartographies of Diaspora: Contesting Identities*. London: Routledge, 1996. Reprint 2003.

Brashear, William M. *Vereine im griechisch-römischen Ägypten*. XENIA. Konstanzer Althistorische Vorträge und Forschungen 34. Konstanz: Universitätsverlag Konstanz, 1993.

Bremmer, Jan N. "The Birth of the Term 'Magic.'" *Zeitschrift für Papyrologie und Epigraphik* 126 (1999) 1–12.

———. "The First Pogrom? Religious Violence in Alexandria in 38 CE?" In *Alexandria: Hub of the Hellenistic World*, edited by Benjamin Schliesser et al., 245–59. Wissenschaftliche Untersuchungen zum Neuen Testament 460. Tübingen: Mohr Siebeck, 2021.

———. *Initiation into the Mysteries of the Ancient World*. Münchner Vorlesungen zu antiken Welten 1. Berlin: de Gruyter, 2014.

Brown, S. Kent. "Egypt, History of (Greco-Roman Period)." In *The Anchor Bible Dictionary*, edited by David Noel Freedman et al., 2:367–74. 6 vols. New York: Doubleday, 1992.

Brunt, Peter A. "The Administrators of Roman Egypt." *Journal of Roman Studies* 65 (1975) 124–47.

Burford, Allison. *Craftsmen in Greek and Roman Society: Aspects of Greek and Roman Life*. Aspects of Greek and Roman Life. Ithaca: Cornell University Press, 1972.

Burkert, Walter. *Ancient Mystery Cults*. Cambridge: Harvard University Press, 1987.

———. "ΓΟΗΣ: Zum griechischen 'Schamanismus.'" *Rheinisches Museum für Philologie* 105 (1962) 36–55.

Carter, Warren. *The Roman Empire and the New Testament*. Abingdon Essential Guides. Nashville: Abingdon, 2006.

Champion, Craige B., ed., *Roman Imperialism: Readings and Sources*. Interpreting Ancient History. Malden, MA: Blackwell, 2004.

Champion, Craige B., and Arthur M. Eckstein. "Introduction: The Study of Roman Imperialism." In *Roman Imperialism: Readings and Sources*, edited by Craige B. Champion, 1–15. Interpreting Ancient History. Malden, MA: Blackwell, 2004.

Cohen, Naomi G. "The Mystery Terminology in Philo." In *Philo und das Neue Testament. Wechselseitige Wahrnehmungen*, edited by Roland Deines and Karl-WilhelmNiebuhr, 173–87. Wissenschaftliche Untersuchungen zum Neuen Testament 172. Tübingen: Mohr Siebeck, 2004.

Cohen, Robin. *Global Diasporas: An Introduction*. London: UCL Press, 1997.

Collins, John J. *Between Athens and Jerusalem: Jewish Identity in the Hellenistic Diaspora*. New York: Crossroad, 1983.

Colson, F. H., et al., eds. and trans. *Philo*. Vols. 1–10. Loeb Classical Library. Cambridge: Harvard University Press, 1934–62.

Cover, Michael B. "Israel's Scriptures in Philo and the Alexandrian Jewish Tradition." In *Israel Scriptures in Early Christian Writings: The Use of the Old Testament in the New*, edited by Matthias Hentze and David Lincicum, 162–87. Grand Rapids: Eerdmans, 2023.

Crowell, Bradley L. "Postcolonial Studies and the Hebrew Bible." *Currents in Biblical Research* 7 (2009) 217–44.

Damgaard, Finn. "Philo's Life of Moses as 'Rewritten Bible.'" In *Rewritten Bible after Fifty Years: Texts, Terms, or Techniques? A Last Dialogue with Géza Vermes*, edited by József Zsengellér, 234–48. Journal for the Study of Judaism Supplement Series 166. Leiden: Brill, 2014.

———. *Recasting Moses: The Memory of Moses in Biographical and Autobiographical Narratives in Ancient Judaism and 4th-Century Christianity*. Early Christianity in the Context of Antiquity 13. Frankfurt: Lang, 2013.

Danker, F. W. *Benefactor: Epigraphic Study of a Greco-Roman and New Testament Semantic Field*. St. Louis: Clayton, 1982.

Dawson, David. *Allegorical Readers and Cultural Revision in Ancient Alexandria*. Berkeley: University of California Press, 1992.

de Jonge, Casper C. "Greek Migrant Literature in the Early Roman Empire." *Mnemosyne* 75 (2022) 10–36.

De Savignac, Jean. "Le Messianisme de Philon d'Alexandrie." *Novum Testamentum* 4 (1960) 319–24.

Delia, Diana. "The Population of Roman Alexandria." *Transactions of the American Philological Association* 118 (1988) 275–92.

Delling, Gerhard. "Philons Enkomium auf Augustus." *Klio* 54 (1972) 171–92.

———. "Wunder–Allegori–Mythos bei Philon von Alexandria." In *Studien zum Neuen Testament und zum Hellenistischen Judentum: Gesammelte Aufsätze 1950–1968*, 72–129. Göttingen: Vandenhoeck & Ruprecht, 1970.

DeSilva, David A. "Jews in the Diaspora." In *The World of the New Testament: Cultural, Social, and Historical Contexts*, edited by Joel B. Green and Lee Martin McDonald, 272–90. Grand Rapids: Baker Academic, 2013.

———. "Using the Master's Tools to Shore Up Another's House: A Postcolonial Analysis of 4 Maccabees." *Journal of Biblical Literature* 126 (2007) 99–127.

Dickson, John P. *Mission-Commitment in Ancient Judaism and in the Pauline Communities: The Shape, Extent and Background of Early Christian Mission*. Wissenschaftliche Untersuchungen zum Neuen Testament 2.159. Tübingen: Mohr Siebeck, 2003.

Diehl, Judy. "Anti-Imperial Rhetoric in the New Testament." *Currents in Biblical Research* 10 (2011) 9–52.

———. "'Babylon': Then, Now and 'Not Yet': Anti-Roman Rhetoric in the Book of Revelation." *Currents in Biblical Research* 11 (2013) 168–95.

———. "Empire and Epistles: Anti-Roman Rhetoric in the New Testament Epistles." *Currents in Biblical Research* 10 (2012) 217–63.

Dillon, John M. *The Middle Platonists: 80 B.C. to A.D. 220*. Ithaca: Cornell University Press, 1977.

Dombrowski, Bruno W. "*HYHD* in IQS and *to koinon*: An Instance of Early Greek and Jewish Synthesis." *Harvard Theological Review* 59 (1966) 293–307.

Dyck, Jonathan. "Philo, Alexandria and Empire: The Politics of Allegorical Interpretation." In *Jews in the Hellenistic and Roman Cities*, edited by John R. Bartlett, 149–74. London: Routledge, 2002.

Edrei, Arye, and Doron Mendels. "A Split Jewish Diaspora: Its Dramatic Consequences." *Journal for the Study of the Pseudepigrapha* 16.2 (2007) 91–137.

Egelhaaf-Gaiser, Ulrike, and Alfred Schäfer, eds. *Religiöse Vereine in der römischen Antike: Untersuchungen zu Organisation, Ritual und Raumordnung*. Studies and Texts in Antiquity and Christianity 13. Tübingen: Mohr Siebeck, 2003.

Eisenstadt, S. N., and L. Roniger. *Patrons, Clients, and Friends: Interpersonal Relations and the Structure of Trust in Society*. Themes in the Social Sciences. Cambridge: Cambridge University Press, 1984.

Evans, Katherine G. "Alexander the Alabarch: Roman and Jew." In *SBL Seminar Papers Annual Meeting 1995*, edited by Eugene H. Lovering Jr., 576–94. SBL Seminar Papers Series 34. Atlanta: Scholars, 1995.

Fascher, E. ΠΡΟΦΗΤΗΣ: *Eine sprach- und religionsgeschichtliche Untersuchung*. Giessen: Töpelmann, 1927.

Feldman, Louis H., and Reinhold Meyer, eds. *Jewish Life and Thought Among Greeks and Romans: Primary Readings*. Edinburgh: T. & T. Clark, 1996.

Feldman, Louis H. *Jew and Gentile in the Ancient World: Attitudes and Interactions from Alexander to Justinian*. Princeton: Princeton University Press, 1993.

———. "Josephus (PERSON)." In *The Anchor Bible Dictionary*, edited by David Noel Freedman et al. 3:981–98. 6 vols. New York: Doubleday, 1992.

———. "The Orthodoxy of the Jews in Hellenistic Egypt." *Jewish Social Studies* 22 (1960) 215–37.

———. "Scholarship on Philo and Josephus (1937–1959)." *Classical World* 54 (1960/61) 281–91.

———. *Philo's Portrayal of Moses in the Context of Ancient Judaism*. Christianity and Judaism in Antiquity Series 15. Notre Dame: University of Notre Dame Press, 2007.

———. "Philo's Version of Balaam." *Henoch* 25 (2003) 301–19.

Fischer, Ulrich. *Eschatologie und Jenseitserwartung im hellenistischen Diasporajudentum*. Beihefte zur Zeitschrift für die neutestamentliche Wissenschaft 44. Berlin: de Gruyter, 1978.

Fisher, Nicholas R. E. "Greek Associations, Symposia and Clubs." In *Civilization of the Ancient Mediterranean: Greece and Rome*, edited by Michael Grant and Rachel Kitzinger, 2:1167–97. 3 vols. New York: Scribner, 1988.

———. "Roman Associations, Dinner Parties and Clubs." In *Civilization of the Ancient Mediterranean: Greece and Rome*, edited by Michael Grant and Rachel Kitzinger, 2:1199–1225. New York: Scribner, 1988.

Forbes, Clarence A. *Neoi: A Contribution to the Study of Greek Associations*. Philological Monographs 2. Middleton, CT: American Philological Association, 1933.

Fraade, Steven D. "Between Rewritten Bible and Allegorical Commentary: Philo's Interpretation of the Burning Bush." In *Rewritten Bible After Fifty Years: Texts, Terms, or Techniques? A Last Dialogue with Geza Vermes*, edited by József Zsengellér, 221–432. Journal for the Study of Judaism Supplement Series 166. Leiden: Brill, 2014.

Frankel, David. "The Deuteronomic Portrayal of Balaam." *Vetus Testamentum* 46 (1996) 30–42.

Frankfurter, David. "Ritual Expertise in Roman Egypt and the Problem of the Category 'Magician." In *Envisioning Magic: A Princeton Seminar and Symposium*, edited by Peter Schäfer and Hans G. Kippenberg, 115–35. Studies in the History of Religions 75. Leiden: Brill, 1997.
Freedman, David Noel, eds. *The Anchor Bible Dictionary*. 6 vols. New York: Doubleday, 1992.
Friesen, Courtney J. P., et al., eds. *The Reception of Philo of Alexandria*. Oxford: Oxford University Press, 2025.
Gafni, Isaiah M. *Land, Center and Diaspora: Jewish Constructs in Late Antiquity*. Journal for the Study of the Pseudepigrapha Supplement Series 21. Sheffield: Sheffield Academic, 1997.
Gager, John G. *Moses in Greco-Roman Paganism*. Society of Biblical Literature Monograph Series 16. Nashville: Abingdon, 1972.
Gambetti, Sandra. *The Alexandrian Riots of 38 C.E. and the Persecution of the Jews: A Historical Reconstruction*. Journal for the Study of Judaism Supplement Series 135. Leiden: Brill, 2009.
———. "The Attack on the Jews in Alexandrian Egypt in 38 CE: Was It a Pogrom?" *Antisemitism Studies* 7 (2023) 370–404.
———. "The Jewish Community of Alexandria: The Origins." *Henoch* 29 (2007) 213–40.
Garnsey, Peter, and Richard Saller. *The Roman Empire: Economy, Society and Culture*. London: Duckworth, 1990 (orig. publ. 1987).
Geljon, Albert C., and David T. Runia, trans. *On Cultivation*, by Philo of Alexandria. Philo of Alexandria Commentary Series 4. Leiden: Brill, 2012.
Goodenough, Erwin R. *An Introduction to Philo Judaeus*. Brown Classics in Judaica. Lanham, MD: University Press of America, 1986 (orig. publ. 1940; 2nd ed. 1962.
———. *The Jurisprudence of the Jewish Courts in Egypt*. 1929. Reprint, Amsterdam: Philo Press, 1969.
———. *By Light, Light: The Mystic Gospel of Hellenistic Judaism*. New Haven: Yale University Press, 1935.
———. "Philo and Public Life." *Journal of Egyptian Archaeology* 12 (1926) 77–79.
———. "Philo's Exposition of the Law and His De vita Mosis." *Harvard Theological Review* 26 (1933) 109–25.
———. *The Politics of Philo Judaeus: Practice and Theory*. New Haven: Yale University Press, 1938.
Graeber, A. *Untersuchungen zum spätrömischen Korporationswesen*. Europäische Hochschulschriften = European University Studies Series 196. Frankfurt: Lang, 1983.
Graf, Fritz. "Excluding the Charming: The Development of the Greek Concept of Magic." In *Ancient Magic and Ritual Power*, edited by Marvin Meyer and Paul Mirecki, 13–27. Religions in the Graeco-Roman World 129. Leiden: Brill, 1995.
Graham. A. J. *Colony and Mother City in Ancient Greece*. Manchester: Manchester University Press, 1964.
Greenberg, Jennifer. "'Ἀγωνιάσωμεν': Philo Judaeus, a Voice of a Colonized Nation." Classic Graduate Theses & Dissertations 5. University of Colorado, 2013.
Greene, John T. *Balaam and His Interpreters. A Hermeneutical History of the Balaam Traditions*. Brown Judaic Studies 244. Atlanta: Scholars, 1992.

———. "The Balaam Figure and Type Before, During and After the Period of the Pseudepigrapha." *Journal for the Study of the Pseudepigrapha* 8.1991 (1991) 67–101.

———. "Balaam: Prophet, Diviner and Priest in Selected Ancient Israelite and Hellenistic Jewish Sources." In *SBL Annual Meeting Seminar Papers 1989*, edited by David John Lull, 57–105. SBL Seminar Papers Series 28. Atlanta: Scholars, 1989.

Gruen, Erich S. "Caligula, the Imperial Cult, and Philo's *Legatio*." *Studia Philonica Annual* 24 (2012) 135–47.

———. *Diaspora: Jews Amidst Greeks and Romans*. Cambridge: Harvard University Press, 2002.

———. "Hellenistic Judaism." In *Cultures of the Jews: A New History*. Vol. 1, *Mediterranean Origins*, edited by David Biale, 77–132. New York: Schocken, 2002.

———. "Judaism in the Diaspora." In *The Eerdmans Dictionary of Early Judaism*, edited by John J. Collins and Daniel C. Harlow, 77–96. Grand Rapids: Eerdmans, 2010.

Gutsfeld, Andreas, and Dietrich-Alex Koch, eds. *Vereine, Synagogen und Gemeinden im kaiserzeitlichen Kleinasien*. Studien und Texte zu Antike und Christentum 25. Tübingen: Mohr Siebeck, 2006.

Hackett, Jo Ann. "Balaam (PERSON) [Heb. Bil'am]." In *The Anchor Bible Dictionary*, edited by David Noel Freedman, 1:569–72. 6 vols. New York: Doubleday, 1992.

Hadas-Lebel, Mireille. *Philo of Alexandria: A Thinker in the Jewish Diaspora*. Studies in Philo of Alexandria 7. Leiden: Brill, 2012.

Harker, Andrew. *Loyalty and Dissidence in Roman Egypt: The Case of the Acta Alexandrinorum*. Cambridge: Cambridge University Press, 2008.

Harland, Philip A. *Associations, Synagogues, and Congregations: Claiming a Place in Ancient Mediterranean Society*. Minneapolis: Fortress, 2003.

———. *Associations, Synagogues, and Congregations: Claiming a Place in Ancient Mediterranean Society*. 2nd, rev. ed., with links to the inscriptions. Kitchener, ON: Philip A. Harland, 2013. https://philipharland.com/publications/Harland%20 2013%20Associations-Synagogues-Congregations.pdf.

———. *Dynamics of Identity in the World of the Early Christians: Associations, Judeans, and Cultural Minorities*. New York: T. & T. Clark, 2009.

———. ed. *Greco-Roman Associations: Texts, Translations and Commentary*. Vol. 2, *North Coast of the Black Sea, Asia Minor*. Beihefte zur Zeitschrift für die neutestamentliche Wissenschaft und die Kunde der älteren Kirche 204. Berlin: de Gruyter, 2014.

———, ed. *Travel and Religion in Antiquity*. Studies in Christianity and Judaism 21. Waterloo, ON: Wilfrid Laurier University Press, 2011.

Harnack, Adolf von. *Die Mission und Ausbreitung des Christentums in den ersten drei Jahrhunderten*. Vierte verbesserte und vermehrte Auflage mit elf Karten. Unveränderte Nachdruck der Ausgabe von 1924. VMA-Verlag, Wiesbaden. No date.

Harper, John-Paul. *Paul and Philo on the Politics of the Land, Jerusalem, and Temple*. Wissenschaftliche Untersuchungen zum Neuen Testament 2/562. Tübingen: Mohr Siebeck, 2021.

Harrison, James R. *Paul and the Imperial Authorities at Thessalonica and Rome*. Wissenschaftliche Untersuchungen zum Neuen Testament 273. Tübingen: Mohr Siebeck, 2011.

Hay, David M. "Philo's References to Other Allegorists." *Studia Philonica Annual* 6 (1979–80) 41–75.

———. "Philo's View of Himself as an Exegete: Inspired but not Authoritative." The *Studia Philonica Annual* 3 (1991) 40–52.

———. "Politics and Exegesis in Philo's Treatise on Dreams." In *Society of Biblical Literature 1987 Seminar Papers*, edited by Kent Harold Richards, 429–38. SBL Seminar Papers Series 26. Atlanta: Scholars, 1987.

Hayward, C. T. R. "Balaam's Prophecies as Interpreted by Philo and the Aramaic Targums of the Pentateuch." In *New Heaven and New Earth: Prophecy and the Millennium; Essays in Honour of Anthony Gelston*, edited by P. J. Harland and C. T. R. Hayward, 19–36. Supplements to Vetus Testamentum 77. Leiden: Brill, 2000.

Hect, R. D. "Philo and Messiah." In *Judaisms and Their Messiahs at the Turn of the Christian Era*, edited by Jacob Neusner et al., 139–68. Cambridge: Cambridge University Press, 1987.

Heilig, Christoph. *The Apostle and the Empire: Paul's Implicit and Explicit Criticism of Rome*. Grand Rapids: Eerdmans, 2022.

———. *Hidden Criticism? The Methodology and Plausibility of the Search for a Counter-Imperial Subtext in Paul*. Wissenschaftliche Untersuchungen zum Neuen Testament 2/392. Tübingen: Mohr Siebeck, 2015.

Heinemann, Isaak. *Philons griechische und jüdische Bildung: Kulturvergleichende Untersuchungen zu Philons Darstellung der jüdischen Gesetze*. Darmstadt: Wissenschaftliche Buchgesellschaft, 1962.

Heinrici, Georg. "Die Christengemeinde Korinths und die religiösen Genossenschaften der Griechen." *Zeitschrift für wissenschaftliche Theologie* 19 (1876) 464–526.

Hengel, Martin. *The Zealots: Investigations into the Jewish Freedom Movement in the Period from Herod I Until 70 A.D.* Translated by David Smith. Edinburgh: T. & T. Clark, 1989.

Herklotz, Frederike. "Aegypto Capta: Augustus and the Annexation of Egypt." In *The Oxford Handbook of Roman Egypt*, edited by Christina Riggs, 11–21. Oxford Handbooks in Archaeology. Oxford: Oxford University Press, 2012.

Henrichs, Albert. "Changing Dionysiac Identities." In *Jewish and Christian Self-Definition*. Vol 3, *Self-Definition in the Graeco-Roman World*, edited by Ben F. Meyer and E. P. Sanders, 137–60. Philadelphia: Fortress, 1983.

Herrmann, P. "Genossenschaft. A. Griechisch." In *Reallexikon für Antike und Christentum*, edited by Theodor Klauser, 10:83–99. Stuttgart: Hiersemann, 1978.

Horbury, William, and David Noy, eds. *Jewish Inscriptions of Graeco-Roman Egypt*. Cambridge: Cambridge University Press, 1992.

Hoftizer, J., and G. van der Kooij, eds. *The Balaam Text from Deir 'Alla Re-Evaluated: Proceedings of the International Symposium Held at Leiden 21–24 August 1989*. Leiden: Brill, 1991.

Horsley, Richard A. *In the Shadow of the Empire: Reclaiming the Bible as a History of Faithful Resistance*. Louisville: Westminster John Knox, 2008.

———. "The Law of Nature in Philo and Cicero." *Harvard Theological Review* 71 (1978) 35–59.

———, ed. *Paul and Empire: Religion and Power in Roman Imperial Society*. Harrisburg, PA: Trinity, 1997.

———. ed. *Paul and Politics: Ekklesia, Israel, Imperium, Interpretation; Essays in Honor of Krister Stendahl*. Harrisburg, PA: Trinity, 2000.

———. *Paul and the Roman Imperial Order*. Harrisburg, PA: Trinity, 2004.

Horst, Pieter Willem van der. *Philo's "Flaccus": The First Pogrom; Introduction, Translation, and Commentary*. Philo of Alexandria Commentary Series 2. Leiden: Brill, 2003.

Hölbl, Günther. *A History of the Ptolemaic Empire*. Translated by Tina Saavedra. London: Routledge, 2001.

Hunt, Jeffrey M., ed. and trans. *De vita Mosis I: An Introduction with Text, Translation and Notes*. Ancient Christianity and Its Context. Waco, TX: Baylor University Press, 2023.

Isaac, Benjamin. "Roman Colonies (Judea)." In *The Anchor Bible Dictionary*, edited by David Noel Freedman, 5:798–801. 6 vols. New York: Doubleday, 1992.

Jördens, Andrea. "Government, Taxation and Law." In *The Oxford Handbook of Roman Egypt*, edited by Christina Riggs, 56–67. Oxford Handbooks in Archaeology. Oxford: Oxford University Press, 2012.

Judge, E. A. "The Social Identity of the First Christians: A Question of Method in Religious History." *Journal of Religious History* 11 (1980) 201–17.

———. *The Social Pattern of the Christian Groups in the First Century: Some Prolegomena to the Study of New Testament Ideas of Social Obligation*. Christ and Culture Collection. London: Tyndale, 1960.

Juster, Jean. *Les Juifs dans l'Empire Romain: Leurs condition juridique économique et sociale*. 2 vols. Paris: n.p., 1914.

Kaiser, Otto. *Philo von Alexandrien: Denkender Glaube—Eine Einführung*. Forschungen zur Religion und Literatur des Alten und Neuen Testaments 259. Göttingen: Vandenhoeck & Ruprecht, 2015.

Kamesar, Adam, ed. *The Cambridge Companion to Philo*. Cambridge Companions to Philosophy. Cambridge: Cambridge University Press, 2009.

Karadimas, Dimitrios. "Alexandria and the Second Sophistic," *Electryone* 2 (2014) 14–36.

Karris, Robert J. "The Background and Significance of the Polemic of the Pastoral Epistles." *Journal of Biblical Literature* 92 (1973) 549–64.

Kasher, Aryeh. "The Jewish Attitude to the Alexandrian Gymnasium in the First Century A.D." *American Journal of Ancient History* 1.3 (1976) 148–61.

———. *The Jews in Hellenistic and Roman Egypt: The Struggle for Equal Rights*. Rev. English ed. Texte und Studien zum antiken Judentum 7. Tübingen: Mohr Siebeck, 1985.

Keener, Craig S. *Acts: An Exegetical Commentary*. Vol. 2, *3:1—14:28*. 4 vols. Grand Rapids: Baker Academic, 2013.

Kiefer, Jörn. *Exil und Diaspora: Begrifflichkeit und Deutungen im antiken Judentum und in der hebräischen Bibel*. Arbeiten zur Bibel und ihrer Geschichte 19. Leipzig: Evangelische Verlagsanstalt, 2005.

Kim, Seyoon. *Christ and Caesar: The Gospel and the Roman Empire in the Writings of Paul and Luke*. Grand Rapids: Eerdmans, 2008.

———. *Paul and the New Perspective: Second Thoughts on "The Origin of Paul's Gospel."* Grand Rapids: Eerdmans, 2001.

Klauck, Hans Josef. *Herrenmahl und hellenistischer Kult*. Neutestamentliche Abhandlungen, N.F., 15. Munich: Aschendorff, 1982

———. *Die religiöse Umwelt des Urchristentums*. Vol. 1, *Stadt- und Hausreligion, Mysterienkulte, Volksglaube*. 2 vols. Studienbücher Theologie 9,1. Stuttgart: Kohlhammer, 1995.

Kloppenborg, John S. "Collegia and Thiasoi: Issues in Function, Taxonomy and Membership." In *Voluntary Associations in the Graeco-Roman World*, edited by John S. Kloppenborg and Stephen G. Wilson, 16–30. London: Routledge, 1996.

———, ed. *Greco-Roman Associations: Texts, Translations, and Commentary*. Vol. 3, *Ptolemaic and Early Roman Egypt*. Beihefte zur Zeitschrift für die neutestamentliche Wissenschaft und die Kunde der älteren Kirche 246. Berlin: de Gruyter, 2020.

Kloppenborg, John S., and Richard S. Ascough, eds. *Greco-Roman Associations: Texts, Translations, and Commentary*. Vol. 1, *Attica, Central Greece, Macedonia, Thrace*. Beihefte zur Zeitschrift für die neutestamentliche Wissenschaft und die Kunde der älteren Kirche 181. Berlin: de Gruyter, 2011.

Kloppenborg, John S., and Stephen G. Wilson, eds. *Voluntary Associations in the Graeco-Roman World*. London: Routledge, 1996.

Klostergaard Petersen, Anders. "Rewritten Bible as a Borderline Phenomenon—Genre, Textual Strategy, or Canonical Anachronism?" In *Flores Florentino: Dead Sea Scrolls and Other Early Jewish Studies; In Honour of Florentino García Martínez*, edited by Anthony Hilhorst et al., 285–306. Journal for the Study of Judaism Supplement Series 122. Leiden: Brill, 2007.

Kooten, George H. van, "Balaam as the Sophist par Excellence." In Philo of Alexandria: Philo's Projection of an Urgent Contemporary Debate onto Moses' Pentateuchal Narratives." In *The Prestige of the Pagan Prophet Balaam in Judaism, Early Christianity and Islam*, edited by George H. van Kooten and Jacques van Ruiten, 131–61.Themes in Biblical Narrative 11. Leiden: Brill, 2008.

Klutz, Todd E., ed. *Magic in the Biblical World: From the Rod of Aaron to the Ring of Solomon*. Journal for the Study of the New Testament Supplement Series 245. London: T. & T. Clark, 2003.

Knott, Kim, and Seán McLoughlin, eds. *Diasporas: Concepts, Intersections, Identities*. London: Zed, 2010.

Koester, Helmut. *Introduction to the New Testament. Volume 1: History, Culture, and Religion of the Hellenistic Age*. 2nd ed. Berlin: de Gruyter, 1995.

———. "ΝΟΜΟΣ ΦΥΣΕΩΣ: The Concept of Natural Law in Greek Thought." In *Religions in Antiquity: Essays in Memory of Erwin Ramsdell Goodenough*, edited by Jacob Neusner, 521–41. Studies in the History of Religions 14. Leiden: Brill, 1968.

Kornemann, E. "Collegium." In *Pauly-Wissowa, Realenzyclopädie der klassischen Altertumswissenschaften*, edited by A. Pauly et al., vol 4.1, cols. 380–480. Stuttgart, 1901.

Koskenniemi, Erkki. *Greek Writers and Philosophers in Philo and Josephus: A Study of Their Secular Education and Educational Ideals*. Studies in Philo of Alexandria 9. Leiden: Brill, 2019.

———. "Philo and Classical Education." In *Reading Philo: A Handbook to Philo of Alexandria*, edited by Torrey Seland, 102–28. Grand Rapids: Eerdmans, 2014.

———. "Philo and Rome: A Dramatic Change in His Thoughts?" *Studia Philonica Annual* 35 (2023) 115–38.

———. "Philo and the Sophists." In *Greeks, Jews, and Christians: Historical, Religious and Philological Studies in Honor of Jesús Peláez del Rosal*, edited by Lautaro Roig Lanzillotta and Israel Muñoz Gallarte, 253–79. Estudios de Filología Neotestamentaria 10. Córdoba: El Almendro, 2013.

Koskenniemi, Erkki, and Pekka Lindqvist, eds. *Rewritten Biblical Figures*. Studies in Rewritten Bible 3. Turku, Finland: Abo Akademi University, 2010.

Kraft, Robert A. "Philo and the Sabbath Crisis: Alexandrian Jewish Politics and the Dating of Philo's Works." In *The Future of Early Christianity: Essays in Honor of Helmut Koester*, edited by Birger A. Pearson et al., 131–41. Minneapolis: Fortress, 1991.

———. "Tiberius Julius Alexander and the Crisis in Alexandria According to Josephus." In *Of Scribes and Scrolls: Studies of the Hebrew Bible, Intertestamental Judaism, and Christian Origins, Presented to John Strugnell on the Occasion of His Sixtieth Birthday*, edited by Harold W. Attridge et al., 175–84. Resources in Religion. Lanham, MD: University Press of America, 1990.

Kuermmerlin-McLean, Joanne K. "Magic: Old Testament." In *The Anchor Bible Dictionary*, edited by David Noel Freedman et al., 4:468–71. 6 vols. New York: Doubleday, 1992.

Laato, Antti, ed. *Rewritten Bible Reconsidered: Proceedings of the Conference in Karkku, Finland, August 24–26 2006*. Studies in Rewritten Bible 1. Turku, Finland: Abo Akademi University, 2008.

Lang, T. J. "Mystery Cults and Christian Associations in Early Alexandrinian Theology. The Case of Clement of Alexandria." In *Greco-Roman Associations, Deities & Early Christianity*, edited by Bruce W. Longenecker, 417–34. Waco: Baylor University Press, 2022.

Lanzinger, Daniel. "Einführung in die Schrift." In *Das Leben des Weisen: Philo von Alexandria, De Abrahamo*, edited by Daniel Lanzinger, 3–30. Scripta Antiquitatis Posterioris Ad Ethicam REligionemque Pertinentia 36. Tübingen: Mohr Siebeck, 2020.

Lazarus, Neil. "Introducing Postcolonial Studies." In *The Cambridge Companion to Postcolonial Literary Studies*, edited by Neil Lazarus, 1–16. First pub. 2004. 5th printing. Cambridge Companions to Literature. Cambridge: Cambridge University Press, 2010.

Lease, G. "Jewish Mystery Cults since Goodenough." In *Aufstieg und Niedergang der römischen Welt*. Vol. 2, *Principat Band 20: Religion 2 Halbband*, edited by Wolfgang Haase, 858–80. Berlin: de Gruyter, 1987.

Leonhardt-Balzer, Jutta. "Diaspora Jewish Attitudes to Metropoleis. Philo and Paul on Balanced Personalities, Split Loyalties, Jerusalem and Rome." In *The Urban World and the First Christians*, edited by Steve Walton et al., 86–98. Grand Rapids: Eerdmans, 2017.

Levick, Barbara. *Roman Colonies in Southern Asia Minor*. Oxford: Clarendon, 1967.

Levison, John R. "Two Types of Ecstatic Prophecy According to Philo." *Studia Philonica Annual* 6 (1994) 83–89.

Lewis, Naphtali. *Life in Egypt Under Roman Rule*. 1983. Reprint, Oxford: Clarendon, 1985.

Lichtenberger, H., and Ulrike Mittmann-Richert, eds. *Biblical Figures in Deuterocanonical and Cognate Literature*. Deuterocanonical and Cognate Literature Yearbook 2008. Berlin: de Gruyter, 2009.

Liddell, Henry George, et al. *A Greek-English Lexicon*. 9th ed. with revised supplement. Oxford: Clarendon, 1996.

Liebenam, W. *Zur Geschichte und Organisation des römischen Vereinswesens: 3 Untersuchungen*. Leipzig: Teubner, 1890.

Lieber, Andrea. "Between Motherland and Fatherland: Diaspora, Pilgrimage and the Spiritualization of Sacrifice in Philo of Alexandria." In *Heavenly Tablets: Interpretation and Identity in Ancient Judaism*, edited by Lynn LiDonnici and

Andrea Lieber, 193–210. Journal for the Study of Judaism Supplement Series 119. Leiden: Brill, 2007.

Lightstone, Jack N. "Migration and Emergence of Greco-Roman Diaspora Judaism." In *Travel and Religion in Antiquity*, edited by Philip A. Harland, 187–211. Studies in Christianity and Judaism 21. Waterloo, ON: Wilfrid Laurier University Press, 2011.

Lintott, A. W. *Imperium Romanum: Politics and Administration*. London: Routledge, 1993.

Llewelyn, S. R. "Flight from Personal Obligations to the State." In *A Review of the Greek Inscriptions and Papyri Published 1984–85*, edited by S. R. Llewelyn, 97–105. New Documents Illustrating Early Christianity 8. Grand Rapids: Eerdmans, 1998.

———. "Tax Collection and the τελῶναι of the New Testament." In *A Review of the Greek Inscriptions and Papyri Published 1984–85*, edited by S. R. Llewelyn, 47–76. New Documents Illustrating Early Christianity 8. Grand Rapids: Eerdmans, 1998.

Loomba, Ania. *Colonialism/Postcolonialism*. 2nd ed. New Critical Idiom. London: Routledge, 2005.

Luck, Georg, trans. *Arcana Mundi: Magic and the Occult in the Greek and Roman Worlds; A Collection of Ancient Texts*. Baltimore: Johns Hopkins University Press, 1985.

Mach, Michael F. "Choices for Changing Frontiers: The Apologetics of Philo of Alexandria." In *Religious Apologetics—Philosophical Argumentation*, edited by Yossef Schwartz and Volkhard Krech, 19–33. Religion in Philosophy and Theology 10. Tübingen: Mohr Siebeck, 2004.

MacMullen, Ramsay. *Roman Social Relations, 50 BC to AD 284*. New Haven: Yale University Press, 1974.

Malherbe, Abraham J. *Social Aspects of Early Christianity*. Rockwell Lectures. Baton Rouge: Louisiana State University Press, 1977.

Malina, Bruce J. "Religion in the World of Paul." *Biblical Theology Bulletin* 16 (1986) 92–101.

Malkin, Irad. "Postcolonial Concepts and Ancient Greek Colonization." *Modern Language Quarterly* 65 (2004) 341–64.

Marrou, H. I. *A History of Education in Antiquity*. Translated by George Lamb. New York: Sheed & Ward, 1956.

Marshall, I. Howard. "The Jewish Dispersion in New Testament Times." *Faith and Thought* 100.3 (1972) 237–58.

Massebieau, M. L. "Le Classement des Oeuvres de Philon." *Bibliothèque de l'école des hautes études: Sciences religieuses* 1 (1889) 1–91.

Mattingly, David J. *Imperialism, Power, and Identity: Experiencing the Roman Empire*. Miriam S. Balmuth Lectures in Ancient History and Archaeology. Princeton: Princeton University Press, 2011.

Mazzanti, Angela Maria. "The 'Mysteries' in Philo of Alexandria." In *Italian Studies on Philo of Alexandria*, edited by Francesca Calabi, 117–29. Studies in Philo of Alexandria and Mediterranean Antiquity 1. Leiden: Brill, 2003.

McGlynn, Moyna. "The Politeuma: Guardian of Civil Rights or Heavenly Commonwealth in Ptolemaic and Roman Egypt." *Biblische Notizen* 161 (2014) 77–98.

McKnight, Scot. *A Light Among the Gentiles: Jewish Missionary Activity in the Second Temple Period*. Minneapolis: Fortress, 1991.

McKnight, Scot, and Joseph B. Modica, eds. *Jesus Is Lord, Caesar Is Not: Evaluating Empire in New Testament Studies*. Downers Grove, IL: InterVarsity, 2013.

McLeod, John. *Beginning Postcolonialism*. 2nd ed. Beginnings. Manchester: Manchester University Press, 2010.

Meeks, Wayne A. *The First Urban Christians: The Social World of the Apostle Paul*. New Haven: Yale University Press, 1983.

Mendelson, Alan. "A Reappraisal of Wolfson's Method." *Studia Philonica Annual* 3 (1974–75) 11–26.

———. *Secular Education in Philo of Alexandria*. Monographs of the Hebrew Union College 7. Cincinnati: Hebrew Union College Press, 1982.

Meyer, Marvin W. "Mystery Religions." In *The Anchor Bible Dictionary*, edited by David Noel Freedman et al., 4:941–45. 6 vols. New York: Doubleday, 1992.

Moberly, R. W. L. "On Learning to Be a True Prophet: The Story of Balaam and His Ass." In *New Heaven and New Earth. Prophecy and Millennium. Essays in Honour of Anthony Gelston*, edited by P. J. Harland and C. T. R. Hayward, 1–17. Supplements to Vetus Testamentum 77. Leiden: Brill, 2000.

Modrzejewski, Joseph Mélèze. "How to Be a Greek and Yet a Jew in Hellenistic Alexandria?" In *Diasporas in Antiquity*, edited by Shaye J. D. Cohen and Ernest S. Frerichs, 65–92. Brown Judaic Studies 288. Atlanta: Scholars, 1993.

———. *The Jews of Egypt: From Rameses II to Emperor Hadrian*. Translated by Robert Cornman, and with a foreword by Shaye J. D. Cohen. Edinburgh: T & T Clark, 1995.

Mongstad-Kvammen, Ingeborg. *Toward a Postcolonial Reading of the Epistle of James: James 2:1-13 in Its Roman Imperial Setting*. Biblical Interpretation Series 119. Leiden: Brill, 2013.

Moore, Michael S. *The Balaam Traditions: Their Character and Development*, Society of Biblical Literature Dissertation Series 113. Atlanta: Scholars, 1990.

Moore, Stephen D. "Paul After Empire." In *The Colonized Apostle: Paul Through Postcolonial Eyes*, edited by Christopher D. Stanley, 9–23. Paul in Critical Contexts. Minneapolis: Fortress, 2011.

Morley, Neville. *The Roman Empire: Roots of Imperialism*. London: Pluto, 2010.

Morris, Jenny. "The Jewish Philosopher Philo." In *The History of the Jewish People in the Age of Jesus Christ (175 B.C.—A.D. 135)*, by Emil Schürer, revised and edited by Géza Vermes et al., 3.2:808–89. 3 vols. in 4 books. Edinburgh: T. & T. Clark, 1987.

Mott, Stephen Charles. "Greek Ethics and Christian Conversion: The Philonic Background of Titus II,10–14 and III,3–7." *Novum Testamentum* 20 (1978) 22–48.

Moxnes, Halvor. "'He Saw the City Was Full of Idols' (Acts 17:16): Visualising the World of the First Christians." In *Mighty Minorities? Minorities in Early Christianity: Positions and Strategies; Essays in Honour of Jacob Jervell on His 70th Birthday 21 May 1995*, edited by David Hellholm et al., 107–31. Oslo: Scandinavian University Press, 1995.

———. "Patron-Client Relations and the New Community in Luke-Acts." In *The Social World of Luke-Acts: Models for Interpretation*, edited by Jerome H. Neyrey, 241–70. Peabody, MA: Hendrickson, 1991.

Muszynski, Michel. "Les 'Associations Religieuses' en Égypte d'après les Sources Hiéroglyphiques, Démotiques et Greques." *Orientalia Louvaniensia Periodica* 8 (1977) 145–74.

Mühll, Peter von der. "Das griechische Symposion." In *Ausgewählte kleine Schriften*, edited by Bernhard Wyss, 483–505. Schweitzerische Beiträge zur Altertumswissenschaft 12. Basel: Reinhardt, 1976.

Mylonas, George E. *Eleusis and the Eleusinian Mysteries*. Princeton: Princeton University Press, 1961.

Najman, Hindy. "The Law of Nature and the Authority of the Mosaic Law." *Studia Philonica Annual* 11 (1999) 55–73.

Nickelsburg, George W. E. "The Bible Rewritten and Expanded." In *Jewish Writings of the Second Temple Period*, edited by Michael E. Stone, 89–156, Compendia Rerum Ioudaicarum ad Novum Testamentum II, 2. Assen: Van Gorcum, 1984.

Niehoff, Maren R. "Einführung in die Schrift (MigrAbr)." In *Abrahams Aufbruch: Philon von Alexandria, De Migratione Abrahami*, edited by Maren R. Niehoff and Reinhard Feldmeier, 3–26. Scripta Antiquitatis Posterioris ad Ethicam Religionemque pertinentia 410. Tübingen: Mohr Siebeck, 2017.

———. *The Figure of Joseph in Post-Biblical Jewish Literature*. Arbeiten zur Geschichte des antiken Judentums und des Urchristentums 16. Leiden: Brill, 1992.

———. "Ist Philon ein typischer Vertreter des Diasporajudentums?" In *Abrahams Aufbruch: Philon von Alexandria, De Migratione Abrahami*, edited by Maren R. Niehoff and Reinhard Feldmeier, 133–46. Scripta Antiquitatis Posterioris ad Ethicam Religionemque pertinentia 410. Tübingen: Mohr Siebeck, 2017.

———. *Jewish Exegesis and Homeric Scholarship in Alexandria*. Cambridge: Cambridge University Press, 2011.

———. "Josephus and Philo in Rome." In *A Companion to Josephus*, edited by Honora Howell Chapman and Zuleika Rodgers, 135–46. Blackwell Companions to the Ancient World. Chichester, UK: Wiley, 2016.

———. "Philo and Plutarch as Biographers: Parallel Responses to Roman Stoicism." *Greek, Roman and Byzantine Studies* 52 (2012) 361–92.

———. "Philo's Exposition in a Roman Context." *Studia Philonica Annual* 23 (2011) 1–21.

———. "Philon als Biograph." In *Das Leben des Weisen: Philon von Alexandria, De Abrahamo*, edited by Daniel Lanzinger, 147–68. Tübingen: Mohr Siebeck, 2020.

———. *Philo of Alexandria: An Intellectual Biography*. Anchor Yale Bible Reference Library. New Haven: Yale University Press, 2018.

———. *Philo on Jewish Identity and Culture*. Texts and Studies in Ancient Judaism 86. Tübingen: Mohr Siebeck, 2001.

———. "Philo's Role as a Platonist in Alexandria." *Études Platoniciennes* 7 (2010) 37–64.

Nikiprowetzky, V. *Le Commentaire de l'Ecriture chez Philon d'Alexandrie: Son Caractère et sa Portée*. Arbeiten zur Literatur und Geschichte des hellenistischen Judentums 11. Leiden: Brill, 1977.

Nock, Arthur Darby. "The Question of Jewish Mysteries." In *Essays on Religion and the Ancient World*, by Arthur Darby Nock. Selected and edited, with an Introduction, by Zeph Stewart, 459–68. Cambridge: Harvard University Press, 1972.

Oertelt, Frederike. *Herrscherideal und Herrschaftskritik bei Philo von Alexandria: Eine Untersuchung am Beispiel seiner Josephsdarstellung in "De Josepho" und "De Somnis II."* Studies in Philo of Alexandria 8. Leiden: Brill, 2014.

Ogden, Daniel. *Magic, Witchcraft, and Ghosts in the Greek and Roman Worlds: A Sourcebook*. Oxford: Oxford University Press, 2002.

Østby, Erik. "Eleusis: Myte, helligdom og ritual." In *Dionysos og Apollon: Religion og samfunn i antikkens Hellas*, edited by Tormod Eide and Tomas Hägg, 59–78. Skrifter utgitt av det Norske institutt i Athen 1. Bergen: Det norske institutt i Aten, 1989.

Pascher, Joseph. Η ΒΑΣΙΛΙΚΗ ΟΔΟΣ: *Der Königsweg zu Wiedergeburt und Vergottung bei Philon von Alexandreia*. Studien zur Geschichte und Kultur des Altertums 17:3–4. Paderborn: Schöningh, 1931.

Patterson, John R. "Colonization and Historiography: The Roman Republic." In *Greek and Roman Colonization: Origins, Ideologies and Interactions*, edited by Guy Bradley and John-Paul Wilson, 189–218. Swansea: Classical Press of Wales, 2006.

Pearce, Sarah. "Jerusalem as 'Mother-City' in the Writings of Philo of Alexandria." In *Negotiating Diaspora: Jewish Strategies in the Roman Empire*, edited by John M. G. Barclay, 19–36. Library of Second Temple Studies. London: T. & T. Clark, 2004.

Perry, Jonathan Scott. *The Roman Collegia: The Modern Evolution of an Ancient Concept*. Mnemosyne Supplements 277. Leiden: Brill, 2006.

Pickering, W. S. F., ed., *Durkheim on Religion*. AAR Texts and Translations Series 6. Atlanta: Scholars, 1994.

Pietersma, Albert. "Jannes and Jambres (PERSONS) [Gk. Iannes, Iambres]." In *The Anchor Bible Dictionary*, edited by David Noel Freedman et al., 3:638–40. 6 vols. New York: Doubleday, 1992.

Pietersma, Albert, and Benjamin J. Wright, eds. *A New English Translation of the Septuagint*. New York: Oxford University Press, 2007.

Poland, Franz. *Geschichte des griechischen Vereinswesens*. Leipzig: Teubner, 1909.

Pucci Ben Zeev, Miriam. "New Perspectives on the Jewish-Greek Hostilities in Alexandria During the Reign of Emperor Caligula." *Journal for the Study of Judaism* 21.2 (1990) 227–35.

Puech, Émile. "Bala'am and Deir 'Alla." In *The Prestige of the Pagan Prophet Balaam in Judaism, Early Christianity and Islam*, edited by George H. van Kooten and Jacques van Ruiten, 25–47. Themes in Biblical Narrative 11. Leiden: Brill, 2008.

Rajak, Tessa. "Jewish Rights in the Greek Cities Under Roman Rule." In *Approaches to Ancient Judaism*. Vol. 5, *Studies in Judaism and Its Greco-Roman Contexts*, edited by William Scott Green, 19–35. Brown Judaic Studies 32. Atlanta: Scholars, 1985.

―――. "Was There a Roman Charter for the Jews?" *Journal of Roman Studies* 74 (1984) 107–23.

―――. "Was There a Roman Charter for the Jews?" In *The Jewish Dialogue with Greece and Rome: Studies in Cultural and Social Interaction*, 301–33. Arbeiten zur Geschichte des antiken Judentums und des Urchristentums 48. Leiden: Brill, 2001.

Reicke, Bo. *Diakonie, Festfreude und Zelos in Verbindung mit der altchristlichen Agapenfeier*. Uppsala Universitäts Årsskrift 1951:5. A.-B. Lundequistska Bokhandeln, 1951.

Reiling, Jannes. "The Use of Pseudoprophetes in the Septuagint, Philo and Josephus." *Novum Testamentum* 13 (1971) 141–56.

Reinhartz, Adele. "The Meaning of Nomos in Philo's Exposition of the Law." *Studies in Religion* 15 (1986) 337–45.

―――. "Philo's Exposition of the Law and Social History: Methodological Considerations." In *SBL Annual Meeting 1993 Seminar Papers*, edited by Eugene H. Lowering, 6–21. SBL Seminar Paper Series. Atlanta: Scholars, 1993.

Remus, Harold. "Moses and the Thaumaturges: Philo's *De vita Mosis* as a Rescue Operation." *Laval théologique et philosophique* 52 (1996) 665–80.
Ricks, Stephen D. "The Magician as Outsider in the Hebrew Bible and the New Testament." In *Ancient Magic and Ritual Power*, edited by Marvin Meyer and Paul Mirecki, 131–43. Religions in the Graeco-Roman World 129. Leiden: Brill, 1995.
Riedweg, Christoph. *Mysterienterminologie bei Platon, Philon und Klemens von Alexandrien*. Untersuchungen zur antiken Literatur und Geschichte 26. Berlin: de Gruyter, 1987.
Riggs, Christina, ed. *The Oxford Handbook of Roman Egypt*. Oxford Handbooks in Archaeology. Oxford: Oxford University Press, 2012.
Ritner, Robert K. "Egyptian Magical Practice Under the Roman Empire: The Demotic Spells and Their Religious Context." In *Aufstieg und Niedergang der römischen Welt: Geschichte und Kultur Roms im Spiegel der neueren Forschung. 2. Principat*, vol. 18. Religion (Heidentum: Die religiösen Verhältnisse in den Provinzen) Band 5, edited by Hildegard Temporini and Wolfgang Haase, 3,333–79. Berlin: de Gruyter, 1995.
———. "The Religious, Social, and Legal Parameters of Traditional Egyptian Magic." In *Ancient Magic and Ritual Power*, edited by Marvin Meyer and Paul Mirecki, 43–60. Religions in the Graeco-Roman World 129. Leiden: Brill, 1995.
Ritter, Bradley. *Judeans in the Greek Cities of the Roman Empire: Rights, Citizenship and Civil Discord*. Journal for the Study of Judaism Supplement Series 170. Leiden: Brill, 2015.
Robertis, Francesco Maria de. *Il Fenomeno Associativo Nel Mondo Romano: Dai Collegi Della Repubblica Alle Corporazioni del Basso Impero*. Naples: "L'Erma" di Bretschneider, 1955.
Roberts, C., et al. "The Guild of Zeus Hypsistos." *Harvard Theological Review* 24 (1936) 39–88.
Romilly, Jacqueline de. *Magic and Rhetoric in Ancient Greece*. The Carl Newell Jackson Lectures 1974. Cambridge: Harvard University Press, 1975.
Royse, James R. "The Works of Philo." In *The Cambridge Companion to Philo*, edited by Adam Kamesar, 32–64. Cambridge Companions to Philosophy. Cambridge: Cambridge University Press, 2009.
Rösel, Martin. "Wie einer vom Propheten zum Verführer wurde: Tradition und Rezeption der Bileamgestalt." *Biblica* 80 (1999) 506–24.
Runia, David T. *Exegesis and Philosophy: Studies on Philo of Alexandria*. Collected Studies Series. Aldershot, UK: Variorum, 1990.
———. "How to Read Philo." In *Exegesis and Philosophy: Studies on Philo of Alexandria*, 185–98. Collected Studies Series. Aldershot, UK: Variorum, 1990.
———, trans. *On the Creation of the Cosmos According to Moses*, by Philo of Alexandria. Philo of Alexandria Commentary Series. Leiden: Brill, 2001.
———. "Philo, Alexandrian and Jew." In *Exegesis and Philosophy: Studies on Philo of Alexandria*, 1–18 Collected Studies Series. Aldershot: Variorum, 1990.
———. ed., *Philo of Alexandria: An Annotated Bibliography 1987–1996, with Addenda for 1937–1986*. Supplements to Vigiliae Christianae 57. Leiden: Brill, 2000.
———. ed., *Philo of Alexandria: An Annotated Bibliography 1997–2006*. Supplements to Vigiliae Christianae 109. Leiden: Brill, 2012.
———. ed., *Philo of Alexandria: An Annotated Bibliography 2007–2016*. Supplements to Vigiliae Christianae 174. Leiden: Brill, 2022.

———. *Philo in Early Christian Literature: A Survey*. Compendia Rerum Ioudaicarum ad Novum Testamentum III,3. Assen: Van Gorcum, 1993.

———. "Philon von Alexandria." In *Reallexicon für Antike und Christentum*, edited by Georg Schöllgren et al., cols. 606–628. Stuttgart: Hierseman, 2015.

Runia, David T., et al., eds. *Laws Stamped with the Seals of Nature: Law and Nature in Hellenistic Philosophy and Philo of Alexandria*. The Studia Philonica Annual. Studies in Hellenistic Judaism. Brown Judaic Studies 337. Providence: Brown University, 2003.

Ryu, Jang. *Knowledge of God in Philo of Alexandria*. Wissenschaftliche Untersuchungen zum Neuen Testament 2/405. Tübingen: Mohr Siebeck, 2015.

Safrai, S. "Relations Between the Diaspora and the Land of Israel." In *The Jewish People in the First Century: Historical Geography, Political History, Social, Cultural and Religious Life and Institutions*, edited by S. Safrai and M. Stern, 184–215. 2 vols. Compendia Rerum Ad Ioudaicarum sec. 1, vol. 1. Assen: Van Gorcum, 1974.

Safran, W. "Diasporas in Modern Societies: Myths of Homeland and Return." *Diaspora* 1 (1991) 83–99.

Salmon, E. T. *Roman Colonization Under the Republic*. Aspects of Greek and Roman Life. London: Thames & Hudson, 1969.

San Nicolò, Mariano. *Ägyptisches Vereinswesen zur Zeit der Ptolemäer und Römer*. Vol. 1. Münchener Beiträge zur Papyrusforschung und antiken Rechtsgeschichte 2. Munich: Beck, 1913.

Sandelin, Karl-Gustav. "Jews and Alien Practices During the Hellenistic Age." In *Attraction and Danger of Alien Religion: Studies in Early Judaism and Christianity*, 1–26. Wissenschaftliche Untersuchungen zum Neuen Testament 290. Tübingen: Mohr Siebeck, 2012.

Sandmel, Samuel. *Judaism and Christian Beginnings*. New York: Oxford University Press, 1978.

———. *Philo of Alexandria: An Introduction*. New York: Oxford University Press, 1979.

———. "Philo Judaeus: An Introduction to the Man, His Writings, and His Significance." In *Aufstieg und Niedergang der Römischen Welt II.21.1: Geschichte und Kultur Roms Im Spiegel der Neueren Forschung. 2, Principat. Religion. [Hellenistisches Judentum in Römischer Zeit: Philon und Josephus]*, edited by Wolfgang Haase, 3–46. Berlin: de Gruyter, 1984.

Sandnes, Karl Olav. *Belly and Body in the Pauline Epistles*. Society for New Testament Studies Monograph Series 120. Cambridge: Cambridge University Press, 2002.

Schaller, Berndt. "Philon von Alexandreia und das 'Heilige Land.'" In *Fundamenta Judaica: Studien zum antiken Judentum und zum Neuen Testament*, edited by Lutz Doering and Annette Steudel, 13–27. Studien zur Umwelt des Neuen Testaments 25. Göttingen: Vandenhoeck & Ruprecht, 2001.

Schäfer, Peter. *Judeophobia: Attitudes Toward the Jews in the Ancient World*. Cambridge: Harvard University Press, 1997.

———. "Magic and Religion in Ancient Judaism." In *Envisioning Magic: A Princeton Seminar and Symposium*, edited by Peter Schäfer and Hans G. Kippenberg, 19–43. Studies in the History of Religions 75. Leiden: Brill, 1997.

Schenck, Kenneth. *A Brief Guide to Philo*. Louisville: Westminster John Knox, 2005.

Schimanowski, Gottfried. *Juden und Nichtjuden in Alexandrien. Koexistenz und Konflikte bis zum Pogrom unter Trajan (117 n. Chr.)*. Münsteraner Judaistische Studien 18. Berlin: LIT, 2006.

———. "Die jüdische Integration in die Oberschicht Alexandriens und die angebliche Apostasie des Tiberius Julius Alexander." In *Jewish Identity in the Greco-Roman World*, edited by Jörg Frey et al., 111–35. Ancient Judaism and Early Christianity 71. Leiden: Brill, 2007.

Schmeller, Thomas. "Zum Exegetischen Interesse an Antiken Vereinen im 19. und 20. Jahrhundert." In *Vereine, Synagogen und Gemeinden im kaiserzeitlichen Kleinasien*, edited by Andreas und Dietrich-Alex Koch Gutsfeld, 1–19. Studien und Texte zu Antike und Christentum 25. Tübingen: Mohr Siebeck, 2006.

Schmidt, Karl Ludwig. "διασπορά." In *Theological Dictionary of the New Testament*, edited by Gerhard Kittel and Gerhard Friedrich, 2:98–104. Translated by Geoffrey W. Bromiley. 10 vols. Grand Rapids: Eerdmans, 1964.

Schmitt-Pandel, Pauline. "Collective Activities and the Political in the Greek City." In *The Greek City: From Homer to Alexander*, edited by Oswyn Murray and Simon Price, 199–213. Oxford: Clarendon, 1990.

Schwartz, Daniel R. "Philo and Josephus on the Violence in Alexandria in 38 C.E." *The Studia Philonica Annual* 24 (2012) 149–66.

———. "Philo, His Family and His Times." In *The Cambridge Companion to Philo*, edited by Adam Kamesar, 9–31. Cambridge Companions to Philosophy. Cambridge: Cambridge University Press, 2009.

Scott, James M. "Exile and Self-Understanding of Diaspora Jews in the Graeco-Roman Period." In *Exile: Old Testament, Jewish, and Christian Conceptions*, edited by James M. Scott, 173–218. Journal for the Study of Judaism Supplement Series 56. Leiden: Brill, 1997.

———. "Philo and the Restoration of Israel." In *SBL Seminar Papers Annual Meeting 1995*, edited by Eugene H. Lovering Jr., 553–75. SBL Seminar Papers Series 34. Atlanta: Scholars, 1995.

Segal, Alan F. "Hellenistic Magic: Some Questions of Definition." In *Studies in Gnosticism and Hellenistic Religions*, edited by R. van den Broek and M. J. Vermaseren, 349–75. Études Préliminaires aux Religions Orientales dans L'Empire Romain. Leiden: Brill, 1981.

Segovia, Fernando F. "Biblical Criticism and Postcolonial Studies: Toward a Postcolonial Optic." In *The Postcolonial Biblical Reader*, edited by R. S. Sugirtharajah, 33–44. Malden, MA: Blackwell, 2006.

———. "Biblical Criticism and Postcolonial Studies: Toward a Postcolonial Optic." In *Decolonizing Biblical Studies: A View from the Margins*, 119–32. Maryknoll, NY: Orbis, 2000.

———. *Decolonizing Biblical Studies: A View from the Margins*. Maryknoll, NY: Orbis, 2000.

Seland, Torrey. "Collegium kai Ekklesia: Nyere synspunkter på de gresk-romerske foreninger som modell for og parallell til de urkristne forsamlinger." *Ung Teologi* (1984) 49–65.

———. "'Colony' and 'Metropolis' in Philo. Examples of Mimicry and Hybridity in Philo's Writing Back from the Empire?" *Études Platoniciennes* 8 (2010) 13–36.

Seland, Torrey. "'Conduct Yourselves Honorably Among the Gentiles' (1 Peter 2:12): Assimilation and Acculturation in 1 Peter." In *Strangers in the Light: Philonic Perspectives on Christian Identity in 1 Peter*, 147–89. Biblical Interpretation Series 76. Leiden: Brill, 2005.

———. *Establishment Violence in Philo and Luke: A Study of Non-Conformity to the Torah & Jewish Vigilante Reactions*. Biblical Interpretation Series 15. Leiden: Brill, 1995.

———. "The Expository Use of the Balaam Figure in Philo's *De vita Mosis*." In *The Studia Philonica Annual/Studies in Hellenistic Judaism* 28. Studies in Honor of David Runia, edited by Gregory E. Sterling, 321–48. Atlanta: SBL Press, 2016.

———. "The Expository Use of the Balaam Figure in Philo's *De Vita Mosis*." In *The Studia Philonica Annual* 28 (2016) 321–48.

———. "Forbønn hos Filo av Aleksandria." In *Teologi på tidens torg: Festskrift til Peter Wilhelm Böckman*, edited by Peder Borgen et al., 155–78. Relieff 23. Trondheim: Tapir, 1987.

———. "Philo and the Clubs and Associations of Alexandria." In *Voluntary Associations in the Graeco-Roman World*, edited by John S. Kloppenborg and Stephen G. Wilson, 110–27. London: Routledge, 1996.

———. "Philo as a Citizen: Homo Politicus." In *Reading Philo: A Handbook to Philo of Alexandria*, edited by Torrey Seland, 47–74. Grand Rapids: Eerdmans, 2014

———. "Philo, Magic and Balaam: Neglected Aspects of Philo's Exposition of the Balaam Story." In *The New Testament and Early Christian Literature in Greco-Roman Context*, edited by John Fotopoulos, 333–46. Supplements to Novum Testamentum 122. Leiden: Brill, 2006.

———. "Why Study Philo? How?" In *Reading Philo: A Handbook to Philo of Alexandria*, edited by Torrey Seland, 57–79. Grand Rapids: Eerdmans, 2014.

Shroyer, Montgomery J. "Alexandrian Jewish Literalists." *Journal of Biblical Literature* 55 (1936) 261–84.

Siegert, Folker. "Philo and the New Testament." In *The Cambridge Companion to Philo*, edited by Adam Kamesar, 175–209. Cambridge Companions to Philosophy. Cambridge: Cambridge University Press, 2009.

Smallwood, E. Mary. *The Jews Under Roman Rule: From Pompey to Diocletian*. Studies in Judaism in Late Antiquity 20. Leiden: Brill, 1981.

———, ed., trans., and comm. *Philonis Alexandrini Legatio ad Gaium*. 2nd ed. Leiden: Brill, 1970.

Smith, Jonathan Z. "Trading Places." In *Ancient Magic and Ritual Power*, edited by Marvin Meyer and Paul Mirecki, 13–27. Religions in the Graeco-Roman World 129. Leiden: Brill, 1995.

Sowers, Sidney G. *The Hermeneutics of Philo and Hebrews: A Comparison of the Interpretation of the Old Testament in Philo Judaeus and the Epistle to the Hebrews*. Basel Studies of Theology 1. Richmond, VA: John Knox, 1965.

Stanley, Christopher D. ed., *The Colonized Apostle: Paul through Postcolonial Eyes*. Paul in Critical Contexts. Minneapolis: Fortress, 2011.

Sterling, Gregory E. "'The Jewish Philosophy': Reading Moses Via Hellenistic Philosophy According to Philo." In *Reading Philo. A Handbook to Philo of Alexandria*, edited by Torrey Seland, 129–54. Grand Rapids: Eerdmans, 2014.

———. "Philo of Alexandria's *Life of Moses*: An Introduction to the Exposition of the Law." In *Studia Philonica Annual* (2018) 31–45.

———. "The School of Moses in Alexandria: An Attempt to Reconstruct the School of Philo." In *Second Temple Jewish Paideia in Context*, edited by Jason M. Zurawski and Gabriele Boccaccini, 141–66. Beihefte zur Zeitschrift für die neutestamentliche Wissenschaft 228. Berlin: de Gruyter, 2017.

———. "The School of the Sacred Laws: The Social Setting of Philo's Treatises." *Vigiliae Christianae* 53 (1999) 148–64.
———. "'Thus Are Israel': Jewish Self-Definition in Alexandria." *The Studia Philonica Annual* (1995) 1–18.
Stern, M. "The Jewish Diaspora." In *The Jewish People in the First Century: Historical Geography, Political History, Social, Cultural and Religious Life and Institutions*, edited by S. Safrai and M. Stern, 117–83. 2 vols. Compendia Rerum ad Ioudaicarum sec 1. vol. 1. Assen: Van Gorcum, 1974.
Strobel, A. *Die Stunde der Wahrheit. Untersuchungen zum Strafverfahren gegen Jesus.* Wissenschaftliche Untersuchungen zum Neuen Testament 21. Tübingen: Mohr Siebeck, 1980.
Sugirtharajah, R. S. "Charting the Aftermath: A Review of Postcolonial Criticism." In *The Postcolonial Biblical Reader*, edited by R. S. Sugirtharajah, 7–32. Malden, MA: Blackwell, 2006.
———, ed. *The Postcolonial Biblical Reader*. Malden, MA: Blackwell, 2006.
———. *Postcolonial Criticism and Biblical Interpretation*. 2002. Reprint, Oxford: Oxford University Press, 2009.
Tcherikover, Victor. "The Decline of the Jewish Diaspora in Egypt in the Roman Period." *Journal of Jewish Studies* 14 (1963) 1–32.
———. *Hellenistic Civilization and the Jews*. Translated by S. Applebaum. A Temple Book. New York: Atheneum, 1970. Reprint, 1985.
Tcherikover, Victor, et al., eds. *Corpus Papyrorum Judaicarum*. 3 vols. Cambridge: Harvard University Press, 1957–1964.
Terian, Abraham. "A Critical Introduction to Philo's Dialogues." In *Aufstieg und Niedergang der Römischen Welt II.21.1: Geschichte und Kultur Roms Im Spiegel der Neueren Forschung. 2, Principat. Religion. [Hellenistisches Judentum in Römischer Zeit: Philon und Josephus]*, edited by Wolfgang Haase, 272–94. Berlin: de Gruyter, 1984.
Thomassen, Einar. "Is Magic a Subclass of Ritual?" In *The World of Ancient Magic: Papers from the First International Samson Eitrem Seminar at the Norwegian Institute at Athens, 4–8 May 1997*, edited by David R. Jordan et al., 55–66. Papers from the Norwegian Institute at Athens 4. Bergen: The Norwegian Institute at Athens, 1999.
Tod, Marcus Niebuhr. *Ancient Inscriptions: Sidelights on Greek History*. Chicago: Ares, 1932. Reprint, 1974.
Torallas Tovar, Sofía, ed. and trans. *Sobre los Sueños; Sobre José*. Madrid: Credos, 1997.
Torallas Tovar, Sofía, and Anastasia Maravela-Solbakk. "Between Necromancers and Ventriloquists: The ἐγγαστρίμυθοι in the Septuagint." *Sefarad* 61 (2001) 419–38.
Tracy, Sterling. *Philo Judaeus and the Roman Principate*. Williamsport, PA: Bayard, 1933.
Trotter, Jonathan R. "Going and Coming Home in Diasporan Pilgrimage: The Case of Philo's Ἱεροπομποί and Diaspora-Homeland Relations in Alexandrian Jewish Perspective." *Journal for the Study of Judaism* 50 (2019) 26–51.
Turner, E. G. "Tiberius Iulius Alexander." *Journal of Roman Studies* 44 (1954) 54–64.
Unnik, W. W. van. *Das Selbstverständnis der jüdischen Diaspora in der hellenistisch-römischen Zeit. Aus dem Nachlass herausgegeben und bearbeitet von Pieter Willem van der Horst*. Arbeiten zur Geschichte des antiken Judentums und des Urchristentums 17. Leiden: Brill, 1993.

Vermes, Géza. *Scripture and Tradition in Judaism: Haggadic Studies*. Studia post-Biblica 4. Leiden: Brill, 1961.

———. *Scripture and Tradition in Judaism: Haggadic Studies*, 127–77. 2nd, rev. ed. Arbeiten zur Geschichte des antiken Judentums und des Urchristentums 17. Leiden: Brill, 1973.

———. "The Story of Balaam—The Scriptural Origin of Haggadah." In *Scripture and Tradition in Judaism: Haggadic Studies*, 127–77. 2nd, rev. ed. Arbeiten zur Geschichte des antiken Judentums und des Urchristentums 17. Leiden: Brill, 1973.

Victor, Royce M. *Colonial Education and Class Formation in Early Judaism: A Postcolonial Reading*. Library of Second Temple Studies 72. London: T. & T. Clark, 2010.

Waltzing, J. P. *Etude historique sur les corporations professionelles chez les Romaines depuis les Origines jusqa la chute de l'Empire d'Occident*. 4 vols. Louvain: Peeters, 1895–1900.

Waszink, J. H. "Genossenschaft." In *Reallexicon für Antike und Christentum*, 10:99–117, 1978.

Weimar, Peter. "Formen Frühjüdischer Literatur: Eine Skizze." In *Literatur und Religion des Frühjudentums: Eine Einführung*, edited by Johann Maier and Josef Schreiner, 123–62. Würzburg: Echter, 1973.

Westermann, William Linn. "Entertainment in the Villages of Graeco-Roman Egypt." *Journal of Egyptian Archaeology* 18 (1932) 16–27.

Wevers, J. W. "The Balaam Narrative According to the Septuagint." In *Lectures et Relectures de la Bible: Festschrift P.-M. Bogaert*, edited by J.-M. Auwers and A. Wénin, 133–44. Bibliotheca Ephemeridum Theologicarum Lovaniensium 144. Leuven: Leuven University Press, 1999.

Wickler, Wolfgang J. H., et al. "Mimicry." s.v. *Encyclopedia Britannica Online*: added by the editors of Encyclopedia Britannica on July 20, 1998; revised by the editors on December 1, 2000; last updated by Melissa Petruzzello on February 27, 2025, https://www.britannica.com/science/mimicry.

Wilken, Robert L. *The Christians as the Romans Saw Them*. New Haven: Yale University Press, 1984.

———. "Collegia, Philosophical Schools and Theology." In *The Catacombs and the Colosseum: The Roman Empire as the Setting of Primitive Christianity*, edited by Stephen Benko and John O'Rourke, 268–91. Valle Forge, PA: Oliphants, 1971.

Williams, Margaret, ed. *The Jews Among the Greeks and Romans: A Diasporan Sourcebook*. Baltimore: Johns Hopkins University Press, 1998.

Wilson, John-Paul. "'Ideologies' of Greek Colonization." In *Greek and Roman Colonization: Origins, Ideologies and Interactions*, edited by Guy Bradley and John-Paul Wilson, 25–57. Swansea: Classical Press of Wales, 2006.

Wilson, Stephen G. *Leaving the Fold: Apostates and Defectors in Antiquity*. Minneapolis: Fortress, 2004.

Wilson, Walter T., trans. *On Virtues*, by Philo of Alexandria. Philo of Alexandria Commentary Series 3. Leiden: Brill, 2011.

Winston, David. "Philo's Ethical Theory." In *Aufstieg und Niedergang der römischen Welt II 21,1: Geschichte und Kultur Roms im Spiegel der neueren Forschung. 2, Principat. Religion: (Hellenistisches Judentum in römischer Zeit: Philon und Josephus)*, edited by Wolfgang Haase, 372–416. Berlin: de Gruyter, 1984.

———. "Two Types of Mosaic Prophecy According to Philo." In *Society of Biblical Literature Seminar Papers,* edited by David John Lull, 442–55. SBL Seminar Papers Series 27. Atlanta: Scholars, 1988.

Winter, Bruce W. *Philo and Paul Among the Sophists: Alexandrian and Corinthian Responses to a Julian-Claudian Movement.* 2nd ed. Grand Rapids: Eerdmans, 2002.

Wolfson, Henry Austin. *Philo: Foundations of Religious Philosophy in Judaism, Christianity and Islam.* 2 vols. Structure and Growth of Philosophic Systems from Plato to Spinoza. Cambridge: Harvard University Press, 1948.

Woolf, Greg. *Rome: An Empire's Story.* Oxford: Oxford University Press, 2012.

Wright, N. T. *Paul: Fresh Perspectives.* London: SPCK, 2005.

———. "Paul's Gospel and Caesar's Empire." In *Paul and Politics: Ekklesia, Israel, Imperium, Interpretation; Essays in Honor of Krister Stendahl,* edited by Richard A. Horsley, 160–83. Harrisburg, PA: Trinity, 2000.

Yamauchi, Edwin E. "Magic in the Biblical World." *Tyndale Bulletin* 34 (1983) 169–200.

Yoder, Joshua. *Representatives of Roman Rule: Roman Provincial Governors in Luke-Acts.* Beihefte zur Zeitschrift für die neutestamentliche Wissenschaft 209. Berlin: de Gruyter, 2014.

Younge, C. D., trans. *The Works of Philo: Complete and Unabridged.* New updated ed. 3rd printing. Peabody, MA: Hendrickson, 1995.

Zahn, Molly M., "Genre and Rewritten Scripture: A Reassessment." *Journal of Biblical Literature* 131 (2012) 271–88.

———."Talking About Rewritten Texts: Some Reflections on Terminology." In *Changes in Scripture: Rewriting and Interpreting Authoritative Traditions in the Second Temple Period,* edited by Hanne von Weissenberg et al., 93–120. Beihefte zur Zeitschrift für die alttestamentliche Wissenschaft 419. Berlin: de Gruyter, 2011.

Zsengellér, József. "Changes in the Balaam-Interpretation in the Hellenistic Jewish Literature (LXX, Philon, Pseudo-Philon and Josephus)." In *Biblical Figures in Deuterocanonical and Cognate Literature,* edited by Hermann Lichtenberger and Ulrike Mittmann-Richert, 487–506. Deuterocanonical and Cognate Literature Yearbook 2008. Berlin: de Gruyter, 2009.

———. ed., *Rewritten Bible after Fifty Years: Texts, Terms, or Techniques? A Last Dialogue with Géza Vermes.* Journal for the Study of Judaism Supplement Series 166. Leiden: Brill, 2014.

Ziebarth, Erich. *Das griechische Vereinswesen.* Preisschriften (Fürstlich Jablonowski'sche Gesellschaft zu Leipzig) 34. Leipzig: Hirzel, 1896. Reprint, Wiesbaden: Sändig, 1969.

Index of Modern Authors

Only authors mentioned in the main text, or in footnotes, are listed in this index.

Adams, Sean A., 51, 170, 205
Ando, Clifford, 30, 31, 205
Applebaum, Shimon, 156, 205, 227
Arnaoutoglou, Ilias N., 144, 205
Ascough, Richard S., 147, 205
Ashcroft, Bill, 9, 14, 19, 20, 21, 29, 141, 205
Assmann, Jan, 167, 206
Atkinson, John, 86, 206
Aune, David E., ix, 167, 169, 206

Barclay, John M. G., 9, 19, 21, 24, 39, 74, 103, 164, 165, 206
Bardtke, Hans, 146, 206
Barraclough, Ray, 62, 65, 66, 82, 100, 206.
Barré, Michael L., 175, 206
Barton, Stephen, 146, 153, 206
Bekken, Per Jarle 36, 206
Bell, H. Idris, 39, 91, 92, 139, 155, 207
Bendlin, Andreas 147, 207
Berchman, Robert M. 167, 173, 207
Berthelot, Katell, 20, 62, 66, 67, 207
Bhabha, Homi K., 19, 140, 207
Bilde, Per, 66, 90, 100, 207
Bird, Michael F., 136, 208
Birnbaum, Ellen, 21, 52, 55, 57, 66, 67, 70, 71, 100, 208

Bitter, Rudolf A., 105, 208
Bloch, René, 80, 208
Boak, A. E. R., 151, 208
Bohak, Gideon, 166, 167, 208
Boissevain, Jeremy, 148, 208
Borgen, Peder, 18, 20, 21, 24, 25, 33, 34, 36, 37, 38, 39, 40, 44, 48, 49, 50, 51, 55, 57, 67, 69, 76, 77, 79, 80, 82, 85, 87, 103, 110, 111, 115, 120, 121, 136, 137, 139, 140, 141, 156, 158, 170, 171, 177, 178, 180, 200, 208–10
Bowden, Hugh, 121, 210
Bradley, Guy, 26, 210, 222, 228
Brah, Avtar, 12, 14, 15, 210
Brashear, William M., 144, 210
Bremmer, J. N., 86, 121, 122, 169, 210
Brown, S. Kent, 30, 210
Brunt, Peter A., 31, 210
Burford, Allison, 31, 146, 210
Burkert, Walter, 121, 210

Carter, Warren, 25, 98, 210
Champion, Craige B., 28, 30, 210
Cohen, Naomi G., 123, 131, 210
Cohen, Robin, 15, 16, 210
Collins, John J., 161, 210, 214

Colson, F. H., 36, 38, 76, 83, 84, 133, 134, 190. 210
Cover, Michael B. 79, 211
Crowell, Bradley L. 8, 211

Damgaard, Finn, 51, 178, 180, 211
Danker, Frederick W., 152, 211
Dawson, David, 67–70, 211
De Jonge, Casper C., 13, 211
De Savignac, Jean, 44, 211
Delia, Diana, 24, 211
Delling, Gerhard, 49, 59, 63, 171, 211
DeSilva, David A. 19, 102, 211
Dillon, John, 53, 57, 208, 211
Dickson, John P., 137, 211
Diehl, Judy, 8, 211
Dombrowski, Bruno W. 146, 211
Dyck, Jonathan, 67, 69, 70, 212

Eckstein, Arthur M., 28, 210
Edrei, Arye, 101, 212
Egelhaaf-Gaiser, Alfred, 147, 207, 212
Eisenstadt, S. N., 148, 152, 212
Evans, Katherine G., 37, 212

Feldman, Louis H., 21, 35, 37, 38, 39, 101, 188, 190, 191, 194, 195, 212
Fischer, Ulrich, 44, 212
Fisher, Nicholas R. E. 146, 212
Forbes, Clarence A., 146, 148, 212
Fraade, Steven D., 178, 212
Frankel, David, 174, 176, 212
Frankfurter, David, 167, 213
Friesen, Courtney J. P., 36, 199, 213

Gafni, Isaiah M., 116, 213
Gager, John G., 189, 213
Gambetti, Sandra, 3, 4, 6, 86, 87, 92, 213
Garnsey, Peter, 30, 213
Geljon, Albert C., 57, 213
Goodenough, E. R., 20, 41, 48, 49, 50, 52, 54–57, 63, 64–65, 66, 67, 73, 74, 75, 78, 79, 80, 82, 83, 99, 100, 106, 119, 127–30, 135, 138, 139, 177, 200, 213
Graeber, A., 146, 213
Graf, Fritz.,, 168, 213
Graham. A. J., 26, 213

Greenberg, Jennifer, 20, 213
Greene, John T., 173, 174, 176, 213
Gruen, Erich S., 4, 107, 214
Gutsfeld, Andreas, 147, 214

Hackett, Jo Ann, 174
Hadas-Lebel, Mireille, 41, 103, 112, 214
Harker, Andrew, 4, 6, 39, 104, 214
Harland, Philip A., 13, 39, 147, 148, 149, 214
Harnack, Adolf von, 99, 214
Harper, John-Paul, 100, 214
Harrison, James R., 20, 73, 82, 214
Hay, David M., 42, 51, 54, 66, 82, 83, 84, 100, 215
Hayward, C. T. R., 192, 215, 220
Hect, R. D., 44, 215
Heilig, Christoph,, 20, 73, 82, 215
Heinrici, G., 146, 215
Herklotz, Frederike, 31, 215
Herrmann, P., 146, 215
Hoftizer, J., 173, 190, 215
Hölbl, Günther, 30, 216
Horbury, William, 16, 215
Horsley, G. H. R., 146, 153, 206
Horsley, Richard A., 8, 45, 215–16, 229
Horst, Pieter Willem van der, 53, 64, 87, 100, 115
Hunt, Jeffrey M., 50, 60, 216

Isaac, Benjamin, 26, 216

Jördens, Andrea, 31, 32, 216
Judge, E. A., 146, 216

Kaiser, Otto, 79, 216
Kamesar, Adam, 216, 223, 225, 226
Karadimas, Dimitrios, 187, 216
Kasher, Aryeh, 34, 39, 40, 103–4, 107, 216
Keener, Craig S., 165, 166, 216
Kiefer, Jörn., 111, 114, 116, 216
Kim, Seyoon., 9, 74, 216
Klauck, Hans Josef, 146, 168, 216
Kloppenborg, John S., ix, 146, 147, 148, 149, 217, 226
Koch, Dietrich-Alex, 147, 214
Kooij, G. van der, 173, 190, 215

Kooten, George H. van, 184–86, 217, 222
Klutz, Todd, 170, 217
Knott, Kim, 14, 217
Koester, Helmut, 45, 55, 217, 218
Kornemann, E., 146, 150, 152, 217
Koskenniemi, Erkki., 33, 34, 35, 41, 60–62, 179, 184, 186–87, 217
Kraft, Robert A., 79, 84, 218
Kuermmerlin-McLean, Joanne K., 170, 218

Laato, Antti, 179, 218
Lang, T. J., 139–41, 218
Lanzinger, Daniel, 60, 218, 221
Lazarus, Neil, 8, 218
Lease, G., 127, 130, 218
Leonhardt-Balzer, Jutta, 112, 218
Levick, Barbara, 27, 218
Levison, John R., 195, 218
Lewis, Naphtali, 30, 218
Lichtenberger, H., 173, 218, 229
Liebenam, W., 145, 149, 150, 152, 160, 218
Lieber, Andrea, 103, 218, 219
Lightstone, Jack N., 13, 219
Lintott, Andrew W., 30, 219
Llewelyn, S. R., 32, 85, 219
Loomba, Ania, 29, 219
Luck, Georg, 167, 219

Mach, Michael F., 79, 84, 105, 110, 219
MacMullen, Ramsay, 38, 219
Malherbe, Abraham J., 146, 219
Malina, Bruce J., 149, 168, 219
Malkin, Irad, 26, 219
Marrou, H. I., 33, 219
Marshall, I. Howard, 101, 219
Maravela-Solbakk, Anastasia, 171, 219
Massebieau, M. L., 55, 56
Mattingly, David J., 28, 30, 219
Mazzanti, Angela Maria, 131, 132, 219
McGlynn, Moyna, 39, 219
McKnight, Scot, 9, 74, 136, 137, 219, 220
McLeod, John, 12, 13, 14, 19, 21, 220
McLoughlin, Seán, 14, 217
Meeks, Wayne A., 146, 156, 220
Mendels, Doron, 101, 212
Mendelson, A., 34, 40, 156, 158, 220

Mélèze-Modrzejewski, Joseph, 3, 39, 103, 115, 220
Meyer, Marvin W., 122, 213, 220, 223, 226
Mittmann-Richert, Ulrike, 173, 218, 229
Moberly, R. W. L., 175, 226
Modica, Joseph B., 9, 74, 220
Mongstad-Kvammen, Ingeborg, 10, 11, 220
Moore, Michael S., 173, 220
Moore, Stephen D., 8, 220
Morley, Neville, 30, 32, 220
Morris, Jenny, 55, 79, 220
Mott, Stephen Charles, 155, 220
Moxnes, Halvor, 25, 98, 148, 220
Muszynski, Michel, 144, 220
Mühl, Peter van der, 161, 221
Mylonas, George E., 121, 122, 127, 136, 221

Najman, Hindy, 45, 221
Nickelsburg, George W. E., 50, 221
Niehoff, Maren R., 7, 48, 51, 52, 53, 54, 57–62, 71, 79, 80, 88, 89, 94, 106–8, 115, 116, 117, 133, 221
Nikiprowetzky, V., 38, 221
Nock, A. D., 130, 221
Noy, David, 16, 215

Oertelt, Frederike, 82, 221
Ogden, D., 166, 221
Østby, Erik, 121, 222

Pascher, Joseph, 128, 134, 222
Patterson, John R., 27, 222
Pearce, Sarah, 39, 103, 107, 108, 115, 222
Perry, Jonathan S., 147, 222
Pietersma, Albert, 111, 222
Poland, Franz, 145, 146, 149, 150, 151, 152, 155, 161, 222
Pucci Ben Zeev, Miriam, 86, 222
Puech, Émile, 173, 190, 222

Rajak, Tessa, 18, 160, 222
Reicke, Bo, 146, 152, 160, 222
Reinhartz, Adele, 43, 222
Remus, Harold, 188, 189, 223
Ricks, Stephen D., 170, 223

Riedweg, Christoph, 131, 135, 138, 223
Riggs, Christina, 30, 215, 216, 223
Ritner, Robert K., 167, 168, 223
Robertis, Francesco Maria de 146, 149, 223
Roberts, C., 146, 152, 223
Roniger, L., 148, 152, 212
Royse, James R., 51, 177, 180, 223
Rösel, Martin, 173, 174, 176, 181, 223
Runia, David T., ix, 20, 36, 45, 52, 54, 57, 80, 139, 208, 213, 223–24, 226
Ryu, Jang, 124, 224

Safrai, S., 102, 205, 224, 227
Safran, W., 16, 224
Salmon, E. T., 27, 224
Saller, Richard, 30, 213
Sandelin, Karl-Gustav, 37, 224
Sandmel, Samuel, 20, 48, 49, 55, 56, 57, 62, 65, 224
Sandnes, Karl Olav, 157, 162, 224
Schaller, Berndt, 80, 224
Schäfer, Alfred, 207, 212
Schäfer, Peter, 92, 206, 213, 224
Schenck, Kenneth, 48, 224
Schimanowski, Gottfried, 24, 37, 224
Schmeller, Thomas, 147, 225
Schmidt, Karl Ludwig, 102, 103, 104, 110, 225
Schmitt-Pandel, Pauline, 148, 149, 225
Schwartz, Daniel R., 4, 36, 37, 39, 41, 75, 103, 219, 225
Scott, James M., 105, 106, 107, 115, 116, 225
Segal, Alan F., 168, 169, 225
Segovia, Fernando F., 10, 11, 12, 25, 29, 98, 225
Seland, Torrey, ix, 4, 6, 7, 8, 9, 15, 20, 26, 37, 38, 39, 40, 44, 45, 48, 62, 66, 76, 86, 88, 93, 98, 121, 133, 135, 136, 141, 144, 146, 153, 156, 165, 167, 172, 173, 181, 199, 206, 208, 209, 217, 225, 226
Shroyer, Montgomery J., 42, 226
Siegert, Folker, 36, 105, 226
Smallwood, E. Mary, 3, 4, 5, 24, 39, 87, 90, 91, 103, 141, 159, 226
Smith, Jonathan Z., 168, 226

Sowers, Sidney G., 45, 226
Stanley, Christopher D., 8, 9, 220, 226
Sterling, Greg E., ix, 40, 41, 42, 49, 50, 52, 179, 180, 187, 208, 226
Stern, M., 24, 101, 227
Sugirtharajah, R. S., 11, 12, 13, 14, 29, 100, 101, 227

Tcherikover, Victor, 16, 24, 33, 55, 56, 91, 227
Terian, Abraham, 38, 53, 227
Thomassen, Einar, 168, 227
Tod, Marcus Neibuhr, 148, 227
Tovar, Sofia Torallas, 171, 227
Tracy, Sterling, 62, 63, 227
Trotter, Jonathan R., 18, 102, 227
Turner, E. G., 37, 227

Unnik, W. C. van, 102, 104, 105, 107, 110, 115, 227

Vermes, Geza, 50, 175, 178, 192, 220, 228
Victor, Royce M., 10, 20, 32, 35, 228

Waltzing, J. P., 145, 146, 228
Waszink, J. H., 146, 228
Weimar, J., 50, 228
Westermann, W. L., 151, 228
Wevers, J. W., 176, 177, 228
Wilken, Robert L., 146, 152, 160, 228
Wilson, John-Paul, 26, 27, 228
Wilson, Stephen G., ix, 37, 146, 217, 228
Wilson, Walter T., 136, 228
Winston, David, 45, 195, 228
Winter, Bruce W., 184, 185, 186, 187, 229
Wolfson, H. A., 34, 35, 40, 41, 123, 130, 132, 139, 140, 141, 155, 195, 229
Woolf, Greg, 25, 26, 30, 229
Wright, Benjamin G., 111, 222

Yamauchi, Edwin E., 170, 229
Yoder, Joshua, 82, 83, 229

Zahn, Molly M., 179, 229
Ziebarth, E., 145, 149, 150, 151, 156, 160, 229
Zsengellér, József, 174, 176, 177, 179, 181, 188, 191, 229

Ancient Document Index

(The abbreviations used are here given in parenthesis.)

OLD TESTAMENT/ HEBREW BIBLE

Genesis (Gen)
Gen	52
2:1–41:24	49
9:20–29	153
30:14–18	170
30:27	172
45:5	172
45:15	172

Exodus (Exod)
7:11	170, 171
7:22	171
9:11	171
15:25	170
19:5	43
22:17	170
23:2	157
33	124
33:7	124
33:9	124

Leviticus (Lev)
19:26	170, 171, 172
19:31	170, 171
20:6	170, 171
20:27	170, 171

Numeri (Num) Numbers
11	125
11:16	125
21:1–2	180
21:16–18	180
21:20–25	180
22–24	165, 173, 174, 175, 176, 180, 181, 191, 192, 197
22:7	172, 175
22:9–12	174
22:20	174
22:22	174
22:31	174
23:9	164
23:10d	177
23:15–16	173
23:23	172, 183
24:1	175
24:2	175
24:3–4	173
24:7	177

Numbers (cont.)

24:15–16	174
24:17	177
25	175
25:3	123
23:5	123
31:8	173, 175, 177, 181
31:9	175
31:16	173, 175, 180, 181, 188, 189

Deuteronomium (Deut) (Deuteronomy)

7:7	42
18:9–14	170
18:10–11	170
18:9–11	170
18:10	171, 172
18:11	171
18:14	172
18:15	194
18:18	194
21:18–21	153
23	134
23:3–5	175
23:5–6	173, 174. 175, 177, 181
23:17	134
24:10–16	85
30:4–5	102
30:4	108, 109
32:7–9	42

Joshua (Josh)

10:2	112, 113
10:12	170, 179
13:22	173, 175, 177, 181
15:13	112
21:11	112
24:9–10	173
24:9	175, 177, 181
24:10	176

Judges (Judg)

16:17	170

1 Samuel (1 Sam)

20:20–22	170
28	170
28:3	171
28:7	171
28:8	171
28:9	171

1 Kings (1 Kgs)

15:12	123
20:33	172
21:6	172

2 Kings (2 Kgs)

2:13–14	170
5:11	170
9:22–23	170
17:17	172
21:6	172
33:6	172

1 Chronicles (1 Chr)

10:13	171

2 Chronicles (2 Chr)

33:6	170, 171, 172
35:19	171

Esther (Esth)

9:19	112

Psalms (Ps)

105:28	123
146:2	102

Isaiah (Isa)

1:26	112
2:6	172
8:19	170, 171
19:3	171
44:25	171
49:6	102
57:3	170

ANCIENT DOCUMENT INDEX 237

Ezechiel (Ezek)

22:18	170

Daniel (Dan)

1:20	171
2:2	171
2:10	171
2:27	171
4:4	171
5:7	171
5:11	171
5:15	171

Nehemiah (Neh)

1:9	102
7:6	111
13:1–2	175
13:2	173, 175

Hosea (Hos)

4:14	123

Micah (Mic)

6:5	173, 175, 176, 177, 181

Malachi (Mal)

3:5	170

APOCRYPHA (DEUTEROCANONICAL)

Tobit (Tob)

13:5	102
14:4b	102
14:5	102

2 Esdras (Esd)

11:9	102

Sirach (Sir)

36:13	102
36:16	102

Baruch (Bar)

2:13–14	102
3:8	102
4:36–37	102
5:5–6	102

2 Macc

1:27	102

3 Macc

3:20	135

4 Macc

4:19	157
18:5	157

2 Baruch

78:7	102

4 Esra (4 Esr)

13:39–48	102

Psalms of Solomon (Ps. Sol.)

8:28	102
11:1–4	102
17:44	102

NEW TESTAMENT

Acts of the Apostles (Acts)

2:5–11	102

PHILO OF ALEXANDRIA

Questiones et Solutiones in Genesin (QG)
(Questions and Answers on Genesis)

QG	48
4:152	139

ANCIENT DOCUMENT INDEX

Questiones et solutiones in Exodum (QE)
(Questions and Answers on Exodus)

QE	48
2:107–163	128

Legum Allegoriae 1 (Leg. 1)
(The Allegorical Laws)

Leg.	48
1:70–71	155
1:89	156
1:108	139

Legum Allegoriae 3 (Leg. 3)

3:10	131
3:100	122, 125, 127
3:151	125
3:155–56	40, 158
3:164–167	34
3:167	34
3:173	125

De Cherubim (Cher.)
(On the Cherubim)

Cher	48
29	150
32–33	165, 178, 181, 182
32	190
40–50	131
42	124, 131
48	124
48c	125
49	120, 122, 125, 126, 127
50	150
91–92	152
124	150

De Sacrificiis Abelis et Caini (Sacr.)
(On the Sacrifices of Abel and Cain)

Sacr.	48
33	122, 125, 127
37	158
48	156
60–62	124
62	125, 127
63	156
94	125

Quod Deterius Potiori Insidiari Soleat (Det.)
(That the Worse attacks the Better)

Det	48
38–39	186
71	165, 178, 181, 184, 190
89	128

De Posteritate Caini (Post.)
(On the Posterity and Exile of Cain)

Post.	48
16	125
89	43
91–92	70
93	43
101–102	186
101	151, 187
133	139
164	125
174	125

De Gigantibus (Gig.)
(On the Giants)

Gig.	48, 153
26	156
54	124, 131
57	131

De Agricultura (Agr.)
(On Agriculture)

Agr.	48
49	150
104	150
136	186
143	186
145	150
160	156

ANCIENT DOCUMENT INDEX

De Plantatione (*Plant.*)
(On Noah's Work as Planter)

Plant.	48, 153
14	151
58	151
59–60	105
100	152

De Ebrietate (*Ebr.*)
(On Drunkeness)

Ebr.	48
1	153
14–95	153
14–15	152
15	153
20–26	155, 156, 158, 163
20–23	153, 157
20–21	158
20	156, 157
21	152
21	155, 157
21b	157
22	157
23	155
24	150
25	157
70	151
82–83	138
94	151
95–96	157
95	157, 158
168	127
177	40, 156

De Sobrietate (*Sobr.*)
(On Sobriety)

Sobr.	48
20	125
41	153

De Confusione Linguarum (*Conf.*)
(On the Confusion of Tongues)

Conf.	48
40	150
56	42
64–66	181
66	190
72	181
77–78	104, 112, 113, 117
97	150, 172
118	105
141	43
159	165, 172, 178, 182, 190
188	150
197	108, 197

De Migratione Abrahami (*Migr.*)
(On the Migration of Abraham)

Migr	48
14	126
26	150
30	150
60	42
63	150
89–93	71
83	171
92–93	109
113–15	165, 178, 181, 182
113	182, 190
114	182, 183
116	156
158	150

Quis Rerum Divinarum Heres Sit
(*Heres*)
(Who Is the Heir of Divine Things)

Heres	48
56	111
98	111
214	139

De Congressu Quaerendae Eruditionis Gratia (*Congr.*)
(On Mating with the Preliminary Studies)

Congr.	48
3	116
12	150
35	40
56–57	105

De Congressu Quaerendae Eruditionis Gratia (cont.)

51	42
62	150
64	186
74–80	34, 158
74–76	40, 156
112	156
166	156
176	139

De Fuga et Inventione (Fug.)
(On Flight and Finding)

Fug.	48
32	150
85	124, 125, 133
94	113
140	150
198	150
212–13	40

De Mutatione Nominum (Mut.)
(On the Change of Names)

38	150
106	171
110	171
179–86	128
200	183
202–203	182, 183, 184
202	165, 172, 178, 181, 190

De Somniis 1 (Somn. 1)
(On Dreams)

Somn.	48
1:41	113
1:123	151
1:125	151
1:164–65	131
1:181	113
1:196	151
1:219–25	64, 66, 100
1:220	171

De Somniis 2 (Somn. 2)

2:10	151
2:57	151
2:127	151
2:139	151
2:277	151

De Vita Mosis (Vita Mos.)
(On the Life of Moses)

De vita Mosis	49, 50, 51, 79, 80, 167, 172, 173, 178–80, 180–96

Vita Mosis 1

1:1	180
1:4	47, 50
1:8–16	60
1:31	35, 157
1:263–99	165, 179, 189, 192
1:263–92	180
1:274	193
1:278	157
1:282	193

Vita Mosis 2

2:185	151
2:216	156, 160
2:163–99	165
2:167	157
2:270	157

De Opificio Mundi (Opif.)
(On the Creation)

Opif.	49
69–71	128
161	150

De Abrahamo (Abr.)
(On Abraham)

Abr.	49, 79
5	44
56	43
66	111
68	111
70	136

72	111	1:315-318	135
77	111	1:317	43
85	111	1:319-323	131, 133, 142
98	42, 43	1:319	183
83	43	1:320	136
126	150	1:321	136
137	150	1:323	133, 135, 136
276	44		

De Iosepho (Ios.) (On Joseph)

Ios.	49, 51, 79
42	43, 45
43	150
85-87	137

De Decalogo (Decal.) (On the Decalogue)

Decal.	49, 79
18	124, 126
89	150

De Specialibus Legibus 1 (Spec. 1) (On the Special Laws)

Spec. 1-4	79
1:7	116
1:14	55
1:41-50	124
1:41	126
1:52	43
1:56	135
1:59-63	197, 202
1:60	172
1:61	196, 202
1:62	167
1:63	164, 172, 183
1:65	194, 195
1:69-70	17, 101
1:69	102
1:77-78	102
1:84-97	128
1:153	55
1:176	159, 163
1:178	150
1:192	162
1:299	158

De Specialibus Legibus 2 (Spec. 2)

2:18-19	35
2:20	151
2:40	150
2:44	42
2:62-63	34
2:62	156, 160
2:79	56
2:90-95	63
2:95	150
2:140	150
2:145-46	162
2:146	111
2:148	162
2:150	111
2:158	111
2:193	150, 152, 162
2:195	162
2:196	162
2:197	162
2:201	126
2:224	158
2:230	156

De Specialibus Legibus 3 (Spec. 3.)

3	57, 74
3:1-6	76-80
3:1-5	41
3:1-3	73
3:1-2	77
3:5	78
3.6	78
3:29	56
3:40	132
3:83-209	85
3:93	171
3:96	150, 152
3:100-102	166
3:100	171

De Specialibus Legibus 3 (cont.)

3:119–23	130
3:126	157
3:135	126
3:155	43
3:157–168	63
3:159–68	85
3:167	86
3:170	150
3:172	150
3:187	150
3:270	150

De Specialibus Legibus 4 (*Spec.* 4)

4:46–47	160
4:48	172, 197, 202
4:49	194, 195
4:61	139
4:134	150, 158
4:159	43
4:178	112
4:179–180	43
4:179	43
4:181	42
4:239	150

De Virtutibus (*Virt.*)
(On Virtues)

Virt.	49, 50, 79
102	43, 112
177	137
179	43, 136
182	162
211–19	137
211	136
219	112
221	136

De Praemiis et Poenis (*Praem.*)
(On Rewards and Punishments)

Praem.	49, 50
1–3	50
1	51
14	79
16–17	112
22	156
60	156, 160
66	34
95–97	165
98	157
115	103, 105, 108, 109
127–152	105
162–66	110
162	158
166	43

Quod Omnis Probus Liber Sit (*Prob.*)
(That Every Good Person Is Free)

Prob.	49
22	156
26	156
74	166
141	40, 156

De Providentia (*Prov.*)
(On Providence)

Prov.	49

De Providentia 1

8	49
58	156

De Providentia 2

2:64	17

De Animalibus (*Anim.*)
(On Animals)

Anim.	49
7	49

De Aeternitate Mundi (*Aet.*)
(On the Eternity of the World)

Aet.	49

De Vita Contemplativa
(*Contempl. Vita Cont. Cont.*)
(On the Contemplative Life)

Vita Contemplativa	127, 160
Cont.	49

ANCIENT DOCUMENT INDEX

Contempl.		136–37	150
18	150	136	143, 150, 151
31	186	137–38	151
40–47	160	137	151
46	152	140	152
40–41	152	142	152
46	152	172	63
52	162	177	172
55	162	281–83	105
68	156	281–82	104
71–72	160	281	99
73–74	160		
80	160	*Legatio ad Gaium*	
83–84	160	(*Legat. Legatio. De legatione*)	
89–90	160	(On the Embassy to Gaius)	
124	150	*Legat.*	59, 106, 110, 112, 114
		1	57, 61
Hypothetica (*Hypot.*)		3	43, 54
Hypot.	49	120–31	5
Hypoth.	49	124	87
Hypothetica	40, 56	130–34	87
		133–34	87
In Flaccum (*Flacc.*)		134	4
(Against Flaccus)		143–61	59
Flacc.	59, 106, 110, 112	155	39
1–5	4	184–348	90
4	150, 160	184–98	6, 88
16–24	4	188	90
24	4	184–86	90
36–39	4	194	90
41–43	90	207–348	6
41	4	281–83	105
43	99	281–82	104, 107, 113–14
45–46	105	281	99, 142, 202
46–47	104	276–329	91, 114
46	14, 97, 99, 107, 113, 116, 118, 142, 202	293	113
		294	113
53–54	4	305	113
53	63	311–17	17
54	5, 87	312	150, 152, 159
55–96	5	316	150, 159
55	39	334–37	91
65–72	87	334	113
73–85	87	337–48	91
75	5	350	88
80	5, 88	352–67	88
136–38	151		

Legatio ad Gaium (cont.)

353	6
357	89
366	89
367	6

Josephus
Antiquitates (Ant.)

4:114–16	102
14:215–16	159
14:216	17
14:235–36	159
14:259–60	159
16:160–66	17
16:162–72	102
18:159	37
18:259	41, 86
18:261–310	90
19:280–85	91
20:100	37

War (Bellum)

2:184–203	90
2:220	37
2:309	37
2:492–98	37
4:19	157
5:45–46	37
6:237	37
18:5	157
7:264	157

LATIN LITERATURE

Pliny the Elder
Historia Naturalis

28–30	166

EARLY CHURCH

Origen
Contra Celsum

6.41	167
7.4	167

Eusebius
Praep. Ev.

7:14	40
7:58	40

RABBINIC LITERATURE

Tosefta

Sukkah 4,6	156

Babylonian Talmud

Sukkah 51b	156

Jerusalem Talmud

Sukkah 5,1	156
Sukkah 55a	156

GREEK LITERATURE

Philostratus *Vita Sophistarum*
(*Vit. Soph.*)
(*Life of the Sophists*) ca 160–240 CE

523	167
590	167

www.ingramcontent.com/pod-product-compliance
Lightning Source LLC
Chambersburg PA
CBHW021938240426
43669CB00047B/269